PRISONERS OF MEMORY

PRISONERS OF MEMORY

A Jewish Family from Nazi Germany

JOAN GLUCKAUF HAAHR

Full Court Press
Englewood Cliffs, New Jersey

First Edition

Copyright © 2021 by Joan Gluckauf Haahr

All rights reserved. No part of this book may be reproduced or transmitted in any form or by any means electronic or mechanical, including by photocopying, by recording, or by any information storage and retrieval system, without the express permission of the author, except where permitted by law.

Published in the United States of America
by Full Court Press, 601 Palisade Avenue,
Englewood Cliffs, NJ 07632
fullcourtpress.com

ISBN 978-1-946989-89-5
Library of Congress Control No. 2021905451

Editing and book design by Barry Sheinkopf

Cover photo, "Obergasse 3, Zwingenberg an der Bergstrasse"

Jews–Germany–Biography–History–1900-1933.
Jews–Biography–Third Reich–Persecution–Germany–Saarland–France–Netherlands–1930-1946. Postwar German Jewish Refugees–New York–Washington Heights–Mexico (1935-1960).

The author gratefully acknowledges permission to reprint a stanza of "The End and the Beginning,"
from *Miracle Fair: Selected Poems of Wisława Szymborska*, Translated by Joanna Trzeciak (W. W. Norton, 2001)

The author gratefully achnowledges permission to cite from the film *The Flat*, written and directed, and co-produced by Arnon Goldfinger (ARTE, Israel, 2011)

For the grandmothers I never met

Martha Rothensies Schack (1885–1941)
and Hanna Rehfeld Glückauf (1880–1942/3)
without whose testimony
this book would not have been possible

> Those who knew
> what was going on here
> must make way for
> those who know little.
> And less than little.
> And finally as little as nothing.
> —Wislawa Szymborska[1]

THE ROTHENSIES FAMILY

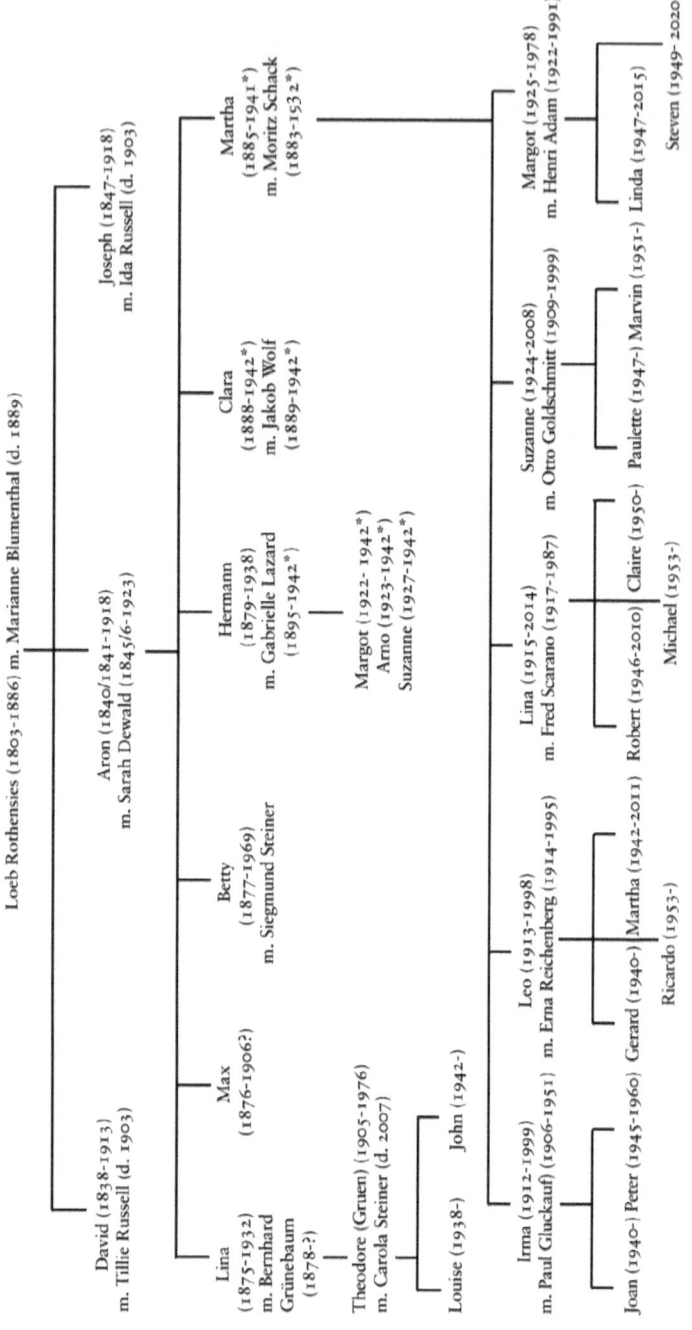

*Murdered by the Nazis

THE SCHACK FAMILY

Nathan Schack (1844-1939) m. Karoline Stern

- Julius (1870-1952, Argentina)
- Lina (1901-1984, Argentina)
- Moritz (1905-1982, Argentina)

Nathan Schack (1844-1939) m. Johanna Kahn

- Simon (1876-1943*)
  m. Rosa May (1875-1942*)
- Karoline (1878-1942*)
  m. Julius Schoenfeld (1877-1943*)
- Moritz (1883-1943*)
  m. Martha Rothensies (1885-1941*)
  m. Selma Strauss (d. 1942*)

THE GLUCKAUF FAMILY

Moses Gluckauf (1844-1919) m. Henriette Tannewald (1844-1905)

- Ernst (1878-1936)
- Emma (1871-19??)
- Rosa (1873-1936)
- Ida (1874-1939)
- Bruno (1876-19??)
- Else (1883-1883)
- Martha (18??-19??)
- Julius (1879-1939)
  m. Johanna (Hanna) Rehfeld (1880-1942-3*)

- Erich (1903-1977)
  m. Gertrude Meier Rolf Glückauf
  m. Edith Jordan (1912-1984)
- Paul (1906-1951)
  m. Elsa Oestreicher (1907-1935)
- Lotte Glückauf (1927-2109)
  m. Irma Schack (1912-1999)
- Werner (1909-1942*)
  m. Selma Mingelgrün (1919-1942*)
- Ilse (1915-2004)
  m. Kurt Kratz (1913-2007)

- Joan Gluckauf (1940-)
- Peter Michael Gluckauf (1945-1960)

*Murdered by the Nazis

Table of Contents

Prologue, i

Part 1: Citizens

Chapter 1: *Zwingenberg an der Bergstrasse, 1*
Chapter 2: Irma and Paul, 23
Saarbrücken, 23
Paris, 45
Amsterdam, 49

Part 2: Victims

Chapter 3: The Parents, 57
Zwingenberg, 57
Frankfurt am Main, 77
Chapter 4: The Children, *102*
Chapter 5: The Glückauf Family, *165*

Part 3: Immigrants and Exiles

Chapter 6: The Early Years, *241*
Chapter 7: The Later Years, *283*
Chapter 8: Aftermaths, *320*

Endnotes, 343
Acknowledgments, 353
About the Author, 357

PROLOGUE

SOME SURVIVORS OF THE NAZI HOLOCAUST never speak of the past, but my mother was not one of them. Again and again she told the stories of her family, assimilated German Jews who, during the disastrous years of 1933 to 1945, unexpectedly found themselves in a world for which nothing had prepared them. She told stories of her childhood in a small village in the western German province of Hesse, of her many friendships with children, Jewish and Gentile, that persisted despite the constant undercurrent of semi-official anti-Semitism that took on such deadly virulence in 1933 when the Nazis came to power. She told of her parents' tragic ends, of beloved cousins in their teens and early twenties when they were deported and killed, of aunts and uncles of whom the only remembrance is the ominous phrase "missing in the East."

I was haunted by her stories. In our house, the ghosts of the victims were always with us, as was the conviction that danger, even death, constantly threatened our commonplace daily lives. Anyone, anything, could be lost in an instant. Yet even as a child I was aware of the corrosive ambivalence my parents and many of their surviving friends and relatives felt toward their former homeland. On the one hand, they maintained an aching love for traditional German culture (Bach! Beethoven! Brahms! Goethe! Schiller!), which they saw as emblematic of the noblest human impulses; on the other hand, they fully understood that the very same Germans who shared their adulation of this cultural heritage had forced them into a nightmare of displacement and exile from which many never awoke. And I too responded paradoxically: despite the horrors they revealed, to me my mother's stories were tinged with an excitement and romance that thrilled me in a way that nothing else did in our prosaic lives in northern Manhattan's Washington Heights.

My obsession with my mother's memories did not vanish after I became an adult and, strange as it may seem, her memories have remained as vivid to me as my own—a phenomenon not as unusual as one might think among so-called "survivors."[2]

Throughout my many years of marriage and motherhood, during my long career teaching literature to generations of young men at Yeshiva College, I planned to write about the things my mother had told me. Now a grandmother myself—having in fact lived longer than the two grandmothers I never met whose fates are recounted in Chapters 3 and 5 and to whom I dedicate this book—I have finally done so. Not really a memoir, though much derives from my own memories of what I was told and what I experienced as the child of survivors, I think of this book as a testimonial: my small effort as the sole remaining repository of these family memories, first, to restore to a semblance of life those who disappeared in the Holocaust and, second, to show something of the crippling effects of their loss on their survivors, the "prisoners of memory" of my title. Eva Hoffman, in *After Such Knowledge: Memory, History and the Legacy of the Holocaust* (New York: Public Affairs, 2004), outlines the responsibility of the so-called "second generation"—my generation and hers—to record and promulgate the narrative of our parents' experiences: "The guardianship of the Holocaust is being passed on to us. The second generation is the hinge generation in which received, transferred knowledge of events is being transmuted into history, or into myth. It is also the generation in which we can think about certain questions arising from the *Shoah* with a sense of living connection."[3]

WHAT ENABLED ME TO TELL THESE STORIES were two gifts from my mother. The first was the large collection of family photographs with which she had filled her suitcase when, in May 1937, she and my father boarded the Belgian freighter that would rescue them from Nazi Europe. These photos of grandparents and great-grandparents, parents and siblings, aunts, uncles, cousins, and friends—a few dead long before the Nazi era, most of the others never to be seen alive again—constituted the only material legacy my parents brought with them from Europe. I came to know my subjects first from their images, some of them remarkably preserved old sepia portraits, others small black and white prints, often bent and cracked from handling.

Even more crucially, however, in addition to saving photographs my mother saved letters. From earliest childhood I was aware of the numerous letters, more than a thousand it turned out, that filled several large boxes on a high closet shelf. A few had been carried from Europe along with the photographs, but most began arriving at regular intervals shortly after my parents' immigration to New York, stopping entirely in 1940 and 1941 – a foreboding signal subsequently confirmed. Mostly written in German, with some in French and a few in Dutch, they were off limits to me for many years, both because my mother denied me access to them and because my German, good enough to understand the simple, everyday conversations of my parents and our relatives and friends, was not up to transcribing and translating the letters' mock-Gothic *Sütterlin* script, made mandatory in the schools from 1915 to 1941 and often illegible to modern readers. I knew that these letters held the treasured voices of my grandparents, of cousins, aunts and uncles whom I would never otherwise get to know, but only after my mother's death and their typed transcription by two native German speakers was I finally able to read them for myself, slowly and laboriously translating them into English. Then, at last, I could hear the writers' voices and follow (insofar as Nazi censorship and the limits of their writing skills permitted) the day-to-day events as they had experienced them. As to the ending there was no suspense: my mother had told me everything.

To my surprise, the book's scope soon began to exceed my original intention. I had planned to focus largely on my parents and their generation of survivors, reluctant immigrants for the most part, whose lives in America remained inexorably imprinted by the traumatic events of their youth. They, after all, were people I had actually known and could write of from memory and observation, my mother's and my own. Ultimately, however, they claimed only the final chapters. For in reading the letters in my mother's collection, which admittedly I began doing with the simple desire for accuracy of dates and events, I found myself captivated by the writers' voices. So, this has also become their story, told wherever possible by the participants themselves: a multigenerational account of the disruption and suffering of one family unfortunate enough to be engulfed by the catastrophic events of the early twentieth century.

The problematic ethics of converting accounts of others' suffering into narrative, whether written or visual, has been a common theme of Holocaust writers and artists. My concern, however, lies not in the philosophy of Holocaust remembrance, a subject of profound and fascinating discussion in its own right, but in the much narrower and more personal realm of family history, in particular the stories of two generations of my family whose lives were irrevocably poisoned by what happened during the few years of Nazi rule. Let me defend my work simply with the hope that, in a small way, my book will resurrect and give voice both to those who died so cruelly and prematurely in Europe and to the survivors lucky enough to escape, who then tried with varying degrees of success to build new lives on this side of the Atlantic.

Part 1
Citizens

CHAPTER 1

Zwingenberg an der Bergstrasse

A FEW DAYS BEFORE HER DEATH, having spent the past three months in a Bronx nursing home, my mother suddenly blurted out: "I want to go home."

"*Home?*" I asked. "*Where is home?*"

"*Zwingenberg*," she said. "*I want to go back to Zwingenberg*," naming the small German village of her birth that she had left in 1930, seventy years earlier, and to which she returned only once for a brief final visit to her family in 1934. The full name of the village, Zwingenberg an der Bergstrasse, translates literally as "Between the Mountains on the Mountain Road," the mountains in question the low hills of the Odenwald, whose many vineyards produce the robust white wines for which the region is famous, and the Bergstrasse the old post road running alongside the mountains between Heidelberg and Darmstadt.

Like many young Jews of her generation with liberal leanings and few resources beyond intelligence and ambition, she had left Germany permanently after the Nazis came to power. But in 1962, while visiting Europe for the first time since her departure so many years earlier, she made an afternoon's stop at her old village. That visit, in its way, reflected many of the ambiguities of postwar German life. Exiting the train, she walked from the station toward her childhood home, but hesitant to ring the bell she continued down the street toward the opposite end of the village. There she encountered an old schoolmate, whom she recognized and who immediately recognized her. He greeted her warmly, informing her that other members of their class still lived in the village and offering to lead her to the house of one of her old girlfriends. Gratefully she followed. They rang the bell, he made the introduction, and, after the excitement of the unexpected reunion had calmed, he left with a hug and a handshake. Imagine my mother's feelings when, as soon as he was gone, her old friend burst out: "*Gott in Himmel!* I was terrified when I saw you coming with the SS!" Shocked, my mother learned that this friendly and helpful man had, during the Nazi period, been a member of the local branch of the SS, the *Schutztaffel*, the military police most responsible for initiating and carrying out Hitler's "Final Solution," the genocide of the Jews. Without doubt he had been a prime persecutor of her parents.

Later that same year, in a visit no less revealing of postwar German complexities, I made my first trip to Zwingenberg. It is the oldest of the several towns and villages along the Bergstrasse, and to this day four- and five hundred-year-old houses edge its narrow,

Zwingenberg—the Obergasse and the Untergasse

cobbled streets. On my first visit, in January 1962, the houses were a uniform drab gray, their half-timbering rotting and deteriorated; the cobbled streets were uneven and treacherous, the stones having lain without repair since before the war. I have been there five times since then, and each time the village looks better, with the bright pastels of the restored stucco houses—now cheerily painted as if in a Disney fairy tale—contrasting boldly with their dark wood half-timbering. And the village now extends far beyond its original boundaries, housing affluent professionals from nearby Mannheim and Darmstadt.

My grandmother's ancestors had owned the house at Obergasse 3 for many generations. It stood then, as it still stands today, on the old market square at the intersection of the two original main streets, the *Obergasse* ("high street") and the *Un-*

tergasse ("low street"). At the time of my initial visit, it was inhabited by the same family of Jehovah's Witnesses who had purchased it for a meager token price in 1939, when my grandparents, like all Jews still remaining in the towns and villages on the Bergstrasse, had been forcibly relocated to the newly established ghetto in Frankfurt. My German half-sister, Lotte, had driven me there from her home in Mannheim. Lotte, ever intrepid, rang the bell and introduced us both to the old woman who answered the door. I was, Lotte announced, the granddaughter of the previous owners, Moritz and Martha Schack. Nervously wiping her hands on her apron, the old woman invited us in, leading us up the stairs and towards the rear while spilling out a non-stop litany of grief, regret, and fear. On and on she rambled: *They too had suffered, lost their business, been forced to rely on the generosity of neighbors for food. Her son had been deported and killed.*

Gradually I realized that she was terrified that I was there to reclaim the house. Only when she understood that my objectives were sentimental, not confiscatory, did she calm down and usher us through the tiny cluttered rooms. As I looked around, I understood why my mother's invariable response to everything antique was a sneering, *"That's just like the old junk we had at home,"* although she used a less polite noun.

WHAT I KNOW ABOUT MY MOTHER'S FAMILY begins with the marriage of my maternal great-great-grandparents, Loeb Rothensies and Marianne Blumenfeld, in the 1830s. The surname Rothensies is an unusual one even in Germany, and there exist two differing recorded accounts of its origin when, in the wake of the Napoleonic secularizing reforms, German Jews—who had hitherto followed Hebrew custom and used the patronymic *ben*, meaning "son of"—were compelled to take secular surnames. In both accounts, a member of the family has been asked by a figure in authority (a municipal official in the first, a teacher in the second) to declare the chosen surname and replies "*Roten sie's*," local dialect for *Raten sie* ("You advise me" or "You guess it"). Whether the response was a failed attempt at levity or derived from ignorance or confusion, the odd name evidently stuck.[4]

Loeb and Marianne had five children: three sons (David, Aron, and Joseph) and two daughters (Betty and Karoline), both sisters dying (as was recorded) "in the prime of life." As family story has it, at some point during the tumultuous years following the 1848 uprisings in Europe, David and Joseph—the eldest and youngest of the Rothensies brothers—fled the German military draft and sailed to New York, eventually settling in upstate Delaware County, where they married two American Protestant sisters.[5]

The middle son, Aron, who remained home, was my great-grandfather. He and his wife, Sarah (*née* Dewald), went on to have six children — Lina (b. 1875), Max (b. 1876), Betty (b. 1877), Hermann (b. 1879), Martha (my grandmother, b. 1885), and Clara (b. 1888). Another son David (birthdate unrecorded) died in infancy.

I have in my possession a remarkable sepia photograph of the children, taken in 1889 or 1890, its occasion unknown. The four girls and two boys, ranging in age from teens to toddlers, gaze intently at the photographer—and at us. At the far left is Lina, fourteen or fifteen, wearing a dark, high-necked dress, its tightly buttoned bodice clearly revealing her developing figure. Her left

The six Rothensies children. Back row (left to right), Lina, Clara, Max, Betty; front row, Martha, Hermann (probably late 1880s).

arm encircles Clara, the youngest, about two, who stands on a chair and stares ahead unflinchingly, her tiny clenched fist the only sign of her unease at the photographer's presence. Beside her, tall and handsome in his school jacket and tie, stands Max, perhaps thirteen; only his large, sad eyes hint at the misery that will lead him, already afflicted with the disease then called St. Vitus Dance (Sydenham's chorea) to commit suicide at thirty. To the near right stands young Hermann, small for his ten years, in a military cadet's jacket, his apparently restless arm stayed by his big sister Betty, to his right. Though only about twelve, she already shows the vigor and determination that will, in a few years, lead her to emigrate alone to America, where she will go on to play the role of family matriarch to her refugee nieces and nephew and their offspring until her death, in 1969, at the age of ninety-two. Only Martha, my grandmother, then a tiny four or five-year-old standing between two older siblings, looks anxious. Her hair (which I know to have been red) is cropped like a boy's. Wearing a white ruff-like collar over her dark blouse, she is the only one of the children to seem intimidated by the evident solemnity of the occasion.

Martha was twenty-six when, in May 1911, she married Moritz Schack, the son of Nathan and Jüttel (Simon) Schack from the tiny farming village of Georgenhausen in the nearby Odenwald, where Nathan's ancestors had lived for many generations. Two years Martha's elder, Moritz had no doubt come to Zwingenberg to be married. Theirs was probably an arranged marriage, as finding suitable Jewish partners surely cannot have easy for those living in the small towns and villages of rural Hesse. Except for their Jewish religion, his family was no doubt indistinguishable from the other small farmers or shopkeepers in their community, with one exception: the undeniable Asian appearance of one or two in each generation, with the characteristic broad faces and ocular epicanthic fold of Asians. I am among them, as is my son and one of my granddaughters. Family legend attributes the Asian look to a purported ancestor from the Caucasus, a Jewish peddler (otherwise unidentified) who was said to have accompanied Napoleon's armies as they returned from their disastrous defeat in Russia and settled in this fertile and pleasant part of Hesse.

As was the case with most rural German Jews, the family's religious practices tended to be moderate, consisting of a loose celebration of the Sabbath and holy days in the local synagogue (if there was one), the standard communal rituals of bar mitzvahs, weddings, and funerals, and a steadfast refusal to eat pork. One family ritual my mother described with considerable amusement: each year before *Rosh Hashonah*, in honor of the coming new year, my grandfather's father, Nathan Schack, would take his annual bath—an extraordinary event that took place in a large tub moved for the occasion to the front yard of his house. As his wife and children ran back and forth to fetch water boiling on the kitchen stove to maintain a constant temperature, my great-grandfather would shout non-stop, his greatest fear being that the "unnatural" immersion would cause him to catch cold and die. Despite the baths, he lived to the age of ninety-five, long enough that his last years were spent under the Nazi regime.

Not that anti-Semitism was unknown to the Jewish citizens of Georgenhausen-Reinheim or to my great-grandfather personally. In the *Frankfurter Israelitisches Familienblatt* of December 13,

1912, a notice appeared explaining the omission of the name of Nathan Schack, honored veteran, winner of two iron crosses for valor, and long-time citizen of the community, from the memorial for surviving veterans of the wars of 1870-71:

> *Darmstadt: In the restoration of the Protestant church in Georgenhausen the name of the surviving Jew Nathan Schack was omitted on the commemorative plaque commemorating the war of 1870/71. The pastor is said to have done so on the grounds that "the name of a Jew does not belong in a Protestant church."*

Yet even after the Nazis were in power, the towns of Reinheim and its neighbors honored him by celebrating his ninetieth birthday. A local Jewish publication, *The Israelite*, published an account of the celebration:

> *Reinheim (Hesse), February 26 (1934): On February 17, the Old Veteran of 1866 and 1870, Mr. Nathan Schack, in nearby Georgenhausen, celebrated in full spiritual and physical well being on his 90th birthday. Not only the whole community took part in the celebration, which was led by the Mayor, but also neighboring communities. . .represented by their boards and teachers. Among the numerous congratulations and gifts was also a letter from President Hindenburg, who sent his picture to the celebrant with a*

handwritten signature. We wish the celebrant a continuing healthy life. Happy Birthday! May he live 120 years!

Even more astonishing, in 1935 (four years before his death), Nathan Schack had an experience that speaks directly to some of the anomalies of Jewish life in 1930s Germany. As the Nurnberg laws were more and more harshly enforced and Jews throughout Germany were increasingly banned from all aspects of economic and social life, a popular illustrated weekly magazine published on its cover a photo of my ninety-two-year-old great-grandfather sitting in front of his house, placidly smoking a traditional porcelain pipe. "*Ein echter Odenwalder Bauer*" read the caption, "a true Odenwald peasant." Captured by a passing photographer looking to illustrate an idyllic vision of an "Aryan" fatherland, the image of an anonymous old Jew with his peasant pipe—intense of gaze, wrinkled of brow, and white of beard—was upheld as a symbol of a racially authentic German.

The village of Georgenhausen no longer exists. With my half-sister as guide, I tried to find it in 2003, driving through the Odenwald to Reinheim, the closest town. Each time we saw a passerby, we stopped the car and asked *"Kennen Sie Georgenhausen?"*—"Do you know Georgenhausen?"—only we pronounced it *"Schorchenhause"* as my mother had done, using the old *Hessische* dialect of her childhood rather than the now more prevalent *Hochdeutsch* with its hard "g's." Most had never heard of it. A few thought the name vaguely familiar but had no idea where it was. Only a couple

"A true German peasant'—Nathan Schack, age 92

of very old men remembered, directing us to an outlying section of Reinheim, into which the once autonomous village had been incorporated in 1979. All that remained of Georgenhausen were two or three old houses and the school.

After their marriage, Moritz and Martha Schack settled in Zwingenberg, one reason no doubt being that when her parents died my grandmother would inherit the family house. With her sister Betty in America, her brother Hermann in Saarbrücken, and her sisters Lina and Clara married and with their own homes nearby, Martha was the only one still living at home. Presumably, too, the larger village of Zwingenberg provided greater scope than his own for my grandfather's ambition, which was to open his own butcher shop. For the first two or three years of their married life, before the First World War, things went relatively well. Then came the war. Like most other young German men, including Martha's brother Hermann, Moritz was drafted into the Kaiser's army. During the first year or so, he was still able to pay occasional visits home. In 1915, however, he was sent to fight on the Russian front. He returned only in 1920, having been wounded and captured by the Russians in September 1917, and spending two years in a Russian military prison. His compensation for those years: two Iron Crosses awarded for valor and his right hand shattered, the fingers partially blown off by shrapnel.

Moritz's useless hand and generally weakened condition after his Russian imprisonment made the butcher's trade no longer feasible, and few other employment options were available during that post-war time of military defeat and economic hardship. He became an itinerant tobacco salesman, selling cigarettes and cigars to taverns and restaurants all along the Bergstrasse. As my mother and aunts recalled, business was poor at best, at least partly because Moritz tended to favor the social aspects of the job, spending more and more time drinking and playing cards with his customers and less and less trying to sell his wares. Eventually declaring bankruptcy –according to the mayoral registry of 1925, my grandfather was fined 300 *Reichsmark* for a violation of the bankruptcy code— the business was for a time registered in my grandmother's name, perhaps as a way of avoiding further fines.[6]

My mother, born in November 1912, was the first of Moritz and Martha's five children—four girls and a boy. Her parents had planned to name her Ilse, but when her eight-year-old cousin Theo emphatically proclaimed Ilse to be a dog's name, she was given the name Irma instead. Two more children arrived soon afterward: a brother, Leo, in 1913 and a sister, Lina, in 1915. Then came the war—and a hiatus—with the two youngest born only after their father's return: Suzanne in 1923 and Margot in 1925. This near-annual arrival of children, however, could not continue. The family's economic situation was too precarious, and my grandmother was yet frailer and more depressed in the war's aftermath than she had been earlier. So following Margot's birth, my grandmother's widowed sister Lina, who lived next door, took matters into her own hands and banished my grandfather from the bedroom. Henceforth he slept downstairs alone.

Never strong, my grandmother was soon overwhelmed by the responsibilities of her growing family. After the birth of her first three children, while her husband was at the front, she had been diagnosed with severe "softening of the bones" and sent for six months to a sanatorium at Bad Nauheim. The children (Lina an infant, the other two barely toddlers) were distributed among various aunts and uncles, my mother going for an extended period to her father's childless sister and her husband in Vilbel, north of Frankfurt. Her *Tante* Karoline was harsh and unaffectionate, and so sparing with food that my mother remembered being constantly hungry while staying there. My Aunt Lina confirmed the meanness. She, too, was sent there for a few weeks one summer, when she was seven or eight but, refusing to stay, left suddenly without even saying goodbye, surprising and shocking everyone by taking the train home alone.

My grandfather and Karoline were the offspring of their father's second wife. The first had died young, possibly in childbirth. My mother and her sister spoke more fondly of a second aunt, *Tante* Rosalie, married to my grandfather's older half-brother, Julius. Warm and expansive, *Tante* Rosalie loved to cook, invariably remarking, as she sat down with the family to enjoy the excellent meal she had prepared, *"Heut muss Ich mir Selbe loben."* ("Today I must praise myself.") As generous as her sister-in-law was mean, she customarily served her guests six eggs each for breakfast, a feast my Aunt Lina recalled with relish to the end of her almost ninety-nine-year life.

JEWS HAD LIVED IN ZWINGENBERG for at least six hundred years and were accepted—if not entirely welcomed—as members of the community. Jewish or Gentile, the men talked business and drank beer together in the dark paneled taproom of the *Altes Brauhaus*, built in 1682 and still open today, the oldest surviving half-timbered house on the Bergstrasse. The women mingled less, the Jewish housewives speaking chiefly with the owners and employees of the shops they patronized and the housemaids and washerwomen they employed to do the domestic dirty work—for, no matter how poor a Jewish family might be, there were always servants to help out, usually needy farmers' wives eager for extra money. Christian and Jewish children were classmates and playmates, suffering together the severities of their often grim and humorless teachers (many among the first to join the Nazi Party) and gathering after school to play in the streets.

The unusual degree of assimilation of the rural Jews of Hesse was noted by Robert Goldman in a book about his childhood as a Jew in Germany:

> *Hessian Landjuden (country Jews) were probably among the most assimilated in Germany's Jewish community of half a million. As small tradespeople, they were not part of the professional and intellectual community, as they were in the larger cities: Berlin, Frankfurt, Hamburg, Munich. They had lived in these villages for centuries. Within a generation or two after the emancipation, when Jews were granted citizenship in the mid-nineteenth century, they became Germans culturally; Judaism was only their religion. Having lived as tolerated usurers and tradesmen in the villages for hundreds of years, the emancipation seemed to set loose a pent-up need or demand for equality. And it expressed itself in a soaking-up of German culture, a demonstrative eagerness to become like their non-Jewish neighbors.*[7]

The separate and not-quite-equal relationship of Jews and Christians in the old villages along the Bergstrasse was symbolized by their cemeteries. Christians were buried in the hallowed ground of the quaint churchyards within the villages; Jews from most of the towns and villages along the Bergstrasse found their last resting place in the isolated, if well-tended, Jewish cemetery at the edge of the village of Alsbach a few kilometers from Zwingenberg. For hundreds of years, its heavy iron gate guarded the fragile sandstone markers, the names of the dead engraved in Hebrew and only occasionally in German. However, even this changed under the Nazis: after the forced relocation to Frankfurt in 1939 of the remaining Bergstrasse Jews, the Jewish dead were buried in the "New" Jewish Cemetery in Frankfurt (the old one too full for more gravesites). The old cemetery in Alsbach fell into ruin, its sandstone headstones crumbling and overgrown with moss. Only recently have the graves been mapped and the cemetery partly restored by a local organization devoted to memorializing the area's vanished Jews.[8]

FROM THE FIRST—AS SHE OFTEN TOLD ME and as her siblings, with varying degrees of resentment or resignation, confirmed—my mother was the brightest star in the family firmament. Not merely the first-born, she was an academic prodigy without peer in village memory. Her earliest school years were spent at the *Kinderschule* run by the Protestant congregation. As she wrote in an autobiographical essay during her seventieth year, she loved both the school and her teacher, Sister Philippine, and still in old age remembered fondly how all the children—whether Christian or Jewish—"would go up to the church at 5 PM" on the Sunday before Christmas.

"There we sang Christmas carols and each child got a basket with goodies, also an apron, or gloves, or socks. Christmas carols are still my favorite songs today."[9]

After three years at Zwingenberg's public primary school, she enrolled in the *Höhere Töchter-Schule*, the *lycée* in nearby Bensheim, where she received a full scholarship for the entire seven years. As always, she was at the top of her class, surpassing her classmates in almost every subject. Her school report, a thin, black book containing all her grades from the ages of ten to seventeen, was—throughout her life—one of her most precious possessions, brought with her to America and often exhibited for me to admire. "*Look,*" my mother would say, holding before my eyes the yellowing pages, with their spidery German script: *Religion: 1, Algebra: 1, Deutsch: 1, Französich [French]: 1, Geschichte [History]: 1, Geographie: 1, Naturgeschichte [Science]: 1.*" "1," of course, stood for "excellent" (which my mother always translated as "perfect"). There were a few "2s," less than perfect marks for drawing, singing, and sewing, but there was only one "3" (merely "satisfactory"), a constant throughout the book: *Turnen* (gymnastics). Physical activity was never my mother's strong suit.

At Bensheim again she loved the school, often speaking of her friendships with the girls in her class, many of whom I felt I knew from the faded sepia photos in her school album. Largely photographed during school outings—weekend hikes in the densely wooded Odenwald or week-long cruises along the Rhine—they show a lively and close-knit group, some of the girls sporting traditional long braids, others—including my mother—with stylish "bobs." A few depict cross-dressing young women playfully mugging for the camera during carnival festivities at Mardi Gras, in which all—Christians and Jews alike—evidently participated. Some of the later photos include men: members of a co-ed class eagerly raising their hands to be called on by the unseen teacher; a picnic in the woods, men and women casually intermingled; a group of laughing men astride a fallen log, the teacher—his "student cap" atop his head—amid them. My mother appears in most of the pictures, arms entwined with one or another of her friends (girls in the early ones, young women or young men in the later), her dark hair and eyes in striking contrast to her classmates' blondness. No doubt, the ease and naturalness of these early friendships intensified my mother's later sense of betrayal. As German Christians came under increasing pressure to distance themselves from Jews, her hitherto close friends (though often with embarrassment, she insisted) one by one let it be known that they no longer desired her company. When, in old age, my mother once more established contact with a former classmate, she treasured their correspondence, reading over and over—often in tears—her old friend Sigrid's accounts of other classmates' losing battles with time.

Nevertheless, my mother's closest childhood friends were two Jewish girls, Liesl (Louise) Mainzer and Rosel David. Both came from families that had lived in Zwingenberg for generations. The three were inseparable, walking (later taking the train) together to school and meeting after school, often passing time in Liesl's father's lumberyard. One episode my mother remembered with glee: the three girls, then about ten years old, overheard a man ordering lumber in specific measurements. When Liesl's father asked what he needed it for, the man replied, "*A coffin for my wife.*"

"*But is she dead?*" asked Herr Mainzer, surprised.

"*Not yet, but she soon will be,*" the man responded, leaving the astonished girls unsure whether he was expressing a threat, a sorrow, or a hope. My mother still giggled when she told the story. Both her friends left Germany in the 1930s and survived. Liesl emigrated to Los Angeles, and she and my mother exchanged birthday cards for many years, arranging to meet occasionally on Liesl's rare trips to New York; Rosel settled in Haifa, Israel.

If my mother's confidence in her abilities grew, so did her ambition. As long as she could remember, she had hungered to escape Zwingenberg, longing for Paris or—if that were impossible—the "little Paris," Saarbrücken, in the independent Saarland. So when, in 1929, she completed her studies at the *lycée*, she did not, as everyone had expected, apply immediately to the Gymnasium, the prelude to university admission. Instead, to the dismay of both family members and teachers, she enrolled in a one-year business school program in Darmstadt, determined to become independent as soon as possible. As she described it: "*I had learned a lot* [at the lycée], *a number of languages, and yet, when the time was up, I decided to go to the Höhere Handelsschule in Darmstadt, which would enable me to make money soon. There wasn't much money at home, and many mouths to feed.*" Although she could not have known it then, this choice probably saved her life. Had she been immersed in a serious academic course of study, it is unlikely that she would have left Germany, as she did on completing the business program.

FEW GERMANS, IN TRUTH, RECOGNIZED THE DANGERS in July 1932, when the Nazis won the two hundred and thirty seats that made them the largest single party in the Reichstag. Short of a majority, their impact seemed temporary, especially in light of their election losses later that year. Even in 1933, when Hindenburg, bowing to Nazi electoral strength, appointed Adolf Hitler as Chancellor, only the most politically sensitive felt danger. Most people—Jews among them—went about their daily business. Many had, in fact, voted for Hindenburg for President, including my grandfather, who—former soldier that he was—venerated the old general, believing in his promises to restore order and prosperity. To the proverbial comment of a wiser friend that *"only the dumbest calves choose their own butcher,"* my grandfather (though once a butcher himself) turned deaf ears.

One after the other, as they finished school, the three older Schack children left Germany. My mother was the first. Restless and eager to strike out on her own, she responded to the first opportunity that came her way. As she later wrote:

Easter 1930 I went to Saarbrücken; I wanted to have a vacation before going to the Oberlyceum, the Gymnasium for girls in Darmstadt, to make the 'Abitur,' into which my cousins Lina and Ludwig Ranis had talked me. But my Uncle Jakob heard of an available job as a 'foreign correspondent,' responsible for writing and translating all correspondence to and from abroad at Ernst Heckel, m.G.H. Drahtseilbahnfabrik [a cable car factory in Saarbrücken]. I applied and got the job. Now I was going to make money! I was seventeen years old and lived with my Aunt Clara and Uncle Jakob, who had a beautiful and large apartment.

As much as the independence and income, she welcomed the urban life readily accessible in Saarbrücken, a city she knew well from fondly remembered childhood vacation visits to her mother's brother Hermann and his family and now the home as well of her mother's youngest sister.

Less than two years later, in April 1933, her brother Leo fled Zwingenberg, suddenly and unexpectedly. Fun-loving, gregarious, and athletic (remembered even now as one of the region's great soccer players), he was warned by one of his many non-Jewish friends that members of the local SA, the *Sturmabteilung*, the so-called "brownshirts"—armed and uniformed members of the Nazi party, notorious for their brutality—were coming to arrest him. Rushed by his friends to the station, he boarded the next train, hoping to reach the border, from where he could then cross on foot into France and get to his uncle in Saarbrücken. He succeeded, and in the early hours of the morning, while it was still dark, my mother met him at a roadside near Forbach, just over the French border. Together they walked the six miles to Saarbrücken, where Uncle Hermann and Aunt Gaby paid for his train ticket to Paris the next day.

Leo never again saw his parents. Eventually immigrating to Mexico, he often returned to Germany in later life, renewing and maintaining contact with many friends, including several of those who had aided his original escape. With Leo in Paris, it was only a short time before their younger sister Lina followed him there, taking a job as a nursemaid for a wealthy French family. By 1934, only the parents and the two youngest girls, Suzanne and Margot, remained at home.

CHAPTER 2

Irma and Paul

Saarbrücken (1930-1935)

MY MOTHER WAS SEVENTEEN WHEN, in the spring of 1930, she moved to Saarbrücken, a city she had come to love during earlier visits with her Uncle Hermann's family. With its rich cultural resources, easy blend of French and German influences, and political independence, it seemed especially hospitable to its Jewish residents, who, though numbering only about twenty-five hundred, provided much of the professional backbone of the city. Generally affluent and comfortably settled, they were doctors, lawyers, judges, and government officials, as well as manufacturers, primarily of shoes and textiles. Many were generous supporters of the flourishing arts scene.

She enjoyed her job at the Heckel cable car factory. Not only did she make many new friends, she experienced her first real romance, albeit with an already married man. When as a curious teen-ager I once inquired about her early love life, she told me of him, pulling out a photo of a handsome, blond young man in a fedora, with a somewhat abashed smile and what we used to call "bedroom eyes." Although the relationship was brief (apparently, he soon dropped her) its impact was lasting, and I have often wondered if my mother's life-long terror of abandonment originated at least in part in that long-ago affair.

She remained at Heckel just over a year. In August 1931 she responded to an advertisement in the *Saarbrücker Zeitung* offering the position of private secretary to the two directors of the *Institut für Microbiologie*, an independent pharmaceutical company that manufactured, in addition to medications, a steady supply of health-related powders, creams, and lotions. With her impressive English and French fluency, she was offered the job, which—as at Heckel—included responsibility for composing and translating all international correspondence. Young and beautiful, she quickly became a favorite of her employers and co-workers alike. She remembered it as an ideal job: "*It was lovely. I had short hours, 9–12, 3–5, and I could do all kinds of sports in my free time. . . . My bosses were wonderful to me; I got raise after raise, and I could live well.*"

She and a friend, another young German Jew named Ernst Kostman, together bought a small paddleboat, and "*every Sunday from Spring into fall we went canoeing to Tübingen, Saargemünd, and into Alsace. We ate at fine restaurants, had deer-roasts, good French food, and it was just delightful.*" My mother described their boat as "*unusual. . .a folding boat*" (that is, collapsible), so that after a few hours' sailing they could easily remove it from the water and pack it up for storage at Ernst's apartment. To my mother, those afternoons on the Saar were among the happiest times of her life. When she recalled them, however, she always added that those calm river journeys were a constant (if, as she always insisted, needless) worry to her own mother, whose pleas that she sell the boat dominated her letters. Most of my mother's stories about those few years in Saarbrücken in the early 1930s described an idyllic life of opera and theater, picnics and parties, of good friends and friendly colleagues, of a mellow pace, and the freedom to live her life as she wished.

For a time, she lived happily in the spacious Saarbrücken apartment of her mother's youngest sister Clara and her husband, Jakob Wolf, but in 1931 her mother's oldest sister, Lina, was diagnosed with cancer, and the Wolfs returned to Zwingenberg to nurse her in her illness. Forced to find new lodgings, Irma moved in with a close friend from Heckel, Hilda Thedy, whose widowed mother ran a boarding house. There, Irma said, she was treated as if she were a second daughter. When Lina, who was her favorite aunt, died the following year, my mother went to Zwingenberg for the week-long *shiva*. Shortly after her return to Saarbrücken, however, Mrs. Thedy, too, suddenly took seriously ill and died, and my mother was forced to move again, this time to a boarding house run by a family named Eichner, who rented rooms to foreigners, many of them German Jews.

One of the tenants was an older man of great personal magnetism. Erich Glückauf was about thirty when my mother met him, handsome, cosmopolitan, and fluent in many languages. When at home, he had a constant parade of visitors, yet he often disappeared for weeks at a time, invariably returning without explanation, jovial and sardonic as ever. All her life attracted to strong, charismatic men, my mother fell madly in love with Erich, who was unlike any man she had met before: more confident, more sophisticated, better traveled. For a short time, she became the woman in his life; as she was soon to find out, she was merely one of many before—and after.

Only then did she learn something about him. Active in leftist politics from his youth, Erich had been elected Secretary to the Communist Party press corps assigned to the Reichstag in Berlin, where he served directly under the Berlin Communist leader Ernst Thälmann. After the Nazis banned the party, in 1934, he was relocated to the Saar Territory on orders from Russia and named chief editor of the *Arbeiterzeitung*, the Communist workers' newspaper in Saarbrücken. With amusement and wonder, even so many years later, my mother described his suitcase, the false bottom of which concealed French, Swedish, Czech, Polish, and Russian passports in a variety of suitable names. Erich made no secret of his wife and son in Moscow, and my mother soon learned of his propensity for pretty women.

Through Erich, my mother, always interested in politics, became directly involved in Saarbrücken's active anti-fascist movement. Many of the activists—Jews, Social Democrats, and other anti-Nazis—were in self-imposed exile in this city, which was German yet not German, a safe haven for members of the Jewish left. Others were there on assignment from the Russian-controlled Communist Party, under instructions to organize a viable anti-fascist movement to ensure that the forthcoming 1935 League of Nations plebiscite did not grant the Saar Territory (with its rich coal and iron resources) to Germany. These included Erich and his friends and acquaintances, who constituted a roll call of those who were to become major players in postwar East Germany, among them Erich himself and his future boss Albert Norden, eventual Chief of the Propaganda Ministry of the DDR with Erich his second-in-command. The group also included a very young Erich Honecker, who, after the war, came to serve as East German Communist Party leader as well as Head of State, and Herbert Wehner, who, having left the party after the war, settled in West Germany and rose to be a high-ranking member of the West German parliament. The rooming house became a center for planning anti-fascist strategy and for supporting endangered democratic movements like that of the Spanish Republicans, whom many of those present, including Erich Glückauf, later aided in the fight against Franco.

For the rest of her life my mother proudly boasted of having carried the Red Flag through the Saarbrücken streets on May Day, marching at the head of the parade organized by her friends. Flattered by her welcome into this group of exiled intellectuals, she felt that she had achieved all she had hoped for in leaving home. That it would soon end was inconceivable. Even though well aware of the looming German threat, she was young enough (only twenty-one in 1934) that the danger from Germany beyond its borders seemed not quite real. What happened afterward made those early years of promise seem a cruel tease.

One morning, when Erich was away on one of his mysterious trips, a slight blondish man with glasses rang the doorbell and introduced himself as Erich's younger brother Paul. He and my mother quickly became friends, sharing common interests in music, politics—and Erich. In the months to follow they were constant companions, sometimes with Erich, when he was in Saarbrücken, more often just the two of them. When my mother left her office for the day, Paul—who soon gave up on what seemed a fruitless hunt for employment—would be waiting for her outside. Intensely private, with a carefully controlled reserve, a cigarette always dangling from his fingers or drooping from the side of his mouth, Paul attached himself to her, joining her and her friends on their evening excursions and walking home with her afterwards, their desultory talk punctuated by long silences. Though my mother told me that she initially resented—and openly mocked—his persistence, she soon got used to his presence. Later, as the political situation became more threatening and Erich left for good, they took comfort in each other's company. I think that Paul, who was my father, probably loved her almost immediately, although he waited a long time to declare his feelings.

Born in 1906 in Wittlich, a small city in the wine-growing region of the Mosel valley between Trier and Cologne, my father was the second of four children, three boys and a girl. Once the Electorate and summer residence of the Archbishop of Trier, by the early twentieth century Wittlich was known chiefly for the large prison that dominated the town physically and economically. The city had a solid Jewish community; the old synagogue—erected in 1910 and still standing—is an imposing gray stone building, its large Romanesque portal topped with a round window (probably once stained glass) and flanked by two stone towers. Paul's parents, Julius Glückauf and Johanna Rehfeld, had arrived in Wittlich in February 1902, both having lived their early years elsewhere: Julius, born in the small, central-German town of Ruhla in Thuringia and raised in nearby Eisenach, where his father, once trained to be a weaver but now a merchant, had prospered; Johanna in the tiny village of Tuchel near the Polish border (and now Tuchola, in Poland). Where they met is unknown, but their marriage was registered in Berlin six months later, on August 22, 1902. The only early photograph of them, though typical of wedding portraits of the time, was taken later in a Wittlich photographer's studio. Why they chose to settle in Wittlich, in the Rhineland, is also unknown, although it is likely that they saw it as a thriving small city in which to establish what they hoped would be a successful business. And this they did, at least for a time. Although Julius had trained as a printer, they chose to open a store selling men's, women's, and children's clothing at cut-rate prices.

Nevertheless, despite their efforts and Julius's innovative and creative advertising,[10] their business seems to have proved disappointing, and they did not remain in Wittlich long. Although their two eldest children were born there (Erich in September 1903, my father, Paul, a little more than two years later), within a few years the family had moved to the industrial Ruhr Valley in North Rhine-Westphalia, first briefly to the small town of Wanne-Eickel, where another son, Werner, arrived in 1909, and then, in 1910, to the nearby large and thriving industrial city of Dortmund where, in 1915, their daughter, Ilse, was born. There they opened a printing business and mint, followed, after the First World War, by several clothing and fine linen stores. And with these they prospered, renting a large apartment on the main street at Hohestrasse 16 behind St. Petri Church and not far from three of their stores.

Their comfortable life was described in 1960 by a witness from Dortmund during the legal proceedings that accompanied the family's claim for restitution:

> *The persecuted couple, Julius and Hanna Glückauf, were known to me personally. They lived on the entire first floor of Hohe Strasse 16, which included 5-6 rooms. . . . [They] had a well-furnished apartment and employed a maid. In addition, the household had two sons, who were employed, and a younger daughter. . . . To what extent the business was boycotted, I cannot say. In my view, it was the*

political situation that led the family to emigrate to Holland. Details of their economic and domestic circumstances I do not know. I cannot describe the home furnishings in any more detail. However, I know that they were very good, they had carpets, good furniture, pictures and good china, etc.[11]

My father's sister Ilse recollected her early years in a letter to me written almost eighty years later:

> *My father was a very good salesman, very charming and well-liked by all his customers. He traveled all over the country, staying home only for short periods. When at home he left all the responsibilities to my mother, who always took care of him and the children, as well as all finances. When there was any problem or need, they all knew that mother could take care of every situation—which she did.*

Paul was a bright, though indifferent student. Following his graduation from the *Realschule*, where he had gained at least some of the skills needed for a career in the family business, his parents enrolled him in a three-year retailing apprenticeship course in Mannheim, a bustling commercial city with a large, prosperous Jewish population, two hundred miles to the south. Their hope was that he might eventually manage a store they planned to open there. The apprenticeship was offered by a well-known Jewish-owned department store on Mannheim's principal shopping street, *Planken*. The store, then called *Schmoller*, remains there still as a branch of the popular retail chain *Kaufhof*. Although unenthusiastic about both the apprenticeship and the prospect of a career in retailing, my father seems to have performed well enough to complete the program. More important to his future, however, was one of the other apprentices: Elsa Öestreicher, a tiny, blond, and pretty native Mannheimer.

It was not at all unusual, in Germany in the 1920s, for Jews and Christians to see each other socially, and Elsa and Paul were soon inseparable both during and after work, despite the open disapproval of both sets of parents. Shortly before the end of their apprenticeships, however, Elsa discovered that she was pregnant.

Marriage seemed the obvious solution, but there were obstacles. Elsa's parents, solid evangelical Lutherans from the conservative suburb of Käferthal, were dismayed at the thought of their daughter's union with Paul, not only because he was Jewish but, perhaps even more, because he seemed to have neither money nor ambition. Yet they pressured Paul to marry their daughter, as that seemed the only way to rescue her from the shame of her situation. My mother always said that Paul and Elsa's literally was a "shotgun wedding," that Elsa's father had pursued my father with a shotgun, although the remark probably reflects her tendency to dramatize more than the reality. Paul's parents, on the other hand, strongly opposed the marriage, seeing the tie to a Gentile shop girl as an unnecessary burden for their twenty-year-old son. They finally gave in, after much pleading and persuasion, but on one condition: they would establish a new store in Mannheim for Paul and Elsa to manage, but Elsa's parents had to finance it. Both families eventually agreed on terms, but there must have been some serious and extended haggling, as the wedding did not take place until 1929, two years after the birth of their child. Unsurprisingly, the financial arrangement proved a continuing source of resentment to the Oestreichers, who were already in debt because of a recently purchased house and had a hard time raising the additional money. The store, *Bielefelder Wäsche Vertrieb* (Bielefelder Linen Distribution), the fifth Glückauf store, sold both men's clothing and fine linens.

Paul and Elsa's child, my half-sister Lotte, was born on the first of February 1927. The only surviving photograph of father and daughter together shows a serious blond girl of about two, tightly clutching her father's hand. She has a Buster Brown haircut and wears a short light-colored dress and dark Mary Janes. My father, hat in his other hand, smiles shyly at the camera and looks uncomfortable. There are other photos of little Lotte: none show her smiling. Even in infancy she looked worried.

And there was reason for worry. For one thing, the store was failing. Paul, evidently preferring to play cards with his friends or go to the cinema (both lifelong passions) to attending to business, left its management primarily to his wife. Poor Elsa, only twenty and with a child to care for, was overwhelmed by the responsibilities of both home and work. The marriage, problematic from the first, soon ended; my father moved out in 1930 and the divorce was finalized in 1933. Lotte and her mother moved in with Elsa's parents in Käferthal.

How did Paul feel about the separation? A single letter, written shortly before Christmas in 1931 and addressed to his four-year-old *"Lottele,"* offers the only evidence:

> *I haven't forgotten you. In my thoughts I am often with you, and I am sad that I can't have you with me. Perhaps it will be possible for us to come together again. When you think of your father, send him a picture of yourself. Please ask your dear Oma to buy you something you really like with the enclosed money. A thousand kisses from your loving Father.*

For almost ninety years, my sister treasured this letter, which represented her sole direct link to her father.

Why did he never write again? Was it indifference or altered circumstances? For there is no doubt that the political climate soon changed. For one thing, what had been an unremarkable relationship in 1926 became a scandal in the early 1930s. Mixed Christian–Jewish marriages, once relatively commonplace, were frowned upon and ultimately prohibited. After the Nazis came to power, Paul surely had little choice but to leave Mannheim quickly in advance of anticipated physical attacks and possible arrest, as the story of his marriage and divorce was widely known throughout the local area. He returned briefly to his parents' home in Dortmund. However, his brother's known Communist affiliations and activism led to all members of the family being frequently summoned by the Gestapo for interrogations and threats. Erich, always on the move, urged his two brothers to leave Germany for Amsterdam.

Following his departure for Dortmund, Paul became the focus of a virulent anti-Semitic attack, first probably in the official Mannheim Nazi newspaper, *Der Hakenkreuzbanne* (The Swastika Flag) and then in *Der Stürmer,* the infamous, most widely circulated of the racist Nazi tabloids and a semi-official organ of the Nazi party.[12] Published weekly by Jules Streicher, the paper generally had the same format from week to week. The front page customarily aimed to incite violence, trumpeting either general anti-Semitic propaganda with titles like "*German Women and Girls: The Jews are Your Destruction*" or outrageous (and often semi-pornographic) attacks on individual Jews in various cities throughout Germany, who were highlighted as examples of Jewish "*sexual criminality*." The stories were usually illustrated with caricatures of leering Jews, large-nosed and slobbering.

Until recently, most of the vast output of *Der Stürmer* remained un-indexed and was available primarily on microfiche. Searching for a way to corroborate the accuracy of Lotte's grandmother's tale of an article attacking our father, I once spent a frustrating afternoon at the New York Public Library hunting through the microfiche archive, but struggling with thousands of pages of small print in the difficult to decipher neo-Gothic *Sütterlin* letters proved too daunting. Now, however, the entire run of *Der Stürmer* from 1923 to 1945 is fully indexed and the indices easily accessible online.[13] And indeed what Lotte had been told was correct. The following article, "*Glückauf, Paul, Dortmund Tragödie eines deutschen Mädchens. Vom Juden geschändet und weggeworfen,*" appears in the 1934/2 volume. Its publication ensured Paul's never returning to Mannheim and soon leaving Germany altogether.

> Paul Glückauf, Dortmund
> The Tragedy Of A Young Woman
> Defiled And Discarded By A Jew.
>
> *In 1925, the girl R. met the Jew Paul Glückauf from Dortmund, Hohe Straße 16. in a department store. The cunning seduction of the Jew was no match for the inexperienced girl. She had no idea about the Jewish question. Miss R. became a mother. She gave birth to a bastard. The Jew Glückauf acknowledged paternity before the Family Court. He agreed to pay 35 marks of child support per month. For two months he fulfilled this duty. Then he did not pay a penny more. For three years he held up promises of marriage to R. and her parents. In the summer of 1928, the elder Jew Glückauf appeared together with his son Paul at the home of the R. family in Mannheim. He dictated the conditions under which his son would marry.*
>
> *If German parents entrust their children to marriage, then this is a serious, holy moment. Nothing is sacred to*

the Jew. The Jew Glückauf sat in the room of the R. family and behaved and haggled as if he were buying a cow from a farmer. He said that R. had to give 4,500 marks to his daughter as a dowry. With this capital, Paul would open a retail store in linens. Then he reached into his pocket and handed R. the following ready-made contract for a signature:

CONTRACT

Bielefeld Laundry Sales, Dortmund, Hohe Straße 20

Owner: J. Glückauf, Westenhellenweg 90 Mannheim, 20.8.28

Between Mr. R, Mannheim, and Mr. Paul Glückauf, Dortmund, the following agreements are made today.

Mr. R. gives Mr. Glückauf 1,000 marks in cash for the opening of his business in Mannheim. Furthermore, Mr. R. undertakes to pay all costs incurred by carpentry and painting, etc., up to a value of 4,500 marks.

Mr R. must also bear the costs of business brokerage. The facility immediately becomes the property of Mr. Glückauf.

If Mr. R. does not fulfill the obligations, Mr. Glückauf is entitled to resign from his private promise [of marriage to R's daughter, note by the editor of the *Stürmer*] *The private promise will be redeemed only if all conditions of this contract are fulfilled. . . .*

Signature R.; Signature Paul Glückauf

The business was founded in Mannheim. Mr. R. fulfilled the terms of the contract. But the Jew Paul Glückauf made no attempt to marry. He agreed with his Talmud, which says: "A gentile girl may disgrace a Jew, but not marry her." (Abobah Sarah 37a) [14]

He had long been weary of the "Goja" [a feminizing of "Goy"?]. In March 1929, the marriage occurred. The Jew Glückauf did not care about wife, child or business. He spent his time playing cards and drinking coffee. And he sought new victims among German girls. All the work was left to his wife. In the Talmud it is written: "The goyim are given a human form only so that the Jews do not have to be served by animals." *

After two years, the business went bankrupt. For three months, the Jew Glückauf let himself be fed by his wife's parents. During this time his brother Erich Glückauf, who was a functionary in the house of the Rote Fahne [the "Red Flag", a widely distributed Communist newspaper] and in the KPD, wrote to him that he should come to him to Berlin. He wanted to draft him into the KPD. Paul Glückauf immediately joined the KPD in Mannheim, immersed himself in the study of the Russian language and later traveled to Berlin. After four months he already informed his wife, whose well-being he did not care about at all, that he was with his parents in Dortmund. She should sell her furniture and with the proceeds start an egg and butter business in a

Dortmund working-class district. When his wife could not decide to do so, he made her understand that without money she was worthless to him.

The haggard woman divorced the Talmudic Jew in January 1933. Since then, her old parents take care of her. A grief-stricken, prematurely aged face and a child growing up at her side, on whom the stamp of racial sin is imprinted, testify to the tragedy of a ruined life.

Thousands of such tragedies are taking place in Germany. National Socialism will put an end to them in the future. The law forbidding marriage of those with German blood to those of other races will bring immeasurable blessings upon our people. The fate of the girl R. from Mannheim will be spared to future German women.

As was usual with *Der Stürmer*, the article contained mostly half-truths and outright lies. Where the initial R. came from is unknown, as Elsa's surname was Oestreicher. The one indisputable fact was that Paul, age twenty, and Elsa, age eighteen, conceived a child and later married, with some negotiation by their parents, none of whom were happy about the situation. We know, too, that the two families, after considerable difficulty, came to an agreement that the Oestreichers would contribute a fixed sum towards setting up a shop for the young couple and the Glückaufs would finance the remainder and supply the shop. *Der Stürmer*'s Talmudic explanation is, of course, pure fiction. In truth, my father's family was not religious, and I question whether either he or his father had ever studied the Talmud.

That Paul proved a less than avid worker I can believe, as lack of interest in his jobs was a lifelong weakness. He always preferred drinking coffee and playing cards. But the claim that he was a seducer of women (a common *Stürmer* line of attack) is laughable. Nor was he ever a Communist, never studied Russian, never even visited Berlin. He and my mother, during their time in Saarbrücken, did support the Communists' anti-fascist agenda, but both were Social Democrats—and liberal Democrats when in the United States—all their lives.

The account of Elsa's subsequent history is largely fiction as well. Although, according to my mother, my father had always assumed that Elsa had later remarried—probably, given the times, to a Nazi or Nazi sympathizer—and concealed her child's true parentage, the actual story was quite different. By 1934, when the article was published, Elsa had indeed remarried, although her second husband was not a Nazi, and she may already have been expecting his child. Lotte's suffering came, of course, not from her mixed parentage or even from her orphaned state (as her mother died in childbirth from that pregnancy) but from the Nazis and their supporters. *(See Chapter 7 for a more detailed account of Lotte's experiences during the Nazi period.)*

On April 19, 1933, moved by fear of attack or arrest on Hitler's birthday the following day, with its promised Nazi demonstrations and violence against Jews and other perceived enemies, my father and his younger brother, Werner, took a train from Dortmund to a town near the Dutch border. Unwilling to risk an encounter with the border police, they waited until dark and stole across the border on foot before resuming the train ride to Amsterdam.

Once having arrived, the two brothers immediately rented a room, living on contributions from home since, as foreigners, they were forbidden to work. Within a few months, they were joined by the rest of the family. Dortmund, notwithstanding its largely working-class population (more commonly a signal of left- rather than right-wing political sympathies), had proven surprisingly hospitable to Nazi ideology, and persecution of local Jews had begun even before Hitler took office. "Don't Buy from Jews" signs were posted on buildings throughout the city and—like other Jewish businesses—the Glückauf family's stores were boycotted and their front windows sometimes smashed. Suddenly without income, the parents listened to their sons' pleas and, in September 1933, sold as much as they could, packed up their furniture and belongings and moved to Amsterdam with their teenage daughter. There they rented a small apartment in a neighborhood south of the city center that already had a substantial German-Jewish population. Paul and Werner moved in with them, although my father—unemployed and restless—did not stay long and soon followed his older brother Erich to Saarbrücken.

On January 13, 1935, however, everything changed for Saarbrücken's Jews and political refugees. A bit of history is in order here. Historically French and considered part of Alsace-Lorraine, the prosperous, industrial Saarland had been annexed by Germany after the Franco-Prussian War of 1878. But with the German defeat in the First World War, under the terms of the 1919 Treaty of Versailles, the Saarland was declared nominally independent. Although the French had hoped to recover the territory as one of the spoils of victory, the British and the Americans objected, and a compromise was worked out: For fifteen years (from 1920 to 1935), the Saarland was to be an "Autonomous Territory" administered by France under League of Nations supervision. France could control its rich coal mines and integrate it into the French customs jurisdiction; but at the end of those fifteen years, a plebiscite would be held to determine the territory's final status. That is, all legal residents would get to vote on whether the Saarland would henceforth remain independent, be formally annexed by France, or become an integral part of Germany.

My mother told the story many times, always with sorrow and anger. The combined anti-fascist forces—she and her friends, together with other like-minded groups—had devoted most of the previous year to supporting the fight against union with Germany, holding rallies and marching, publishing anti-German leaflets, and buttonholing citizens on the streets. Certain of victory (and for most, it didn't matter whether the results favored a French or an independent Saarland), they were dumbfounded at the outcome: more than 90 percent of the population of the Saarland voted for National Socialist rule under Germany. My mother's explanation was always passionate and unambiguous: The Nazis had stolen the election!

But here the story gets confused: my mother's account, which I heard so often and which I had always accepted as truth, was not corroborated by what I learned during a visit to the Historical Museum of the Saar, which tells a different story, one that testifies to Germany's massive—and effective—campaign for annexation. Lavishly displayed in all writings on the subject are the posters and other materials that formed the core of the publicity campaign. In one striking poster, a Christ-like Hitler emerges from heaven, his arms wide open in welcome, with a swastika rather than the star of Bethlehem shining in the sky above. "*Deutsch ist die Saar/ Deutsch immerdar*" is the most frequent slogan: "German is the Saar, German forever." "*Die Saar ist frei*" is another, accompanied in one poster by the picture of a worker breaking his chains, the omnipresent swastika prominently displayed. Still another poster, picturing a grazing cow, plays on the double meaning of the word *Rindvieh*:

> *Ein Rindvieh frisst viel Heu u. Stroh,*
> *Ein Esel nur wählt status quo.*
> [A cow/idiot eats lots of hay and straw,
> An ass just chooses "status quo."]

The accompanying photographs suggest that the Nazi campaign found a highly receptive audience. The victorious Germans were greeted by thousands of Saarlanders cheering in the streets. Retaliation for those who had opposed German annexation soon followed: their windows were broken, their businesses destroyed, the walls of their properties covered with hostile graffiti. In some of the smaller villages, the virulence of their fellow citizens' attacks drove people to suicide. Within a few days of the election, some 8,000 people left for France, many of them Jews. By 1940 about 90 percent of the Saarland's approximately 5,000 Jews had left the country, most escaping to France, others to Holland or Luxembourg. As we know, however, those countries too were soon occupied by the Germans, and many of the Saarland's Jews ultimately perished in Auschwitz, Majdanek, and Treblinka. Among them were my mother's elegant aunt Gaby and her three beautiful and accomplished children.

The night of the plebiscite, all was chaos. Yet while battles between pro- and anti-German forces raged on the streets, my mother lay in a hospital bed, having been admitted the previous day with an alarmingly high fever, the diagnosis diphtheria. Paul and Erich fled immediately, joining the frantic exodus of Communists, Socialists, and Jews who crammed the trains for France that night, in full knowledge that German annexation of the Saarland would probably mean their immediate arrest. Not too ill to recognize her own danger, my mother signed herself out of the hospital the next morning, planning to go to her brother in Marseille. She described what happened next: "*I went to the railroad station; I wanted to ask for a ticket to Marseille, but then and there I said: 'No—please give me a ticket to Paris.' Erich and Paul had gone to Paris, and so I went there also.*" Both met her at the station; it was my father's twenty-ninth birthday. Their first stop was the office of an ear specialist, who drained the accumulated pus from my mother's ear.

Paris

(January 14–August 31, 1935)

WITH THE HELP OF COMMUNIST FRIENDS of Erich, Irma and Paul found rooms in Belleville in the nineteenth arrondissement, then, as now, a depressed, working-class section of the city. They loved the city and the freedom it offered, and their days in Paris fell into a similar pattern. Often walking from one end of the city to the other, they met with other exiled friends and, stopping for aperitifs at their favorite cafés, usually ended the day with what my mother always spoke of as wonderful meals at one of the cheap bistros in their friendly, gritty neighborhood.

How were they able to live? Neither could work, of course. In a time of economic depression and mass unemployment, the immigration of foreigners, refugees or not, was seen by the French political right and left alike as posing a threat not just to the economy but to their way of life. Nor did the French government look sympathetically on those, like my father, without any regular means of support.[15] Every month Paul had to report to police headquarters at *La Cité*, and every month he was refused the permit needed for legal residency. Desperate for funds, he wandered from one refugee agency to another, imploring them for aid. He even appealed to the Communists, but their response, while memorable, was a dead end. My mother described his pleas to the party thus: "*What have you done for us?*" they wanted to know.

"Well," my father said, "*I did some work for the party in Saarbrücken, helping my brother distribute propaganda.*"

"*Have you blown up any trains?*" they asked. "*Sabotaged any government offices? No? Then get lost.*"

What saved them both was generosity from an unexpected source: my mother's former employer, Dr. Erich Christensen, co-director of the *Institut für Microbiologie*. Married with children, in his fifties, handsome and distinguished, an eminently respectable burgher and a political liberal, he was horrified at the sudden turn of events that had made Saarbrücken, his beloved and cosmopolitan city, an outpost of the German Reich. He was also evidently in love with my mother, who had been his personal secretary since her start with the firm four years earlier. A little more than a month after their arrival in Paris, she received a letter from him:

February 22, 1935
Chère amie!

Mrs. K. returned to work yesterday and has given me your address. I take the occasion of a stop at Kédange, my future address of dispatch in France, to express to you in writing my wish to stay in contact with you, to keep you as a friend, and to help you as much as I can. I am not only a businessman, more or less successful, but also an incurable romantic, a bit of a poet, whose dreams embody themselves in you as the last refuge of liberty and humanity! I have to tell you this so that you will better understand my slightly paradoxical attitude. You probably think I am a little crazy that I begin to show my affection for you just at the moment you are leaving me. However, it was impossible before, as I was your 'boss.' Write to me what you are doing and want to do, your worries and your sorrows, your opinions, your dreams and your desires. I shall be at Kédange very often and will answer you regularly. Especially if you change your address, write to me about it immediately so the 'contents' within my letters will not get lost. On the first day of March I shall travel to Luxembourg to discuss with friends the possibility of doing something for you.

At the Institute, little by little, we repress ourselves, but we fear the beginning of the new system. . . . In April I count on being able to go to Paris for several days to resolve the financial questions and to see you again, or to help you come there if you are somewhere else.

Much, much friendship and just as much tenderness as you will accept on my part,

Your Christensen

Address your letters to Mme. Elisabeth D. . . . Kédange/Morell, in double envelopes please.

What followed was an extraordinary series of letters over a period of more than two years, some in French, most in German, all mailed from Kédange, just over the French border from Saarbrücken. Yet of the 126 letters from Erich Christensen in my possession, the above letter is the only one that my mother herself, in her own hand, translated (from French to English). Initially addressed to my mother alone (as *Ma cherie*, or *Meine liebe*, or, most often, *Liebe Freundin*), later—after my parents' marriage—all Dr. Christensen's letters were addressed to both Irma and Paul. His final letter, in 1938, was sent to New York. Every letter included a substantial sum of money.

For my mother, understandably, the letters were and remained a source of discomfiture. Forced by circumstances to accept her former employer's gifts, she was nevertheless embarrassed by his attention. When, years later, I asked her why she had not nominated him as one of the "righteous gentiles" honored at the Holocaust memorial, *Yad Vashem*, in Jerusalem, she shrugged, saying that she hadn't wanted to distress his family with the knowledge of his affection for her.

Now that I have read the letters—many of them clearly love letters—I understand her unease. Nevertheless, my parents lived on those regular payments during the seven months they were in Paris and then for almost two years in Amsterdam. That income, in the guise of payments to a "dummy" cosmetic business, saved my mother from the persecution of the French authorities, who granted her (though not my father) legal residence for a time. To further secure her status, moreover, Dr. Christensen worked to establish, first my mother, then my father, as formal sales representatives of the *Institut* itself, to make it appear that they had legitimate employment. A complete (probably mostly fictional) correspondence was maintained, detailing supposed continuing business transactions.

Nevertheless, the French authorities' patience with my father's irregular status inevitably came to an end. In September 1935 he was deported to the Netherlands, where his parents had been living for the past two years as resident aliens, and my mother went with him.

Earlier that year, on the 24th of May, my parents had become officially engaged. As they sat one day in the Buttes-Chaumont, the large, wooded, hilly park in their neighborhood (now reputed to be a favorite gathering place of Islamic extremists), my father asked my mother to marry him. She told me that though she had (as she later phrased it) "*some trepidations*," she accepted, not knowing what else to do under the circumstances. Both felt abandoned by Erich and generally forlorn, and they turned to each other as much because they had no one else as out of deep love. At least that's what my mother intimated to me years later. What my father felt I don't know. He died at forty-five, when I was eleven—long before I was old enough to ask that kind of question. My impression is that he loved her and never stopped hoping that she would, somehow, become the affectionate and generous person he wanted her to be.

Amsterdam

(September 1935–May 1937)

INITIALLY MOVING INTO A ROOM in the boarding house run by his mother, Paul and Irma—like the other tenants—paid rent, which came from the continuing flow of funds from Dr. Christensen. However, they soon became uncomfortable in the role of paying guests served by other family members and, although they continued to join the family for dinner each evening, they rented their own small apartment nearby, at Waalstraat 80.

They were married on September 10, 1936, in a communal, civil ceremony in Amsterdam's City Hall, which was followed by a modest celebratory breakfast consisting of the Dutch obligatory array of smoked fish, meats, and cheeses. The guests were few: my father's parents, his brother Werner and sister Ilse, and some friends from the boarding house. Nor did anyone from my mother's family attend the wedding, although her mother was able to visit Amsterdam for what she referred to in a letter as *"a few lovely days"* later that fall, then meeting Irma's new family for the first and only time. After lunch, the newlyweds, together with Paul's parents, took a tram to the popular beach at *Zandvoort aan Zee*, west of the city, where they spent the afternoon and where a few photographs were taken. There were no photographs of the actual wedding; no one had thought of it.

Although Dr. Christensen established another business for them, my father was no more successful in Amsterdam than he had been in Paris. And although neither of my parents really wanted to immigrate to the United States, it was becoming increasingly clear to them that life in Europe offered little future to either Jews or any member of the political left. In Holland, as in France, Paul was unable to get official permission to stay. So they decided to seek entrance to the United States, to join my mother's sister Lina, who had been living in New York for the past two years. As had been the case with Lina, they were aided in acquiring the necessary papers by my mother's cousin Theodore Grünebaum (who, since his immigration to New York, was calling himself "Teddy" Gruen) and their wealthy distant cousin Julius F. Roten\, a long-time New York resident. In the early spring of 1937, about a year and a half after their arrival in Amsterdam, their American affidavits came through.

In the months before their departure, occasional letters arrived from Irma's family in Zwingenberg. Her mother—torn between sorrow about their impending departure and relief about their imminent escape—tended, as usual, to focus on practical concerns: *"Perhaps you have already sold the furniture. . . . Or do you have a mover? You wanted to take things with you, but I guess it's very expensive. Have you bought your tickets? Lina's cost 320 marks . . . . From Amsterdam it will probably be cheaper."* Her feelings about the separation are barely acknowledged:

> *I want to thank you for your loving invitation. However, I will not be able to come. I am happy that I was able to be with you in the fall. Dear Irma, you know very well that I am not a hero when it comes to good-byes. I prefer 'hello agains.' And, as I brush myself off, I am also reminded that for such a trip I would need a coat. . . . Your dear parents, Paul, will find it hard to say goodbye, too.*

Another letter seems equally stoical:

Now the big trip really looks serious, though I can't understand that you still don't know the boat you want to sail with. God willing you will have a safe trip and that you, dear Irma, won't feel your usual motion sickness. Aunt Betty was saying that it's important to eat moderately, to have some nourishment. Lina wasn't seasick and hopefully you won't be either. But I can't believe that I won't see you again for such a long time, perhaps ever. But one can't change things and shouldn't waste time in regrets, forgetting what's really important. It must have been very hard to say goodbye to Paul's parents. I think they have taken care of you to the extent possible. So one has to thank God. Please let us know if you are staying for a couple of days more. Your loving mother.

In both letters, in speaking of Paul's parents' sorrow she surely was reflecting her own.

Below their mother's words, Irma's young sisters added their own short greetings, clearly welcoming the possibility of soon being able to join their older sisters in New York. Fourteen-year-old Suzy, who begins with a formal "*Now you are about to embark on your voyage over the big water,*" signs off with "*I will follow you soon.*" Eleven-year-old Margot displays her customary exuberance: *Dear all of you! We received your letter and realized that you want to leave Holland soon. Please greet my Linesse, Aunt Bessie, Uncle*

Sigmund, Theodor, Carola, Uncle Edmund, Aunt Clementine, etc. and tell them I'll see them soon! For today heartfelt greetings and 100000000000000 kisses"—repeating at the end, *"I'll be over there very soon!*

About the actual situation of Moritz and Martha Schack and their two youngest daughters, those outside Germany could only guess based on hearsay and the testimony of what became a constant stream of refugees. Some of Martha's letters of 1937 hint at more pressing fears, largely about money. There is talk of a sum of 60 *Mark*—to be sent from either Holland or America by way of Moritz's family in Georgenhausen—that without appropriate affidavits would be confiscated by the authorities. My grandmother urges my mother to acquire and submit the affidavits before she leaves: *"Have you heard anything from Georgenhausen? Please find out what you can about the affidavit and sign it, so that we will get the 60 Marks, because if not, the government will get it. I wish I could have sent it to you for the trip."* A postcard repeats the request and a second postcard, sent just before Irma and Paul were to sail, shows Martha's urgency in a postscript addressed to Paul's parents: *"Dear Family Glückauf, Should the children already be gone when this letter reaches you, please send it to them immediately. Thank you so much. With best wishes, Martha Schack."* What the matter entailed or whether or not those sixty Marks were ever delivered is unknown.

Irma and Paul sailed from Antwerp, Belgium on the 20th of May 1937: she was twenty-five, he thirty-one. Two of six passengers on the Belgian freighter Mercier, all designated *Premiere Classe*, they were honored each night to sit at the captain's table. Years later, after the war, they learned to their sorrow that on June 10, 1941, the Mercier had been torpedoed and sunk by a German U-boat. Of the Mercier's fifty-seven crew members, seven were killed and six wounded. Among the dead was the captain, Maurice Lambé (an especially gracious gentleman, my mother recalled), who insisted on going down with his ship. One of the surviving crew members described his end: *"The last we saw of him he was standing on the bridge waving. He was terribly calm."* After the war, the Belgians posthumously awarded him the Croix de Guerre and, in 1946, named another merchant ship the *Capitaine Lambé* in his honor.

Paul and Irma Glückauf arrived in New York on June 1, 1937.

Photo Gallery

Marianne Rothensies (née Blumenthal) and Loeb Rothensies

Sara Rothensies (née Dewald) and Aaron Rothensies.

Clara Rothensies, later Clara Wolf

Martha Rothensies, later Martha Schack

Hermann Rothensies as a military cadet

Betty Rothensies, later Bessie Steiner

Martha and Moritz Schack

Moritz Schack in army uniform (photo taken in Riga, Latvia)

Leo and Irma Schack (c. 1914)

Suzy Schack's first school day (1930)

Margot Schack

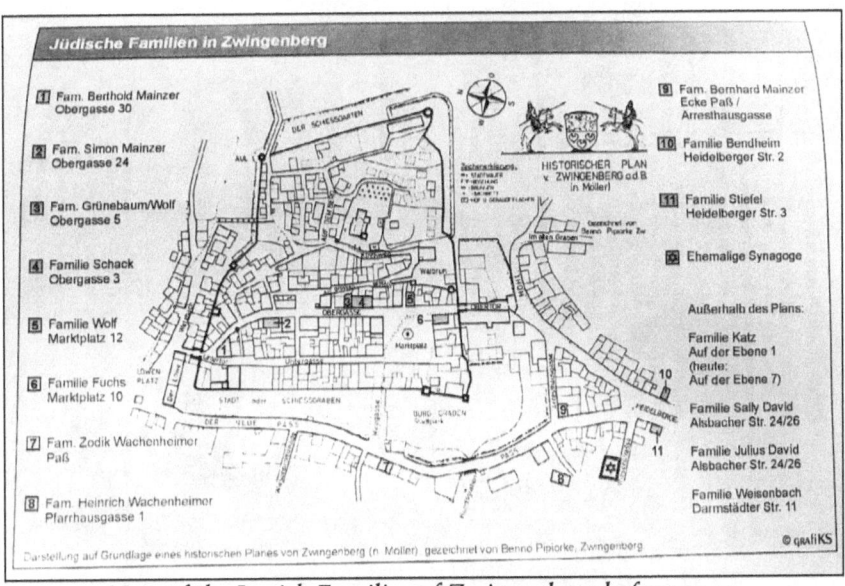

Map of the Jewish Families of Zwingenberg before 1933.
Benno Pipiorke as it appears in Fritz Kilthau's Mitten Unter Uns.

Margo and Lina Schack (early 1930s)

Alsbach Jewish Cemetery in 1993, the burial place for all Jews from the Bergstrasse until 1939

Irma Schack at the Höhere Töchterschule in Bensheim in 1922 (top row, rightmost)

Irma Schack (top row, third from left) and classmates in middle school (c. 1924)

Irma Schack (second row, second from left) in high school with schoolmates (c. 1929)

Left to right, sisters Lina, Suzy, and Margot Schack with Aunt Lina Grünebaum and mother, Martha Schack (1930)

Leo Schack (in white shirt) playing soccer

Leo Schack (right) with a teammate

Irma Schack, with a chic modern haircut (Saarbrücken or Paris)

Leo Schack

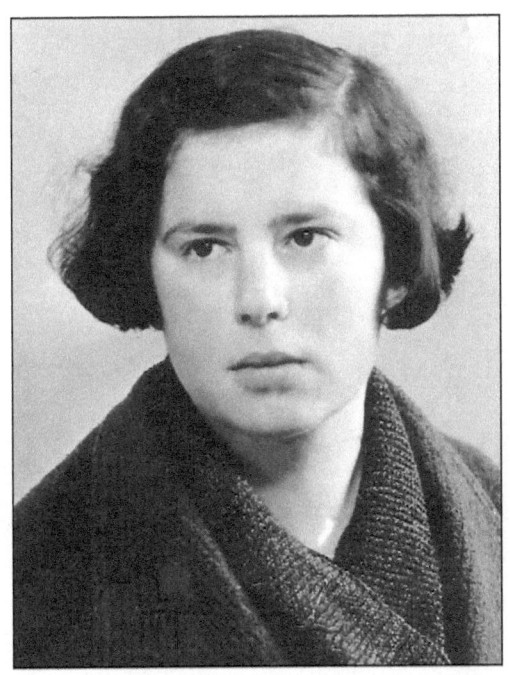

Lina Schack, 1939

Hermann Rothensies with children Arno and Margot

Margot, Arno, and Suzanne Rothensies in Saarbrücken (c. 1929-1930)

Margot Rothensies, first day of school (c. 1928)

Clara and Jakob Wolf in Saarbrücken

Jakob Wolf in the doorway of his tobacco store

Irma (second from left, her head turned away from us) with classmates in the Odenwald

Irma (right) with friends

Leo and Irma in Paris

Irma with Leo's friends in Paris

A little kiss in the Bois de Boulogne

August 1934, Irma's last visit home. Moritz Schack recently released from Dachau. Front row, Lina, Suzy, Margot. Behind them, Martha (hidden), Irma. In window, Jakob and Clara Wolf

Erich Glückauf

Irma in Saarbrücken (October 12, 1932)

Paul Glückauf in Saarbrücken

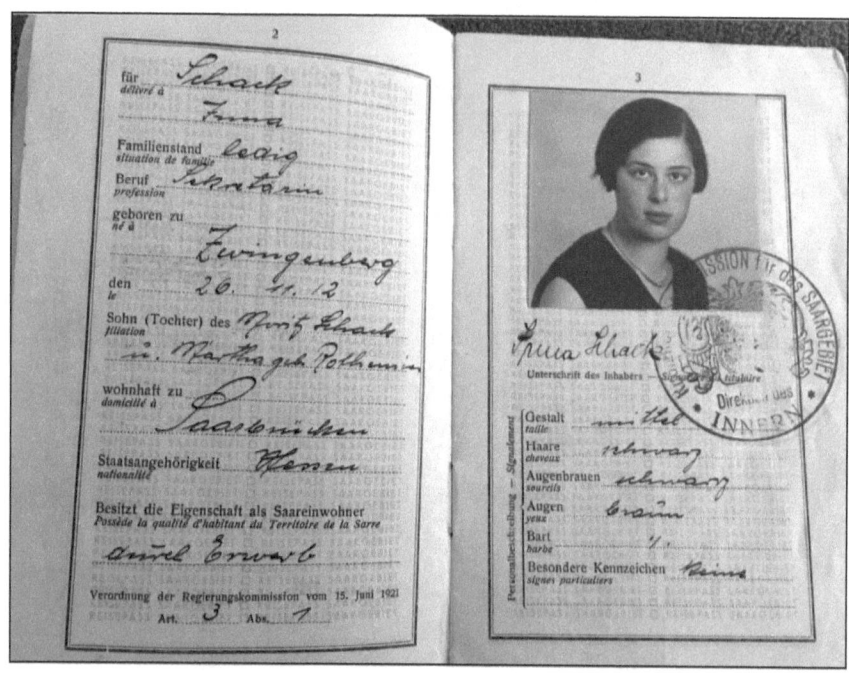

Irma Schack, Saarbrücken carte d'identité

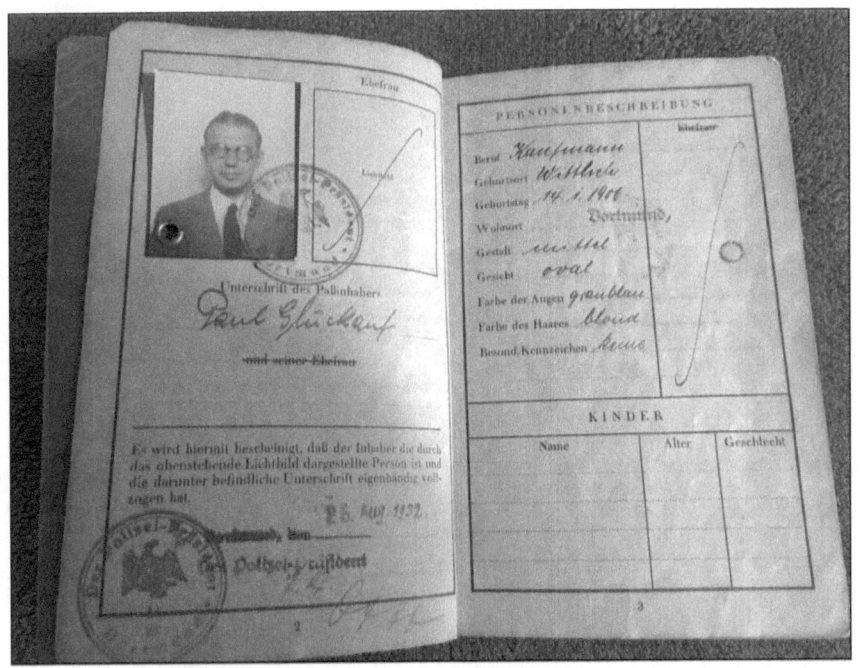

Paul's German passport, issued August 26, 1932.

Irma's employer, Dr. Erich Christensen (Institut für Microbiologie, Saarbrücken).

Saarbrücken, the 1935 plebiscite. *Deutsch die Saar immerdar*
("May the Saar be German forever.")

Deutsch ist die Saar. Deutsch immerdar.
("The Saar will be German forever.")

Paul, his daughter Lotte, and her cousins in Mannheim (c. 1928–29)

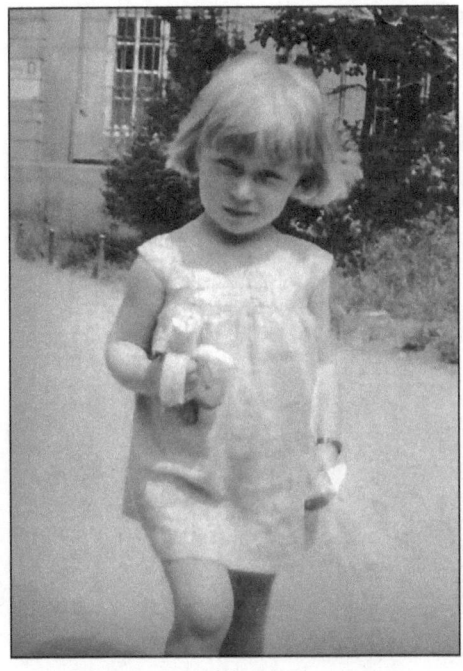

Lotte Glückauf (age 4 or 5)

Julius and Hanna Glückauf, possible marriage photo (1900–1902)

Hanna Glückauf with her oldest son, Erich

An advertisement for the Glückauf clothing store in Wittlich

Hanna Glückauf with her son, Paul

Julius Glückauf (Paul's father)

Irma and Paul at Zandvoort aan Zee (west of Amsterdam)

Irma with Dr. Erich Christensen.

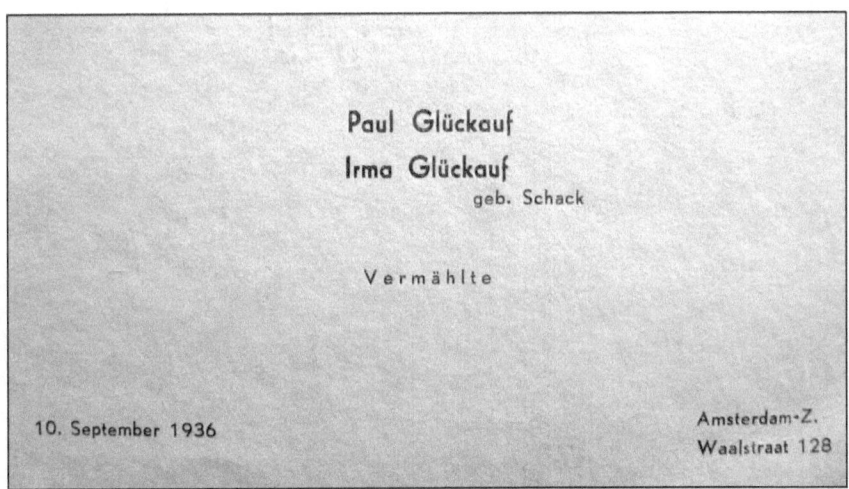

Marriage announcement of Paul Glückauf and Irma Schack

A ticket to America aboard the Belgian freighter Mercier

The Mercier

Aboard the Mercier

Aboard the Mercier

Irma with other refugee passengers

Irma with Captain Maurice Lambé

Part 2
Victims

CHAPTER 3

The Parents

Zwingenberg (1933-1939)

IN THE EARLY AUTUMN OF 1932, in the small Hessian village of Zwingenberg an der Bergstrasse, a local newspaper, the *Bergsträsser Bote*, ran three short notices about the Jewish high holy days:

October 1: Today our Israelite fellow citizens are celebrating their New Year's holiday; according to their reckoning, it is 5693.

October 8: Our Israelite fellow citizens will celebrate their highest holiday, the Day of Atonement, next Monday.

October 14: For the Israelites, the Christian month of October is the month of most holidays. Accordingly, on the 1st of October they celebrated their New Year (the first month of the Israelite year is called "Tischri"), from the 15th to the 22nd October they celebrate the "Feast of Bowers" (Sukkot). On the 23rd of October—with the day of the "Joy of the Laws" (Simchas Torah)—the circle of special holidays is completed.[16]

These notices, in their very ordinariness, reveal much about Jewish–Gentile relations in small-town Germany before the Nazi era. Although considered somewhat exotic, the Jews were "fellow citizens." Though their customs needed some explanation, their celebrations were accorded respect.

Things changed with astonishing rapidity after the Nazis took power early the following year, on January 30, 1933. Merely two months after (on March 31 and April 1, 1933), as part of a general action against Jewish-owned businesses throughout Germany, the SA (the storm troopers, commonly known as "brown shirts") and the SS (the black-uniformed elite paramilitary corps of the Nazi party) shut down all Jewish firms in nearby Bensheim and arrested their owners. On the following day, the *Bergsträsser Anzeigeblatt* described the action in language very different from that of its rival paper the previous fall:

> Yesterday morning in Bensheim, too, Jewish businesses were shut down, as an angry population confronts a danger to peace and order. The dreadful Jewish propaganda, the boycott of German goods, and the persecution of our Ger-

man countrymen abroad [responding to published reports of Nazi actions against the Jews] have brought the population to the highest pitch of agitation.

As with many subsequent actions against Jews throughout Germany, what was in fact a well-planned attack was portrayed as a spontaneous demonstration of popular will. Moreover, as was to become commonplace, the arrest of the Jews was said to be for their own protection. On March 11, the *Bergsträsser Bote* quoted Hitler's close associate and a Nazi party leader, Hermann Göring:

As the state of provocation against Jewish inhabitants is continually growing, there is nothing to do but place more and more Jews in protective custody. They are being brought to the district jail, where they will stay.[17]

Three weeks afterward, on April 6, a fire at the headquarters of the local Nazi party was attributed to arson set by local "Jews and Communists." A day of demonstrations by local Nazis culminated in the arrest, that same night, of several Zwingenberg Communists and Social Democrats, as well as one forty-two-year-old Jewish resident.[18]

Throughout Germany the number of Jewish businesses shrank rapidly. At the same time, Jews were progressively banned from communal activities. *Jews Not Wanted* signs went up in shops, cafes, sports arenas, and swimming pools. An advertisement in the

May 19, 1934, *Bergsträsser Bote* reads: "*Visit the swimming pool in Bensheim: A Jew-free family pool.*"[19] In August 1935, the Zwingenberg town council passed the following resolution, which laid out new prohibitions:

> *Jews are forbidden to immigrate to our community. The police will accept no more applications from Jews. Likewise Jews are forbidden from buying new houses or properties within the village. Jews may no longer use the common village scales or the cattle stalls. This is also true of Jewish agents and commissioners. At this time Jews and their agents are banned from leasing public lands and auctioning wood. Everything having to do with public property is denied them. Whoever of the German public has to do with Jews, either in business or privately, loses the right to the support of the community. Those who maintain contact with Jews will find no consideration regarding tax extensions and requests for other forms of public assistance.*[20]

Police investigations of attacks on Jews were pro-forma at best. Violators of the anti-Jewish statutes, on the other hand, were swiftly punished, usually with fines.[21] As a result of the increasing persecutions, most Zwingenberg Jews sold their property and possessions, usually at a fraction of their value, and left. While some moved to larger German cities, where they hoped to be less conspicuous, those fortunate enough to acquire visas emigrated abroad.

Among the few who remained in the village after 1935 were my grandparents, Moritz and Martha Schack, and their two youngest children, thirteen-year-old Suzanne (Suzy) and eleven-year-old Margot. The three older Schack children had all left and appeared to be safe. Lina sailed to New York in 1935. My mother, Irma, was living in Amsterdam with my father's family, and both were soon to join Lina in America. Leo had been living and working in Marseille.

For the most part, the letters from Zwingenberg saved by my mother (most from her mother, a few from her father, aunt, and sisters) convey little substantive information. Nor do they reveal much about the writer's state of mind. Most were dated from 1937 onward, written after my parents were in the United States, and consist largely of greetings to family members in New York and queries about their well-being, with only a few hints, carefully disguised, of their increasingly desperate situation. The reason is not hard to discern: the cryptic markings of the Nazi censors embellish the upper left corner of almost every page. After 1939, the letters become increasingly shorter (at the end they were primarily postcards) and focus entirely on inquiries about the health of the family in America, brief, non-committal references to my grandparents' health, and increasingly faint expressions of hope of eventual emigration, as their "number"—that is, their ranking on the list of applicants for admission to the United States—was impossibly high, and thus admission was unlikely. Of their poverty, isolation, and dread of the future there is little mention; their experiences must be pieced together from the scant evidence in their letters and in others' later accounts, most notably that of my Aunt Suzy, who, at the request of her children—in 1995, when she was seventy-two—recorded her experiences in an hour of oral testimony for Steven Spielberg's Survivors of the Shoah Foundation.[22]

At least as fateful as direct persecution, as we know now, during the mid- and late-1930s the Jews of Germany were slowly being starved. Forbidden both to work and to patronize non-Jewish merchants—and what Jewish merchants there were could no longer do business with non-Jewish suppliers—most found it increasingly difficult to buy enough food to satisfy their hunger.[23] In my grandparents' case, my grandmother's small tobacco shop (by then the family's main support) had gone bankrupt in 1934, as "people just did not dare buy anything anymore"; nor were they able to hire any household help. As Suzy testified many years later: "*Prior to* [the Nurnberg laws of 1934], *we had maids, cleaning, washing, ironing [but] this was all not possible anymore.... We no longer could keep any kind of non-Jewish help in the house, and of course no Jewish help was available.*"

According to my mother, their father was so desperate for money that he accepted the offer of the local pharmacist to buy the two Iron Crosses he had been awarded for exemplary military service during the First World War. Shamelessly, the pharmacist subsequently displayed them conspicuously in his store and claimed the honors as his own.

The August 1935 statute had deprived the family of the small garden plot at the village's edge that had previously provided potatoes, cabbages, carrots, and other vegetables that they stored for the winter and lived on for much of the year. Sympathetic neighbors (usually Communists) occasionally helped out, leaving a head of cabbage, a few potatoes, some butter, a few eggs, or a loaf of bread anonymously at the doorstep. Even when there was something to put on the table, my grandmother herself ate little, preferring to give what there was to her husband and daughters. As a result, she grew increasingly thin, and her once abundant red hair faded to dull beige. Nor could worn clothing be replaced, and clothes looked even shabbier hanging from emaciated frames.

The two girls suffered daily humiliations. Barred in 1934 from attending their old school, they were sent instead to a Jewish school in nearby Darmstadt. As Suzy testified:

> *We boarded the train every day and the fear we had going on that train was just horrendous because we faced beatings every day; we faced being thrown from the moving train every day by children also going to Darmstadt who weren't Jewish. Once we arrived in Darmstadt, we literally ran a gauntlet from the train station to the school; we were constantly menaced and beaten up. There were many times we wondered if we would get back home, what we would find when we got back home, because it was very tenuous.*

The events of what became known as *Kristallnacht* also had a serious impact. *Kristallnacht* (often called "The Night of Broken

Glass") loosely refers to the days immediately preceding and following November 9, 1938, their events ostensibly precipitated by the assassination in Paris of a young German diplomat, Ernst vom Rath, by a seventeen-year-old Jew. According to a report of one Zwingenberg resident: "*The campaign against the Jews that went through the whole of Germany also affected our community. On the 10th of November 1938, there occurred brutish and violent demolitions of all the Jewish residences in the town, and pieces of furniture were set afire. Schoolboys smashed in the doors and windows of Jewish homes.*"[24]

Fritz Kilthau documents these events in Zwingenberg, drawing on the detailed testimony delivered before the Darmstadt District Court in 1947 during the trial of those responsible for the local attacks. According to the witnesses, in the early morning hours of November 9th to 10th, four SS men, carrying hammers and axes, left their headquarters and headed towards the Schack family's house on Obergasse 3. Though the front door was locked, the first-floor tenant heard the commotion and opened it. The SS men stormed upstairs, burst through the entry of the apartment, and attacked the furnishings, smashing dishes, porcelain, and glass, and tossing the broken furniture into the street. My grandmother, in her nightgown, and the two girls emerged screaming from their bedrooms. According to one witness, "*Frau Schack and the children screamed so terribly, that I thought that they were being beaten.*" The SS men then slashed open all the down comforters and shook their contents into the street. The result, a witness testified, was that

"The whole street was full of goose feathers; it looked as if it were snowing."[25] They then set fire to the bedclothes.[26]

Having finished at Obergasse 3, the SS men went next door to Obergasse 5, where my grandmother's sister Clara and her husband, Jakob Wolf, lived above their small dry goods shop. They began by ransacking the shop at the front of the house and then attacked the upstairs apartment, again smashing all the glass and furnishings. Clara and Jakob, by then both slight and frail, were taken into custody and brought downstairs to watch the destruction of their property from the street. Several other residents stood by observing, and according to the testimony of a witness, some did more than just look, grabbing what merchandise they could and running off with it. A photo, taken the following day, shows about twenty people standing around the Marktplatz in small groups—adults as well as children. Most gaze towards the Wolf's ransacked house; a few men sit on the edge of the fountain chatting. The scene looks eerily calm, more like a casual social occasion than the aftermath of violence and terror.

The four SS-men then moved on to a third Jewish house on the Marktplatz, similarly destroying the furnishings and, in a dramatic finale, tossing the bathtub into the street through the window. The bathtub in the street was an event so memorable that it was still recalled by several surviving Zwingenberg citizens half a century later. Afterwards, the SS continued their work in the neighboring village of Alsbach. Later that night, an unidentified Zwingenberg Jew was forced to scrub the Marktplatz with a toothbrush.[27]

In her Shoah Foundation testimony, Suzy described her own memories of the events of November 9th and 10th. In the early hours of the morning of November 10th, at five A.M., the family heard the sound of breaking glass and rushed to the kitchen. Like their bedrooms, it was on the second floor of the house, which was built into the hillside leading up to the church. She described the break-in:

> [W]e heard breaking glass, and I ran to the kitchen where there was a window leading out to the foyer, and I saw a black arm coming through with an axe to smash this window in. Now as a child I dreamt that this would happen, when I was a little girl I dreamt that a black arm would come and smash this window in, and it really happened. My father was taken away, and I went to the Bürgermeisterei, to the Mayor, across the street to the city hall, and I said, "Why would you do this to me? My father was a veteran of the war and he was injured and why would you do this to me?"
>
> So he picked up his newspaper and said, "Look what they did to this young man," referring to vom Rath, who was assassinated in Paris. "That's why they are doing this to you because this beautiful young man was killed by your kind."
>
> I said, "We have nothing to do with it." I was only fourteen and a half, going on fifteen, and he only had ex-

cuses for what was done to us; he had absolutely no compassion. I went back home; my mother was trying to pick up the pieces of glass. They had smashed our office looking for letters from my brother; they couldn't find any of course because we disposed of them as soon as we got them.

Notwithstanding the morning's events, Margot insisted on going to school that day, although Suzy stayed home to help their mother clean up the mess.

"When [Margot] got to Darmstadt she saw everything was burning: the school was burning, the synagogue was burning, everything was on fire. But she made it home again by train, I don't know any more how she made it, I am wondering to this day how did she come out of town?"

The next day, November 10th, was their mother's birthday. It was then that they learned that their father was in the next town, about to be sent to the concentration camp, Buchenwald. Their mother ran all the way there and saw him on a truck, about to be taken away. Later in her testimony, Suzy said that, notwithstanding the sixty years that had gone by, she often still thought of the events of *Kristallnacht*.

This was not Moritz Schack's first arrest. There exist no letters to confirm the dates, but sometime during the years 1933–1935 he had spent time in a concentration camp, most likely Dachau. He returned from the camp, weak, sick, and with his right arm broken. On his return, someone photographed the family: my grandparents and their four daughters (Leo was by then settled in France). It was probably the last time that my mother and Lina, who was soon to embark for America, visited home. My grandfather, his arm in a sling and his head shaved like a prison inmate, looks like a haunted man.

According to Kilthau, however, the *Kristallnacht* deportation did not occur until two days afterward, on November 12th. Nor was Moritz Schack the only deportee: in the aftermath of *Kristallnacht*, many Jews throughout Germany were sent to prison or concentration camps. In addition, my grandfather was relatively fortunate to be released on December 2nd, less than three weeks later, a beneficiary of a regulation that Jewish World War veterans with military distinction were to be freed as soon as they showed evidence of that distinction. His brother-in-law, Jakob Wolf, was not as lucky. Arrested on November 15th, he was sent to Dachau and held until December 21st. A postcard to the family in New York from his wife Clara, dated November 30, cautiously alludes to the two men's absence: "*We are glad to hear from Irma that you are all well. I can say the same of us, likewise of both brothers-in-law, whom we expect back from their trip in the next few days.*"

A second incident, told me by my Aunt Margot, is also briefly mentioned in Suzy's Shoah Foundation testimony. A few days before *Kristallnacht*, their mother had sold some items of furniture to a neighbor, among them a sofa and a small cabinet. Such a commercial transaction between Jew and Christian was, of course, illegal. Her eyes filling with tears, Suzy described what followed. The

SS men banged on the door, demanding entry. Then "they dragged my mother out of the house and burned the sofa in front of her on the marketplace. My mother had to pick up the burning wood, and I wanted to help her, and they wouldn't let me."

The episode is further amplified in Kilthau's *Mitten unter Uns*, based on interviews with surviving eyewitnesses more than half a century later:

> *Someone informed the head of a local committee that went by the name of "Action against the Jews," who demanded that the purchaser return the goods at once. This the "offender' promptly did, wheeling the items back in the same handcart in which he had picked them up. After this occurred, the furniture was burned on the Marktplatz by the SS men. According to an unnamed witness: "The Jewesses Schack and Wolf, who had been held back by* [name omitted], *after this action were forced to sweep the Marktplatz clean* [i.e., sweep up all the ashes] *while under* [SS] *observation.*

There is still more to the story. According to Kilthau, the would-be purchaser, still alive in the 1990s, recalled the following:

> *A few days afterward, I was stopped by the Jewess Schack, who wanted to give me back the 18 Reichsmark that I had paid for the furniture.... Some days later, Frau Schack again came to my house and offered me the money*

again. She looked as if she were being followed. . .and I went with her all along Annastrasse to the cemetery, from where she continued alone to her house.[28]

No one ever learned whether the money was returned; as far as is known the attempted sale brought no money. I wonder whether the purchaser really played the noble role he describes in his account offered sixty years later.

In 1947, the Darmstadt district court sentenced three of the four SS men implicated in the Zwingenberg *Kristallnacht* destruction to prison: the leader got two years, the others between four and eight months. The fourth had died in the war. All were later pardoned.

While *Kristallnacht* saw the destruction and burning of synagogues all over Germany (the name derives from the broken glass of the synagogue windows), the synagogue in Zwingenberg on Wiesenstrasse 5, although damaged and desecrated, remained relatively intact, its ritual objects having previously been sent to Frankfurt for safekeeping. A bizarre set of circumstances contributed to its survival. There was a small apartment in the synagogue, formerly used by the Hebrew teacher but at that time occupied by a certain Frau Anthes, who was serving as the *"shabbos goy"* (the non-Jew hired to do all necessary physical work on the Sabbath, when Jews were prohibited from working). On the previous day, November 8th, her severely depressed son had shot himself to death, and his body was laid out in the apartment. On the night of November 9th, as news of the destruction elsewhere became known, her neighbors confronted the authorities, demanding that the building not be attacked. Although some vehement words passed on both sides, the townspeople were eventually given assurances that the synagogue would remain untouched. Soon afterwards, however, as recollected by a witness who was six years old at the time, trouble began:

> *Nighttime noise was not unusual at that time in Zwingenberg. That night, however, there was heard not only the clanging of machines but also the confused voices of many agitated people. It seemed very threatening to me, and I became anxious.*

A mob of local SA men converged on the synagogue, tearing the Star of David from its post in front of the building and smashing the windows over the main entrance. According to witnesses, one young man was explicitly ordered by his superiors to destroy the two main windows, one with the Ten Commandments, the other with an engraving in golden Hebrew letters of the Talmudic exhortation *"Know before whom you are standing."*[29]

The following morning the authorities officially declared my grandfather Moritz Schack *"the last Jew in Zwingenberg"* and forced him to sell the synagogue to a private citizen for 6,000 RM.[30] The preliminary documents of sale taken care of, my grandfather entered the building. When he failed to return, the officials overseeing the transaction stormed in after him and found him hanging from a pipe in the bathroom.[31] Quickly cutting him down (the privilege of ending lives prematurely evidently reserved for the authorities alone), they then placed him under arrest. On December 15th, following an inspection of the synagogue property, Moritz Schack was compelled, as "board members" of the "Israelite Congregation," to be present at a "Notary Lamb's" office in Bensheim for signing of the official sale documents. There he was alsoo forced to pay all transaction costs, even though those were customarily paid by the purchaser, not the seller.[32]

In addition (an example of the many absurdities imbuing Nazi regulations), a question had arisen as to the legitimacy of the transaction, as the sellers were of course Jews, and any Jewish commercial dealings with non-Jews violated the first statute of the Nurnberg Laws. The issue was resolved by the authorities asserting that, because the synagogue had already been stripped of its interior furnishings and only the walls remained (a manifest untruth, as post-war testimony was to reveal), the transaction could go forward as planned. However, when the money was finally paid six months later, on June 10, 1939, it was given not to *"the hands of Moritz Schack or to his delegate,"* as had been stated in the contract, but placed into an escrow account *"which can be withdrawn only with the approval of the national government."*

Except for a couple of oblique references to their husbands' otherwise unexplained absences, these events were not mentioned in either my grandmother's or her sister's correspondence. However, the obviously deteriorating situation in Germany created new urgency in the rest of the family that Suzy and Margot, who, as minor children, were still eligible to emigrate, somehow escape from Germany. In brief notes written more than a year earlier to my parents in Amsterdam, who were then on the verge of leaving for New York themselves, the two girls had already expressed the hope of soon seeing them and other family members in America. Two weeks before *Kristallnacht*, the girls again expressed hope of joining their sisters, both now in New York, with Suzy outlining her hope for a new future: "I would like to learn to be a hairdresser. What do you think? Are they needed there?" Suzy's situation was especially critical, as in less than three months, when she was to turn fifteen, she would no longer be eligible for the more liberal emigration permit available to children. Their mother's accompanying letter, apparently uncensored (as it bears no mark), reveals her concerns:

> *My dearest children! Lina writes us that she is working on getting papers for Suzy. Can she get permission to work at all before the age of 16? I would not want her to become a burden to you. As Suzy tells you, she would like to learn to style hair, and I believe that she has the skills for it (as well as for sewing). Please let us know what you think. Unfortunately, Margot has a high number, as you know. However, maybe we can work around that. Think about it.*

That "high number," of course, made all too slim the likelihood of Margot's gaining entry to the United States.

Although the fate of the children was a huge concern, there were other pressing reasons for Martha to be anxious. One was the recent death of her brother Hermann in Saarbrücken. In addition, an unusually explicit caution at her letter's end hinted at their awareness of the constant surveillance maintained over her family: "*On Friday an official came to Clara and asked what relatives we have in St. Avold, because Aunt Gaby had enclosed a 20-mark bill in a letter—and this, of course, is not permitted. Therefore, please be warned.*" St. Avold, a small town in the French province of Lorraine, was home to Clara's in-laws.

After *Kristallnacht*, Martha's letters became even more circumspect. A birthday postcard to Irma, dated November 17, 1938, only hints at the current disaster—Moritz's arrest and deportation five days earlier—and no longer refers to the possibility of emigration at all: "*I hope that you are all happy; we are too. . . . Papa is momentarily not here, but he also sends greetings and congratulations.*"

Yet in the aftermath of *Kristallnacht*, what was to be done about the two girls became even more critical. Entry to the United States seemed unlikely to be granted at any time soon. Three weeks after *Kristallnacht*, thirteen-year-old Margot refers briefly and vaguely to a possible solution: "*Suzy and I may soon travel to Paul's parents.*" The reference to travel seems almost casual, and the potential destination (Amsterdam) is unnamed. A fruitless invitation to join them in Holland, where Jewish refugees were, for the most part, no longer being granted entry, had indeed come from Paul's parents, who were making what efforts they could to aid Irma's family.

My grandparents' desperation is revealed only after the fact, when, in an unusually long letter from early February 1939, they described the girls' departure from Germany and safe arrival in France. Heeding the pleas of their relatives in France, the two girls left Germany on children's passports on February 1, 1939, just one day before Suzy's fifteenth birthday when she would have become ineligible for emigration. The evident relief expressed in the letter is clearly tempered by their parents' grief at what they feared might be a permanent separation. Martha wrote first:

> *This afternoon your letter to Suzy arrived, and all of us were very happy as always to see that you are all well. . . . I can report the same from us. Small troubles are to be expected, and one can only be glad when it's nothing worse. I am very happy that everything worked out so nicely for the two children, even though it was very hard for me to send them away so young. Nevertheless, one has to thank God. Margot wrote that they have already written to you, and she is going to write you a big 'megille,' because she likes writing, compared to Suzy who writes as little as she can get away with. Moritz accompanied the children to Saarbrücken. Everything had to go fast. Saturday we received the letter from Gaby, telling us that children under the age of fifteen will be permitted to enter France. We immediately requested the emigration. Monday we again wrote a letter to St. Avold. On Tuesday, Moritz went to the consulate, and Wednesday*

morning at half past six they were gone. Now they have already written us twice, seemingly very happy. They will stay in St. Avold only for a couple of weeks, then continue to Leo [in Marseille]. We are waiting for news from him. I guess he told you about his marriage on January 15th.

And in a small hint of what was soon to be their future, Martha mentioned a visit to their old friends, the Schoenfelds, in Frankfurt. "*They are very nice people. . . .*" At the end of his own brief account of the girls' departure, Moritz ends desolately: "*We are now the ones left behind.*"

Suzy, in her testimony for the Shoah Foundation many years later, tearfully described their parting in greater detail:

My father escorted us to Forbach, which was on the border, and I remember that when we tried to say goodbye the Nazis pulled him back, calling him "Saujud," "Jewish pig." My father had a paralyzed arm . . . and when we tried to say goodbye to hug him they wouldn't let us. After that we were physically searched to see if we had any diamonds or gold hidden anywhere to take out of the country. My mother's brother [Hermann] had meantime passed away, and there were my aunt [Gaby] and the three children. . . . They came to pick us up in Forbach and took us to St. Avold where we stayed for about ten days until there was enough money—my brother sent the money—to send us to

Marseille. We traveled up to Lyon, and in Lyon my brother's then friend, now brother-in-law, picked us up and escorted us back to Marseille so we didn't have to travel alone to Marseille. We didn't speak French then yet, so this man picked us up. That was in mid-February.

Although Lina had periodically been sending money to her parents from New York via cable, after the girls' departure Martha explicitly requested that she send no more: *"Dear Lina, You ask in today's letter if we received the money you sent us per telegram. On December 28 the Dresdner Bank sent us RM 40, and I have already written you that. . . . However, I ask you not to send anything anymore, because now we are alone and the expenses are not that high."* An oblique and unexplained reference (*"Besides, we have to sell the furniture, as we can't take it with us"*) is the first indication that they, too, will soon be leaving the village where Martha's family had resided for hundreds of years.

Frankfurt am Main

(1939–1941)

MARTHA'S CASUAL REFERENCE to selling the furniture seemed incidental; it was not. What the rest of the world did not know was that rural and small town Jews throughout Germany were being forcibly relocated to large urban ghettos. For those remaining in the towns and villages of the Bergstrasse, that meant the city of Frankfurt am Main, some fifty kilometers to the north. Once the girls were gone, Martha's references to visits to Frankfurt became more frequent.

The earliest hints came from her sister, Clara. With an impossibly high "number" (*"for our sins. . .59,900"* Clara wrote to Lina in New York), the likelihood of emigration for Clara and her husband, Jakob, was virtually nil, although they continued to hope for "*easements*" on immigration from "*the young, remote islands (Virgin) or South America.*" In a postcard to her sister Betty (Bessie) in New York dated just a few days after *Kristallnacht*, on the day that was to see her husband's arrest and imprisonment in Dachau, Clara alluded to separate—ostensibly casual—visits to Frankfurt by both Jakob and Martha "*to see how things are in Frankfurt,*" adding, "*They seem to be pleased with the life there.*"

Preparations for the move to Frankfurt had begun even before Suzy and Margot's departure. With the girls gone, events moved quickly. Early in 1939, Moritz and Martha were forced to sell their house—owned by Martha's family for more than three hundred years—to the family of Jehovah's Witnesses living in the rental apartment on the ground floor. In an undated letter to New York following the sale, Martha described the current situation: "*The house is sold, and the legal work was completed Thursday eight days ago. I think I have told you that the Schüchs, Gärtners and Schneigers. . .are the buyers.*" Although evidently ignorant of the details, she seemed aware that some legal involvement was required of the family abroad, adding, "*Now I ask you kindly to inform us if and what we should send you. Please inform yourself about the regulations; the house should be paid for on March 15 or April 1."*

There is an interesting postscript to the sale of the house, the money for which seems never to have been paid in full, if at all. Several years after the war's end, in November 1949, their son Leo, now living in Mexico City, received a surprising, ostensibly friendly letter from one of the purchasers, their former neighbor Leo Schuch. After sending greetings *"to you and your dear sisters"* and expressing the hope that nostalgia for *"the beautiful Bergstrasse"* not erase *"the memory of all your suffering in this country,"* Schuch noted the wartime suffering of his own family—his son having died in battle and son-in-law in Dachau. The motivation behind the letter became clearer as it progressed. Avoiding all mention of the forced nature of the sale, Schuch wrote: *Dear Leo! As you know, according to the wish of your parents, we bought the house on the Obergasse. Your parents, in their time, offered us the house, as they knew that [as Jehovah's Witnesses] we were decided opponents of the Nazis...."*

Only then, however, did his real purpose become evident. The occupation government was permitting former Jewish owners of such properties to reclaim them. For the Schuchs to retain ownership of the house, it would be necessary for Leo and his sisters to make a legal declaration that they had no intention of claiming the property and send a notarized statement to that effect. *"I would be very thankful to you, dear Leo, if you would sign such a one.... I would not want to ask to take possession from you and your sisters, if I did not know that your unfortunately deceased parents would give that certificate. If you have any expenses for this, I would compensate them. For your pains I give you my most heartfelt thanks."*

What the Schuchs feared, of course, was losing the house. However, as no one in the Schack family had any interest in reclaiming the property, the Schuchs were able to retain possession and were still living there when I first visited in 1962.

Ever since Suzy and Margot's arrival in France, Leo had been trying to gain French entry papers for his parents so that they too could settle in Marseille, which still seemed a safe refuge. In the late spring of 1939, he had traveled once more to Paris to make inquiries on their behalf. With the outbreak of war in September 1939, however, his ability to do anything for his parents came to an abrupt end, as he—along with all other native Germans, whether Jewish or not, whether pro- or anti-Nazi—was almost immediately interned by the French as an enemy alien. Now his chief concern became his own survival and that of his wife (who was expecting their first child) and his two young sisters in Marseille.

Although my grandparents' great hope had been to join their children in France, like others among their neighbors and relatives throughout the Bergstrasse their immediate destination would be Frankfurt. Clara and Jakob had already moved there and, as Martha wrote (whether she was trying to relieve her children's anxiety or her own), *"They like it very much, as Clara said today."* And although my grandparents continued to hope that the move would be temporary, and that at least one of their children would—despite all odds—succeed in getting the requisite papers for their emigration, that never came to pass.

One early casualty of the forced relocation seems to have been Moritz's nonagenarian father, Nathan Schack, who—to escape the virulent anti-Semitism of his home village—had since the previous year been living with his daughter and son-in-law in the resort village of Vilbel, a few miles north of Frankfurt.[33]

Anti-Jewish violence in his home village of Georgenhausen had begun shortly after the Nazis came to power. A 1933 "action" described by Georg Allman, a non-Jewish member of the Socialist Workers' Youth, illustrates the cruelties visited upon the local Jews by their fellow residents from the start:

It was Friday evening, the Jews were in the synagogue and were now praying their sabbath. The SS man Hentschel said to me, "Go in and get rid of all the stinking Jews, and they'll all do the washing up under your command. The women and children can go home!" Again I refused to do that, and Hentschel came up against the front door and pushed me in. Here everyone was crying because they had heard what was going on outside, and the men came up to me, because I knew them all very well. I told them what was going to happen, the women and children were crying, and the men were going with me, do not ask what was going on, because everyone wanted to be the biggest Jew-haters. . . . Like the Jews, I held a bucket in my hand, and took the small funereal procession of twelve Jews, mostly older men, to the top of the Gasthaus 'Zur Spritze over to the baron garden on the outskirts to Gross-Bieberau. The whole time we were accompanied by a hysterically hooting crowd. Everybody got a bucket of water and had to wash up the flat roof. The popular entertainment was obviously very large, because some were already afraid to climb the ladder. But the SS helped them up. Since it was getting dark, headlights assisted the onlookers so the fun didn't have to end. The Jewish men all wore black suits and soon looked for mercy. . . . Their hats were impaled with rubber truncheons and thrown among the crowd. The supervising SS gangsters always kicked the Jews on the fingers or against their feet to make them slip, and the fun became ever cruder. I can just say that an SS man hit the Jew Blum, a bald man, with his rubber truncheon on his head, causing the blood to spurt. I will never forget the screams of this man, and for a moment it became quite quiet amongst the people.[34]

News of their grandfather's death in early February came to the children in a postcard from their mother:

We must send you a sad message. A while ago a telegram came that our dear grandfather has died. He was not feeling well for some days, and I hope he did not suffer much. But this is probably the best thing that could happen. Friday would have been his ninety-fifth birthday, and I wanted to go there next Sunday. Father intended to drive over tomorrow, since they wanted to move to Frankfurt the following day. Now he and I will drive over this evening for the funeral. It goes in a hurry.

Preparations for their own move to Frankfurt continued, with the plan (as Moritz noted in one of his postscripts) "*to rent a room in Frankfurt for June 1st.*" They were still in Zwingenberg in early April when they received news of the death, in Amsterdam, of Paul's father from complications of diabetes and sent "*deepest condolences*" to Paul and Irma. Martha, who remained religious to the end of her life, tried to console them: "*[Y]ou have to comfort yourselves in the thought that God wanted it this way and did it to ease the suffering of the beloved dead. For your dear mother it is certainly a comfort that Werner* [her youngest son] *is with her and that he helps her in her pain.*" Recalling Julius Glückauf's high spirits and kindnesses during her visit to Amsterdam two years earlier, when she had met her son-in-law and his family for the first and only time, she lamented: "*One would never guess that two years ago your dear father was so lively and amusing. I remember him accompanying me to the train, and even buying me the ticket for the trip.*" Only at the end did she mention that she and Moritz had visited Frankfurt "*and we liked it.*" About their life in Zwingenberg, there is no word.

Thirteen-year-old Margot, however, revealed more of her parents' daily reality. Writing to her sisters the following month from

Marseille, she relayed what she knew, having obviously been in closer touch with them.

> *Our parents wrote this week. They are moving to Frankfurt. They have gotten a room at Appels, exactly like Uncle and Aunt. Furniture that was not destroyed during the "Aktion"* [that is, during the Kristallnacht marauding] *was partially sold, since they are unable to take any furniture with them. Papa wrote they have not yet received the money from the house, and this is bad for them. I am glad they will live in Frankfurt, because there they can have a little rest. I wrote Mama and told her she should not drive herself so meshugge with cleaning the house. Our parents are quite alone, and no one dares help them. That is very sad. Papa no longer goes out on the street at all, because Neubauer (Kissel) harasses him whenever he can.*

The identity of my grandfather's persecutor was a mystery to be solved, and Fritz Kilthau, who had earlier identified the man as the Mayor, Georg *Adam* Kissel, was kind enough to do further research at my request. In an email to me, he described his findings:

> *Today I phoned several people and at the end I spoke to the granddaughter of Neubauer Kissel. She looked up some family documents and it seems in all probability that*

> *Neubauer was Georg Friedrich Kissel living in the same street as the former mayor. She told me that her grandfather was not the mayor. . . . [Regarding] the person of Georg Friedrich Kissel: He was a rich farmer. He was one of the five persons who destroyed Jewish houses in Zwingenberg during the Reichspogromnacht (i.e. Kristallnacht). After the war there was a trial in Darmstadt and Kissel was sentenced two years prison due to compulsion in four cases. Witnesses testified that Kissel demolished Jewish properties, which were then burned at the Zwingenberg marketplace. Comparing the sentence of Kissel with those of the other participants, Kissel was the leader of the actions against the Jews in Zwingenberg.*

By late June 1939 my grandparents were settled in a Frankfurt apartment at *Uhlandsstrasse 60*, a nondescript five-story apartment house—still standing on the corner of a busy street—where they would live until my grandmother's death in 1941 and my grandfather's arrest and deportation the following year.

From the start, Martha tried to put a positive spin on their new residence with its two tiny rooms. Shortly after their arrival, she described their current circumstances:

> *My dear children! On Thursday we will have been here fourteen days already, and we are very happy to have achieved the first phase. The move and the many prepara-*

tions were easier than I had expected, and I had never thought that I could so easily separate myself from the house and all. Here we have a very pretty two-room apartment on a pretty street. It even looks out on some greenery, and inside there are a couple of plants. . . . One of the rooms has a nice gas cooker, and we have water in the kitchen. . . . We were able to bring an armoire, a sofa, and (from Aunt Lina) a bed and a few chairs. I had written to you that I sold our bedroom furniture already some time ago. We could have brought along all kinds of other nice furniture, but it was too heavy and now remains in Aunt Lina's ground-floor apartment with all our other storage. All in all I am very happy that we have our move behind us. I still have to ship all kinds of stuff, but that will happen later. We often take walks in the evenings. Yesterday evening we were at the [river] Main and saw some paddle boats. Dear Irma, this was once your great pleasure.

Moritz's words seem almost as encouraging: "*We have a beautiful apartment and live with very nice people. I am very glad that we are away from Zwingenberg, and hopefully we will soon get some of our money.*" They enclosed a photograph of their old house "*as a memory.*"

Lack of money, however, was a serious problem, especially as the house payments did not come. In a mid-August letter, Martha reveals additional concerns:

It is not at all hot now, and even the evenings are pretty cold. . . . Today I was in the city with Tante Clara and we bought some things. We still have not received the money for our house, and we will not get it in time for when the mortgage must be registered. . . . Don't worry about us. When we have been short lately, he [unknown: possibly their nephew Theodore Gruen in New York or their son, Leo, in France] *has sent us what is needed. . . . In my previous letter, I wrote that we also have received an entry permit* [for France], *but we are not proceeding, because we cannot afford to buy our stuff. I have written to Leo to buy what we need whenever we get our money. . .but we still have not received any answer, and I will write him again.*

The picture she gives of their living conditions is brief but noncommittal: "*Here people are constantly moving in. . . . We live here with some very nice people on our floor. . . . In the past one would not have believed it possible to get along with so little room,*" although her letter ends with the acknowledgement that "*everywhere there is fear.*"

This was the last substantive letter of 1939. For the remainder of the year only a few postcards arrived from Frankfurt, generally offering brief congratulations and good wishes on birthdays, anniversaries, or Jewish holidays, reports of mail sent or received (or, too often, not received, a persistent cause of worry), joy over Irma's pregnancy with what would be their first grandchild, and vague assurances not to worry. The following, addressed to both daughters in New York, is characteristic both for the parents' obvious concern for their children's well-being and in its silence about their own situation:

> *My dear children! We were very happy when on Saturday morning your letter, dear Glückaufs* [i.e., Irma and Paul], *from the 19th arrived, and especially again in the afternoon when your letter, dear Lina, from September 27th arrived, especially to see from both letters that you and all in our beloved family feel fine. And I can tell you also that we are healthy. Do not worry about us. Today my writing is directed especially to you my dear Irma. For your 27th birthday* [on November 26] *I want to send you my warmest congratulations. Stay healthy and may the dear God fulfill all your wishes.*

Their father added a few words (some illegible): "*Dear Irma and Paul! We have received your letters and, as always, we were very happy to hear that you too are happy...thank God.... For your birthday dear Irma I congratulate you very much and I hope ...health....*" Similar spare greetings constitute the sum and substance of their communication throughout the year.

The following year, 1940, brought few letters. The earliest was a response to the welcome telegram announcing my birth on January 18th, their first grandchild. The congratulatory reply from the new grandparents was addressed to Paul alone, presumably because

Irma was still in the hospital, the normal hospital stay for new mothers then being ten days.

Moritz wrote with uncharacteristic emotion and effusiveness:

> *My dear children! You can surely imagine how great was our happiness when we received your telegram this morning.... How I would love to be with you now, but I am sure that you are well taken care of. Last night I almost couldn't sleep and I was thinking of you and Irma again and in my dream I saw a little child. So I think there really is some connection of thoughts. I almost forgot the important thing because of the excitement: my warmest congratulations on the arrival of your little daughter to Irma. May you and we always get great joy from her.*

Martha's comments, while they also express her joy at the birth, seem somewhat more subdued, perhaps because of her growing despondency and ill health:

> *Dear Paul, You must be very proud to be a father. But I am proud as well in my own dignity. What is the little princess' name in German? Also to you my dear Irma and to the entire family I send congratulations.... I will transmit the happy news to the children* [in Marseille] *tomorrow evening. So all my warmest greetings and kisses from your loving mother and grandmother.*

"*The little princess*" was me, named Joan (an Americanization of the German "Johanna"), in part after my father's mother, in part (I am sure) because the name was, in the late 1930s, very popular and borne by several Hollywood stars.[35]

Exactly one week later, Martha wrote again, this time merely a series of brief, disconnected comments and questions:

> *My dear children! I hope you received the letter we sent you last week after the reception of your telegram. I am thinking so much, especially about you my dear Irma, and I hope you are feeling better every day and that the family is doing well too. We have had no mail from you for a long while now and hope to receive a report very soon. Hopefully you, young mother, did not have to wait as long. We would have loved to congratulate you by telegram; however this is impossible. I wrote to your mother, dear Paul. Of course the children are very happy about the news.*"

In early March there arrived the unexpected, if very welcome, news from their daughter Lina that fifteen-year-old Margot might soon be leaving Marseille for New York. Simultaneously anxious and relieved, Martha responded quickly:

> *I was surprised to read from your letter, dear Lina, that you are expecting Margot very soon. We have known nothing about this the entire time. Yesterday we finally received a letter*

from the children after a long while. Thank God everything is fine. Erna [Leo's wife] wrote to me and Margot too writes happily, that she is ready; Suzy would also be ready when Margot leaves, but as you, dear Lina, write, you think that Suzy will be able to follow in the fall. You tell us you also sent clothes to M[argot]. I hope they will fit. I can do nothing from here.... She did not write when she is leaving. We hope she will have a reasonably good trip. As I said, the only thing I can do from here is to pray for her.... Please write soon.

Margot's travels, however, did not occur as soon as everyone had anticipated. Nor was there any progress towards the parents' escape. In an end-of-the-year birthday letter to Lina, whose birthday fell on December 25th, Martha seems to have given up on the possibility of escaping to Paul's parents in Amsterdam, and it seems clear that Lina—always seeking ways to circumvent the barriers impeding her family's emigration—was having no luck in arranging affidavits for either Leo and his family or her parents. It seems, too, that most mail, in either direction, was no longer getting through. Only two additional postcards arrived from Germany in 1940—one in April, one in May—and in both Martha laments the dearth of mail that *"makes us always worried."*

Contact between the children and their parents was becoming more and more fragmentary. The following year, 1941, brought only a few brief letters and postcards. In February Martha told of news from France: *"Today we got mail from aunt Gaby, Leo, and Erna...."*

Leo writes that everyone is doing fine, so I assume Suzy and Margot are included." She asks Lina, evidently unemployed at the time, to send no more money, and, in an afterword, writes their own "number," 48,000, and concludes by advising her *"not to worry about anything."* A damaged postcard dated May 9 and addressed to Bessie and Sigmund [return address with the now mandatory Jewish identifier Moritz *Israel* Schack], includes Martha's thanks for a letter and photographs received, as well as welcome word of Margot: *"Yesterday we received...news...in Lisbon."* On the reverse side, in faint, almost illegible script, Moritz adds that that they had heard from Margot before she left on her *"great journey,"* and that they hope for her *"good arrival."* Two weeks later, a letter from Martha to Lina gave thanks for providing the affidavit and money for Margot's trip, and offered further news about Margot, who *"left Friday May 16th on a freighter, because all other seats were taken. She is traveling via Cuba and that will take longer, but she is looking forward to seeing a lot."* Expressing her gratitude that *"Erna and Leo are taking such good care of Suzy"* who—at seventeen—was still with them in Marseille, the letter ends cryptically, with the unfinished sentence, *"My finger doesn't want to...."* A subsequent letter from Clara noted that Theo Gruen had contributed to the cost of the voyage.

And so ends all communication from my grandmother, Martha Schack. The remaining correspondence from my grandfather consists of just three letters. The first, written in May or June, says only, *"Your dear mother is not entirely well, but she should soon be better again."* However, a month later, on July 28th, Moritz—

ending his long silence on the subject—at last revealed that Martha had been seriously ill for some time.

> *My dear children and everyone! We were all made very happy by your letters and pictures, especially that you are doing well and are healthy. Yesterday there arrived a letter from dear Lina and Margot, with pictures from July 10, 1941, which gave us great joy, and dear Mama was very happy to read Margot's description of the beautiful passage. I just want to tell you how it is with us. In May 1940, I permitted your dear Mother to be operated on; she was in the second-class section of the hospital, as you can imagine what that all cost. Everything went well until November 5, 1940. On that day, I called the doctor again, and so it is I consulted several doctors and had your dear mother cared for, had her treated with radiation, did everything that the doctors said I should do, let her be X-rayed, but all was in vain and she did not improve. She developed a high fever and on Monday April 21 I had her hospitalized; she is still there, and nothing has improved. As it has now been fourteen weeks, you can also understand how all our money is gone. . . . As for our emigration, you can continue to proceed as you were doing. . . ."*

Here the letter ends; the bottom of the page is missing.

Martha died in the hospital, the *Krankenhaus der Jüdischen Kultusvereinigung* on August 9, 1941. According to what I was told by my mother and aunts, although the ultimate cause of her death was tuberculosis, the immediate cause was starvation, both unavoidable (there was little food) and self-induced (at some point she had stopped eating altogether). The hospital where she spent her final days had been owned by the Frankfurt Jewish community until 1939, when it was sold to the Reich as part of the compulsory Aryanization process. In the course of the next three years, it became a deposit zone for the sick, the aged, the mentally ill, and orphaned children from many other homes and hospitals in the region until it was evacuated in 1942 when most patients and nurses (the latter largely Jewish holdovers from the original hospital) were deported to Theresienstadt and the death camps.

News of Martha's death arrived from her sister Clara who, in a series of highly emotional letters, described her sister's last days. The first was written the day after Martha's death:

> *My dears! It is so hard for me to write, yet it must be done. We wanted to spare you this news about your dear mother and not be cruel, so I wrote you about improvement and for a long time did not write at all, so as not to make you uneasy. My dear sister* [Bessie], *how my thoughts are with you and once again you must be strong and help the dear children bear their great pain. I know that with you and dear Sigmund they have a home and if God wants it, dear Suzy will soon be with you. Then things will all come together, and dear God will not leave you. How confidently*

we saw our dear Martha going into the hospital, but the X-rays showed only that the illness is incurable. Thank God your mother never knew how heavy her suffering was. The last ten days I was able to be with her all day long, and we spent difficult but also beautiful hours together. The latter particularly occurred when your letters came, and we looked at the photos. Dear Bettchen, dear children, I need not write to you how I feel.... Later I will write you in greater detail, I am unable to do any more now, please all be brave.

Later I will also write dear Leo and Suzy, who have already been prepared.... Your dear father was always there, thank God he is calm, what can he do; it is hard for him, but there are such good people in the apartment, they do everything for him and he eats with Tante Lina [presumably his older sister Karoline Schönfeldt]. *Please let all relatives and friends know. Most heartfelt greetings and kisses, your dear Clara.*[36]

Three weeks later, on the last day of August, Clara wrote a detailed account of Martha's final days in the hospital, where she seems to have been kindly treated:

It was very difficult for me to go to our dear Martha, though, God be thanked, I managed to get there daily the last week. The treating physician permitted it; he saw that I did not excite her. As I wanted only to report good news to her, I would practice making a pleasant face, though it was very difficult. Dear Martha was exactly as undemanding in her illness as she always was, and very popular with all the physicians and caregivers. I had spoken with the night nurse (the department was not large) to spend all her free time with her, and she said to me directly that she does it gladly, because she knows her as a good patient from previous times. I would gladly have stayed the last night, but that could not be, also she got an injection and mostly slept. I do not think I imagine it if I say she calmed down when I was there. If I asked, 'what should I bring you tomorrow,' she answered, 'only yourself.' I was allowed to be there already around 9.30 and to stay until evenings. If I was there during dinner in those last days, the sisters [nurses] even brought me meals. . . . Only on the last morning was I unable to go up any longer, [although] I was there Friday evening until 8:30; dear Martha however slept the entire day. I always thought she resembled our dear mother herself. Yet I ordered an extra night nurse, who had been her earlier day nurse, as she was so fond of her. She said: go home now and calm yourself, if I am there everything will be done. That was only a small amount. On the morning of the Sabbath our beloved one died, and when Moritz came at his usual time she had calmly gone to sleep.

There is little additional correspondence from Frankfurt. In late September, Clara again wrote to express condolences:

> *It is a very hard fate that you all have suffered, but on the other hand, for your good and brave mother, death was really a release. It may bring you some comfort if I assure you again that everything was done that could be done by human hands. She did not remain uncared for and fell asleep gently and without any awareness. We must now think that dear God willed the best for her.*

Three months later, in what was to be her final letter, Clara was still focused on Martha's death: *"The leaves are gone from your dear mother's grave. I would gladly have brought her flowers, but that would not make sense."* Birthday wishes to Irma seem an afterthought: *"Dear good Irma, you have a birthday. All good things imaginable just as your good mother would have wished, and a birthday kiss. Aunt Clara."*

Moritz's final letter, now torn and with several parts missing, was written earlier that same month. In it, he still seems hopeful of a rescue that will reunite him with his children in America. I have pieced it together as well as I can:

> *We are still all healthy, which is the main thing. Your letter, received this week dear Lina and Margot, tells me that my emigration is accelerating, for which I thank you very much, but how long will it take until we are with you? Yesterday we had a telegram from Betty, for which I also give thanks and hopefully it will come to pass. Today I got*

back a letter, dated June 28, that I had mailed to Irma, marked that Paul Glückauf could not be located. I will include it here, as you can see.

As your mother can no longer write, I have written several letters and hope you have received them, especially the letter with the pictures of your mother. I have sent it registered mail to assure myself that it has arrived. Now your dear mother has been dead for thirteen weeks, which is good for her as she is spared a lot, she is better off than I am, because I stand alone at this time, and I would prefer to be with her, but that I have the hope of coming to you. If only it would soon come true, I think that I could then put my life in order. But I am so well assisted by my housemate Sophie Kahn and Fräulein Nanny Kahn. As I have already written to you, Fräulein Sophie Kahn was your blessed mother's closest friend.

His last words, the letter's final sentence, were: "*No news from Leo and Suzy.*"

Additional correspondence from Frankfurt never arrived. Yet notification must have been received by someone of an unexpected addendum to the life of Moritz Schack. A May 1943 letter from Leo from Mexico City makes mention of their father's unexpected remarriage but shows no other knowledge of his fate:

From Europe we haven't heard any news for a long time, which concerns us; of course one can only get airmail.

That dear Papa has married again, was a surprise to me, but I will not say anything about it, it is perhaps worst for himself. Simply having to attack the problem of living is terrible, besides everything else, and even the best morale disappears.

All that appears in the records about Moritz's second wife is that she was born Selma Strauss in the village of Storndorf in northern Hessen, that she was six years his junior, and that they were married in Frankfurt on May 28, 1942.[37]

THE TRUTH WAS THAT ON TUESDAY, September 16, 1942, just four months after the marriage, a train bearing 1,378 passengers (Transport XII/3) departed from a station near Frankfurt's eastern harbor, headed for the Theresienstadt concentration camp in Czechoslovakia. Most of the passengers were older people, who, two days earlier, had been gathered at Frankfurt's Gestapo detention center, although there were also forty-two children, ranging in age from twelve months to fourteen years. Among the assembled officials was one of the heads of the local Gestapo, Ernst Holland, who was observed to be especially brutal in his treatment of the prisoners.

The train left the ghetto the following day. A survivor described the journey:

Standing or squatting on trucks on our bundles, we were transported to an open railway track near the eastern harbor. During the whole trip we were insulted and ridiculed by a cheering crowd. . . . Long, long we stood, until at last a train came, which received us: 1,300 people—old and young and many very young, anxious, already knowing their fate, and their mothers huddled. . . . Finally we reached our destination: the station Bauschowitz. We had a number of dead to mourn—some had taken their own lives during the trip." (Ferdinand Levy, c. 1955) [38]

Of the 1,378 passengers deported that day, most died in Auschwitz. Only 105 survived to see liberation.

Among the passengers were Moritz and Selma Schack, he number 1063 and she number 1064.

An outline of my grandfather's subsequent fate can be pieced together from fragmentary evidence gleaned from a few sources: a chance word-of-mouth account, a post-war letter, and Nazi deportation and death records. In *Mitten unter Uns,* Fritz Kilthau tells of a fellow Zwingenberger, a soldier stationed in Ukraine during the war, who told of seeing his old neighbor Moritz Schack doing road work in Kiev and there spoke with him.[39] Whether this was before or after his deportation to Theresienstadt is not known. Strangely, it is possible that Moritz was imprisoned at Theresienstadt at the same time as his older brother, Simon, and his wife Rosa. Perhaps the two brothers met during their yearlong imprisonment. Nazi records attest that Simon perished in Theresienstadt in February 1943 and his wife the month before. One month earlier, on January 23, 1943, Moritz and his wife had been transported from Theresienstadt to Auschwitz in Transport no. 1622, where both presumably were murdered upon arrival.

No one on the other side of the Atlantic knew of any of this. Leo, in the May 1943 letter cited above, expressed hope for all those left behind, fearful of what might be the case but clearly unaware that everyone but Suzy was by that time already dead. "*Hopefully we will see them all soon again, besides dear Papa, dear Aunt Clara and Uncle Jakob, dear Suzy, dear Aunt Gaby and her three dear children, and all the others. What a tragic situation!*"

Not until after the war did the true extent of the family's losses became known to the survivors.

CHAPTER 4

The Children

Marseille

THE FATE OF THE CHILDREN IN MARSEILLE—my mother's siblings Leo, Suzanne, and Margot—is as dramatic, if not as tragic, as that of their parents. With a few exceptions, I have drawn on both written and oral evidence: contemporary letters and other documents, family memories and, in addition, the Shoah Foundation testimony of Suzanne (Suzy) and her husband, Otto Goldschmitt.

Leo

IN 1956 MY MOTHER'S BROTHER, LEO, VISITED New York on business and asked my mother, his widowed older sister, to join him for an evening's entertainment. Depressed and agoraphobic at the time, she refused, as she did all invitations, and offered me—then sixteen—as a companion instead. So, wearing my best dress—a navy blue "princess" style with scooped white collar purchased for me by one of mother's friends for her son's recent *bar mitzvah*—I took the subway downtown to meet my Mexican uncle at the Hotel Shelburne on Lexington Avenue and Thirty-seventh Street, then a popular accommodation for Latin American businessmen visiting New York. I approached the desk timidly, was announced and directed to the elevator. My uncle welcomed me with a kiss. "*A drink?*" he asked. I shyly refused.

"Where shall we go for our evening on the town?" he continued in his fluent, slightly accented English. I shrugged. I had no idea. "Aah," he said. "I know, then. El Chico." And with his arm guiding me, we left the hotel for the club.

Uncle Leo was a dream date, handsome and distinguished, the gray hair on his temples lightly touched with white, solicitous and affectionate—perhaps somewhat too affectionate, in retrospect. Dinner went by in a haze of good food and wine. As the evening went on, we danced cheek-to-cheek to the Latin music on the small round dance floor, Leo whispering sweet words of affection in my ear. No one had ever treated me that way before. To a sixteen-year-old, this was living! He had, however, promised to get me home before midnight and was true to his word. We rode the subway to Washington Heights in quiet, the roar of the uptown IRT drowning out any efforts at conversation. My mother was waiting up nervously. I remember the evening, probably the most romantic of my life up to that time, with great fondness. As, evidently, did Leo. The following February, announcing a forthcoming trip to California, he wrote to my mother: "*A shame that dear Joan cannot be with us. It would surely be as lovely as in 'El Chico.' I think of that often and fondly*". ["*Schade das lb. Joan nicht dabei sein kann. Es ist bestimmt so schön wie in "EL CHICO." Oft und gern errinere ich mich daran.*]

The sole boy among the five Schack children, he had been an irrepressible child, always in trouble and driving his mother to distraction. "She worried about him all the time," my mother told me. "She never had a minute's peace." When he was two or three, he and a friend had disappeared from their usual play area on the *Marktplatz* in front of the house, setting off an all-night search. Only in the morning were they discovered in the village churchyard where they had been locked overnight. Little Leo was calm, though showing obvious disappointment, and he greeted his rescuers with the lament that they had seen no ghosts. One of the best students in the *Oberrealschule* in neighboring Heppenheim, he was also one of the most popular, not least because of his passion and talent for soccer.

That popularity was probably what saved his life. As Leo detailed in a 1997 letter to Fritz Kilthau, who then recounted the story in *Mitten unter Uns*, on April 19, 1933 (the eve of Hitler's birthday following his assumption of the chancellorship), Leo was playing cards with two non-Jewish friends in the apartment above the bakery owned by one friend's family. As was to occur annually thereafter throughout the Third Reich, celebration of Hitler's birthday was marked by the arrest and detention of many Jews and other so-called "enemies of the state." When word came that the SA was on its way to arrest him, his friends, without hesitating, rushed him to the train station, giving him no opportunity either to take leave of his parents and younger sisters or to collect any possessions. They put him on the next train, its destination Mannheim; there he connected to a train to Saarbrücken. Getting off just before the border, he crossed over to the Saarland on foot, where he was met by my mother, who then accompanied him to their uncle Hermann's house in Saarbrücken. The next day his aunt and uncle bought him a ticket to Paris.

Immediately on his arrival in Paris, he appealed for aid to the Jewish Assistance Committee in the Rue Lamarque which, among other services, distributed work permits to foreigners. His timing was fortunate. More than a hundred other German-Jewish refugees were making similar appeals, but all were given money, food vouchers, and permission to remain overnight. Later, as the number of Jewish refugees grew larger, they could no longer be lodged in a single place and soon were scattered in small hotels throughout Paris. And then the committee dissolved altogether, making it impossible for those without official permits, already severely limited by French quotas for foreigners, to get any work at all.

Destitute, with neither job nor assistance from any other refugee agency, how did he survive? In conversation with me several years ago, his older son Gerardo shed some light on this. Once, when Gerardo and his father visited New York, they came upon a Salvation Army man soliciting funds outside their hotel. Seeing Leo put a large bill in the can, his surprised son asked the reason. Leo's reply? "I would have starved in Paris were it not for them."

In addition, as I learned from Gerardo, in his usual enterprising way Leo found another solution to the money problem. Having acquired a job selling floor wax door-to-door, he took a phone book and carefully made note of all the Jewish names. He then visited Jewish family after Jewish family, recounting his story and more-or-less pressuring them to buy. Unaware, however, of the extent to which people abandoned Paris in the summertime, he was surprised to find his income drying up in August, leaving him once again without a *franc* in his pockets.

One of his new friends in the same situation—Ludwig (Louis) Reichenberg, originally from the town of Marköbel, north of Frankfurt—had heard that there was work in Marseille, and the two decided to hitchhike to the south of France. Luck was with them. Fritz Kilthau cites Leo's account:

> *The last part of the trip was through the Rhone district in a truck with fruits and vegetables, and I was lucky enough to have been the top French student when I was at school, and during the five months in Paris my French had gotten even better; the wholesale firm in fruits and vegetables needed an employee, and I was hired.*

Gerardo added to this many years later: Evidently, with no one else available to unload the truck on its arrival in Marseille, the boss had asked them to do it. They did such a good job that he offered them both work.

The first few years in Marseille went well, his adjustment no doubt aided by his adaptability and almost flawless French. Within a few years he was manager of a business, presumably the charcuterie *Alimentation Alsacienne* at 1 Rue Vacon, in the center of the city, whose letterhead graces a letter he sent my parents in mid-1939. A photo Leo sent me in 1995, along with a copy of his letter to Kilthau, presumably is of the same shop. Boasting a large sign reading "*Specialités Alsaciennes, Alimentation*," the shop is fronted by two wooden tables and a few barrels displaying a large selection of cheeses as well as some breads and produce. In the window there hangs an array of würsts and other meats. Two salespeople—a man and a woman—in white uniforms pose in the center, while a few customers examine the merchandise.

On December 31, 1938, Leo married his friend Louis' sister, Erna, and they moved into the apartment above the shop. Among their many friends were former members of the International Brigades who had fought with the Republicans in the Spanish Civil War. Now in exile from Franco's Spain, several later followed Leo and Erna to Mexico.

Increasingly anxious about his parents and two teen-aged sisters still in Germany, Leo began to try to get them out even before the terrifying events of *Kristallnacht* on November 9-10, 1938. After that his efforts accelerated. However, in late 1938 word came to Morris and Martha from Uncle Hermann's widow Gaby. With her three children, she had returned after her husband's death to her hometown of St. Avold in the French region of Lorraine and had learned that France was willing to admit German refugee children through the age of fifteen. With Suzy to turn sixteen on February second, their parents had no choice but to get the girls out as quickly as possible [See Chapter 3]. The girls left Germany for France on children's visas in early February although Leo had no success in gaining exit visas for his parents. In a June 1939 letter sent from Paris to Irma and Lina in New York, he seems irritated at their apparent impatience with his progress at getting the necessary papers:

> From Z[wingenberg] good news at least as to their health, in spite of your constant reproaches that it is taking so long to get our parents out. But believe me, I am working at it. I sent for the papers already in August 1938 and have had assurances for a while now that they will be here within a month. I am waiting with longing. And every day I walk to the Committee in the Ministry.

In his defense, he cites the equally frustrating, if different, experience of old friends from Zwingenberg: Despite their efforts to bribe French ministry officials for an entry visa, they were unable to get one, finally crossing the border illegally with no idea of what lay in their future.

Yet Leo's characteristic optimism and pursuit of *la bonne*

chance shows even here, as he ends the letter describing what he sees as an extraordinary business possibility:

> *Something else: A friend who is in British East Africa (Kenya) wrote me about starting a bomb business with the juice of the grenadilla, also known as passion-fruit. This is apparently well known in North America, and as Kenya is the sole producer in the world of this item, it might be a good deal. Do you know this fruit or its juice? It is described in this way: It looks like a big egg, but chestnut brown (like a plum), the shell is hard and inedible. Inside it is very juicy and is very tasty meat (an herb-like taste).*

Unsurprisingly there is no subsequent mention of this "opportunity."

Suzy and Margot arrived in Marseille early in February 1939. And, as their mother wrote to Irma and Lina, for a time things seemed to go well enough:

> *Erna and the children send good reports. . . . I see from their letter that they are helping Erna in the business. That is good, now that Leo is not at home. Margot wrote that they cry out their wares on the street* [presumably in front of the shop] *because the street is where business takes place.*

But the hope, as always, was to get the girls to New York, and to that end they had to learn some English. This plan, however, evidently did not go smoothly, as their mother acknowledged a month later:

> *Margot does not want to go to school. I have already written her that she absolutely must go to school, and also Leo and Erna want it. Maybe you can ask them about it, but not that I have written you about it. As far as I know, Suzy gets some hours* [of English] *but still cannot write a lot. I had them send Margot's affidavit* [presumably for entry to the U.S.] *from Stuttgart and will send it to Marseille. Maybe it will go faster over there. So you need not write in English. I think that if they can only learn the language, then they can study something else. One does always worry when everything is so far away and one cannot do anything about it.*

With the German invasion in 1940 and the imposition of the Petain-led Vichy government on the whole of France, ominous changes began to be felt. Marseille, though long a haven for foreigners, had never fully welcomed them. The most recent influx had consisted largely of refugees fleeing either the Nazis in Germany and Austria or Franco's regime in Spain after the Republican defeat. These people, by and large, brought with them few economic resources, especially the German and Austrian Jews: those with money were generally able to immigrate to the Americas. Long before Vichy, the police had kept them under surveillance. Among the many refugees who spent time in Marseille were prominent anti-Nazi cultural figures like Heinrich and Golo Mann, Lion Feuchtwanger, and Walter Benjamin.

One German refugee, Hans Fittko, later described the incongruity of French attitudes:

> *The age old hatred of the archenemy, les boches* [the "Krauts"], *weighed heavily on all of us. To the French we émigrés were simply Germans. We came from there, we spoke with the despised accent boche. Even during the years of emigration we always remained, in the eyes of many Frenchmen, the "sales boches"* ["dirty Krauts"]. *And now—we were prisoners, so we must be spies.*
>
> *Indeed, before the war we had been reviled as warmongers, because France didn't want to hear about Hitler's plans for aggression. But now it was wartime and the gross distinction between Nazis and anti-Fascists was no longer recognized. We were the enemy.*[40]

Even before the invasion, things had begun to change drastically after the declaration of war in September 1939. Although they had been among the earliest victims of Nazi persecution, thousands of foreigners (among them many Jews) were interned by the French as enemy aliens, often in concentration camps like the notorious

Gurs near the Spanish border. Among them were Leo and his brothers-in-law.

The first indication that things were not going well in Marseille came in a September 1939 letter from Erna to New York:

> I did not really want to write about us. But otherwise you will perhaps hear it from others. Dear Leo and my two brothers are interned for over one month already ... they reported voluntarily in August. I undertake everything possible but so far to no avail, and unfortunately little hope. As you will surely understand, I no longer have the business. Suzy, despite her good will, cannot work because she is not allowed to and the same is true for me. The children [Suzy and Margot] understand everything too well. I would very much have liked the St. Avold family to take them, but it is currently not in my power. Then they would happily have a place to live and free food from the state, yes [those in St. Avold] are better off than we are.

No further news arrived from Leo until November 1939 when he again wrote to Irma and Lina, this time from Aix-en-Provence. First expressing his concern about the *"lack of news about our parents,"* he then poured out what he referred to as a *"litany of distress."* This may be the only time Leo's usual optimism failed him, when he and his brothers-in-law, having tried to enlist in the Free French army to help fight the hated Germans were instead interned as "enemy aliens" with no idea when they would be released from detention. As he described the consequences:

> *My job that was pretty good is lost, my money is blocked by the bank. Neither my wife nor my two sisters have a sou. . . . How will they live without income? And on top of all that, if you permit me to be straightforward, I don't mince words; my dear Erna expects a happy event in the month of April, which will make it impossible for her to work.*

What follows is a fervent plea for help:

> *I am not accustomed to cry or to beg, but can you possibly send them $30/month, that will permit her and my two sisters to survive? I don't want you to make me a gift; I will return it when I can, that is when my account is unblocked and when I can earn again. It is useless to discuss the reasons for my detention, and superfluous to speak of the errors we have made before these tragic days. If I appeal to you at this unhappy moment, it is because I feel the weight of responsibility for my wife, responsibility I assumed on the day of our marriage, which obliges me to assure her a dignified and honorable life. And if I address myself to you, it is because I suffer the material impossibility that makes it necessary.*

Placed in the army auxiliary used for general labor, Leo and his brothers-in-law were assigned to construction of the Maginot Line in the southern French Alps. Yet even then, after the long account of his sorrows, powerless yet responsible for the survival of his wife and two sisters in Marseille, he still was able to write, *"Maybe this year will prove to be only a bad dream; an old law of nature says, yes, 'after the rain the sun must shine.'"*

Under other circumstances, the statement of obligation (*"to assure her a dignified and honorable life"*) might seem pompous and self-serving, an almost comic expression of dignity in such a young man. But retrospect permits another reading, and even Leo did not know how dire the situation actually was. Moreover, he had real reason for regretting *"the errors we have made."* A few years earlier, his sister Lina had appealed for assistance in getting him entry to the United States via Julius Roten, the wealthy distant cousin of their mother who had deep roots in New York and who had been instrumental in her own immigration. An oil company executive, Roten had managed to acquire affidavits for Leo and his family, personally signed by New York's Governor Lehman and United States Secretary of State, Cordell Hull. To his obvious current regret, Leo had responded to the offer: *"Thank you for the affidavit; I prefer to stay in France."* According to Lina, Leo's refusal had yet greater repercussions. With Roten's help, affidavits for entry to the United States had evidently also come through for their parents, but they refused to leave without Martha's sister Clara and her husband. Lina felt that had Leo emigrated at that time, their parents might have followed, as *"he had so much energy."* Leo spent the next two years interned as a *prestataire*, a uniformed auxiliary soldier, performing outdoor labor for the army. His letters from the Basses-Alpes, where he was assigned, most in French, some in German, reveal his anger and frustration at the continuing internment: *"Life is a bad joke! There I had no right to be a German, here I am confined like this. What is the logic?"* In addition, his anxiety about his wife and sisters led to increasingly desperate appeals for money. Not once does he complain about his own physical situation. It is only from Erna's letters that we know of his hunger and the constant pain caused by the cold and harsh conditions. Some excerpts from his letters from his time of internment follow. Most are translated from French, a few from German.

Marseille, Dec. 10, 1939:

The time passes, but nothing changes of the boredom of my internment. It is a crazy riddle. . . . Now that [my family] have most need of me, now it is necessary that I mope around in this camp. . . . The only thing that gives me hope is the possibility of leaving here with permission to emigrate to an American country. Is it possible to get an affidavit? Maybe it would be the "baton of salvation." Now our only right is that of despair. For me life is still bearable from a material point of view. I eat and I sleep. But what will happen to Erna? And the two little girls? How will a solution to that be found? And Uncle Roten, what does he think about my case? Is he angry with me? I have wronged him. But when one is young one makes foolish mistakes. And for now let us hope for a miracle. . . . I embrace you in the hope of good news.

Volx (Basses-Alpes), 156e RR, 14 Compagnie, Feb. 19, 1940:
Here all is bien à bord; as you see from my address, I am assigned as a worker in a regiment that is now in Les Basses-Alpes. We are in a pretty good cadre, our place of residence the valley of the Durance, we eat pretty well, but I spend my time waiting for a furlough. It will soon be six months since I left our house. But there are always rules to subject us, that is to say us refugees; we are almost soldiers, but have none of the advantages, at least as of now. . . . Erna has written me that Margot will leave perhaps at the beginning of March; Suzy still waits for an affidavit, as do our parents. They are all well, the three. The rest of the family is also in good health, which is some satisfaction in these hard times. I wish, together with the French people among whom I have lived for so long and have spent the best years of my life, where I will soon, perhaps, be a citizen, that this war ends soon with a complete and crushing defeat of that Germany which I hate, before the hecatombs are filled up, as a result of total war, with innocent flesh and blood. It is my dearest wish. I await your good news and embrace you.

Manosque (Basses-Alpes), March 23, 1940:

It's been a long, long time since I heard from you. I hope that you are all well. By us all is "G.S.D." [Gott Sei Dank or Thank God] well, which I am comforted to hear from dear Erna's letters. I am happy when I read that Erna feels in as good health as possible, given her condition. And soon, this month, we will have the joy of the birth of our young child. We have heard nothing of our parents in a long time.... I only hope that they are well.... When will the war begin? Perhaps in a short time you may get a photo of your brother as a poilu [an infantryman, literally "hairy one"]. That wouldn't be so bad!

Suzy helps a lot in the house, doubly needed at this time. Margot now is waiting only for her birthday [September 28], when the Red Cross will pay for her departure. Her number is on file. She is happy that she will soon see you again. If only all three could get to safety in this way. Marseille is very close to Italy. Too close.[41]

Once more, before I mail this letter which must be sent to Marseille in the morning when the deliverer goes there, the only request I am making of you: as my [emigration] number is so impossible, look out for dear Erna and Suzy (and Margot as long as necessary). I appeal to you all, the next month will be the hardest, there has to be some end. I am counting on your help, otherwise from where should it come?"

Leo's and Erna's son, Gerard, was born on March 20, 1940, in a private hospital, the Clinique Paradis, and Suzy notified her sisters: "Hereby the joyful news: An heir has arrived. He is named Norbert Gerard. Mother & child are doing fine. . . . He was born on 6:35 Saturday afternoon of the 30th March 1940, weighed 3.90 kg and immediately laughed.

Leo was granted a brief leave to attend his son's circumcision. Immediately following his return to his base, he wrote at some length to his sisters in New York:

Manosque, April 9, 1940:

Little Gerard has a good strong voice (which we heard more often than I can count). I have tried to inform our parents of the good news and will try again. . . . Our luck goes from bad to worse; our having a son doesn't make a reunion any likelier. Is it possible in this life to have happy days alternating with unhappy ones? That is my hope. But why doesn't the war start? Yesterday the boches brutes invaded the defenseless Scandinavian countries; it is shameful. What more will have occurred by the time this letter is in your hands?

I am uneasy about the future of our family, and I tell you once more, to assure their survival which I consider my duty, listen here: In an earlier letter I wrote: "I believe, I am not a beggar; I am simply unfortunate at the moment. Here is the remedy, essential if my family is to survive: you four families [presumably Irma, Lina, Theo and Carola, and Julius Roten] send Erna $20-$25 a month, that is as little as $6 from each of you a month. Is that a great sum there? Do it quickly! Think of my sweet baby, of my wife, also of Suzy and Margot. . . . I do not want to analyze the reasons that I have to repeat this; I don't understand it. Beforehand, the fruits of my labor always covered at least my bread, at least our necessities. When I have left this unit, with tears in my eyes, to return God knows when, my only thought, my only care, is to assure their lives. Try to imagine that one of your relations, a voluntary soldier fighting for freedom, has not a single pleasure greater than receiving good news about those he loves and cherishes. To have contributed to that is a great work, material cares obstruct the night's sleep, there needs no other raison-d'être.

I hope that you are all well. Your letters are a godsend to me. Yesterday when I was home, Irma's letter arrived with Margot's affidavit. Now all has arrived. Did you receive the confirmation from me, by airmail, of the $10 check for the month of January? That is, simply to say that the money arrived and is paid.

Leo occasionally mentions small amounts of money received from New York, but the total cannot have been much. My father and Lina were for the most part unemployed, unable to find jobs in New York's depressed economy, and my mother, with a baby at home, was otherwise employed. The restaurant that Paul and Lena had opened and that represented a hope for a steady income had lasted only a few months.

On May 10, 1940, Leo's regiment of auxiliaries was sent to Dunkirk. Unable to write during the two months of presumably heavy combat, he finally managed to get through the German lines —a journey that took four days, the last part via military train from Bordeaux—and return to Marseille. In a long letter, his last written from France, he describes his experiences and once more begs for help:

> *Marseille, July 24, 1940:*
>
> *I was together with Louis and Salli* [his brothers-in-law] *in the same regiment. During the last two months in Northwest France, we made our way through hazardous marches, with endless pains; often we were surrounded. Under that terrible fire, we lost Salli: that is, for five weeks we had no news of him. Yesterday morning we received a telegram that he is in England.*[42]

Now, however, having managed to return to Marseille, Leo could once more address his family's needs. The rest of the letter illuminates his fears, anger, regrets, and hopes:

> *I am here, for the time being, together with Louis, for a few days' furlough, which for us seemingly is not yet past. My dear wife, also our son, who is a little Goldkind are, G.S.D., both in good health.... Suzy and Margot are both at home, as they have no papers; both are well. Margot will*

be able to emigrate, but her visa hasn't come yet. One must have patience. . . . We haven't heard from our parents in a long time; we hope that all is going as well as possible. Tante Gaby wrote me this week from Poitiers; her health is fine but she is terribly unhappy. Her sister Alice has had no news of her two sons for a long time. You must know what that means. Nor is there news of the Salomon son [Minna's husband and Blondine's son-in-law from St. Avold].

Now I must mention some facts that oppress me terribly. I mean no reproach nor possibility of correction, just pure dismay. All three of us have been mobilized.[43] *Our savings were not large, and are partly in Paris, thus in German hands. Ten months of war have used everything up. Life becomes more expensive from day to day. I eat in the barracks. Suzy and Margot have been at home for the last two months, the little one is there, you know what that means, and my wife gets 435 Fr. a month military allocation. Do you know what it means, when a liter of oil costs 13 francs? One word: that is "hunger." I myself would have a cure for that in normal times, when I could work, even though friends or near-relatives refuse* [my plea], *especially since the sum that can help is so terribly high* [presumably sarcastic]. *A monthly subsidy divided by four relatives of $20 = $5 each; that sum would for now and the near future support a humane life for both your sisters and* your brother's wife and baby. In a short while I must go away again and leave my wife alone in her misery. I am powerless, I can change nothing. Like a common beggar on my knees, I can only beseech for alms, hoping that it is not for too long anymore.

The single and final thing remaining depends on me, I think, and it is easy: to fulfill my role, so that this year should be only a bad dream; an old law of nature says, after the rain the sun must shine. But other questions arise: Will we be able to stay here? I have to consider everything. No event should surprise us. Where shall we go? The letters I have enclosed, which I ask you please to send further via airmail, may perhaps provide a solution. Better to attempt too much than too little. Or might there perhaps be a way to the U.S.A. or some country where you or your acquaintances have family? Please write soon and give me your advice. What does Theo think, what does Uncle Roten, who knows everyone, everywhere? Or if I weren't so far away, over here, couldn't Uncle Roten write a good recommendation for me to a large firm, one or another branch. That doesn't cost very much, and I would definitely show myself worth his trust. If I only had some money, I could easily find my way back on my feet. All of this in the hope that I shortly will have no more military obligations to fulfill. Perhaps, when the letter gets to you that will already be the case. Chi lo sa?" [Who knows? (Italian)]

Yet even while acknowledging his own desperate situation, Leo never lost his optimistic visions for a better future:

> *I don't want to do the same thing I did before the war. I would prefer working either in a large firm or in some kind of administration where there is a future, either as an employee, or in my own business. I always go forward; when no one helps me, I must take whatever comes. I have no illusions about finding a produce firm like my last "landing." I am no such child of luck. My life has always been touched by pitch, always pressed by necessity. I always have to march through harsh conditions. And as I once again must start anew, please excuse me if I am looking to do something comme il faut. I know very well that I have Uncle Roten's enmity, as I didn't accept his generous offer of 1936. Those papers are always in front of my eyes. The times have only proved him right. But I looked at the world through rose-colored glasses and thought I had a real future here. And when circumstances permit, I would still believe in a future for myself here. . . .*
>
> *Then, to conclude according to logic, I will also have completed my duty here as a soldier. But I have grown so skeptical. A lost war is the opposite of one that is won. And all principles are topsy-turvy. Would I have received some small recognition of my service, if it weren't for the alien laws? From what I can see and hear up to now, [it*

will be] *very hard. After having written about everything at such length and in such detail, I believe that you also understand me. I have a lot to summarize, many possibilities in mind. I must do it. With loving greetings and kisses to all of you and your loved ones. P.S. A technical question: If, in response to the first paragraph of my litany of distress, you send money, please either write with the dollar notes inside or do it as you've been doing it up to now.*

According to the autobiographical letter Leo wrote Fritz Kilthau in June 1997, he continued in the wholesale business after his demobilization and return to Marseille, then still in the unoccupied *zone libre*, the Free Zone south of German-controlled Vichy. With his prior company now defunct, he writes of having created his own at the same location *"with great success,"* although his sister Suzy's Shoah Foundation testimony paints a less rosy picture of a *"daily struggle to stay alive, not knowing whether the Germans would come or not."*

With fear increasing throughout 1941 that southern France would not remain unoccupied for long and that the Germans and Italians would soon invade Marseille, Leo—along with many others—resolved to escape with his wife and son to North Africa. As with most refugee emigration from Marseille, the arrangements were made through a composite agency named HICEM, which had been created in 1927 to aid the emigration of European Jews. The acronym was an amalgam of the three disparate agencies:

HIAS (Hebrew Immigrant Aid Society) based in New York, which, together with the American Joint Distribution Committee, continued to provide most of the funding; ICA (Jewish Colonization Association) located in Paris but registered as a British charitable society; and Emigdirect (United Jewish Emigration Committee) based in Berlin. Prior to 1933, HICEM had largely helped Eastern European Jews, subject to frequent anti-Semitic pogroms, to find more hospitable homelands. After the rise of Nazism, however, HICEM served as an umbrella organization serving all refugee Jews, trying to find countries willing to accept them, arranging the necessary papers and then paying the $420 per passenger fare for their passage. Following the fall of France in 1940, HICEM's main headquarters moved to Lisbon, in neutral Portugal, and the French office was relocated to Marseille in the French free zone.

With a large staff of more than eighty employees, which it was able to maintain until legal emigration ended after the German occupation of Southern France, the Marseille office of HICEM, often working with other rescue agencies like the American Friends Service Committee, managed to help more than six thousand Jews leave France and gain entry elsewhere (largely the United States, Central and South America, and China). Many Jews were also helped indirectly, as HICEM worked to reconnect separated families, give assistance, and deliver packages to the French camps in the Unoccupied Zone (in several of which full-time HICEM representatives went to live), and pressure governments to admit refugees. In all, the organization helped more than 40,000 refugees acquire visas and tickets for passage, usually by getting them first to Lisbon and then onto neutral Portuguese ships. Those who were able to pay the necessary money did so themselves. Those who could not were supported through contributions, largely from HIAS or wealthy Jewish philanthropists.[44]

In October 1941, Leo, his wife, and their young son boarded a ship for Algiers; from there they took a train to Casablanca. The previous May, Margot—at fifteen still legally a child and thus able to leave France—had received an American visa, largely through Lina's efforts. Under the auspices of HICEM, she had traveled alone first to Lisbon and from there to New York, where she was now safe.

What to do about eighteen-year-old Suzy, however, was a problem. Too old to receive a children's visa, she was wholly dependent on her brother. Most likely unable to acquire enough money to pay for an additional exit visa beside their own and their baby's (and perhaps reluctant to take on responsibility for a stubborn and often uncooperative young adult), Leo and Erna decided to go without her, leaving Suzy to fend for herself in Marseille. For his own family, Leo had acquired two exit visas: one for China, the other for Mexico, and he resolved that they would board the first ship arriving in Casablanca that accepted refugees. Their future was determined when the *Serpa Pinto*, arrived from Lisbon bound for Veracruz, Mexico.

According to a bulletin put out by the Jewish Telegraphic Agency, dated October 15, 1941, the *Serpa Pinto* left Lisbon on

October 25 carrying 600-700 refugees "*to new homes in North and South America*" and was scheduled to stop in Casablanca to "*pick up the last 200 refugees who sailed from Marseille last Spring and have been detained in North African internment camps ever since, as well as about 75 more emigrants from unoccupied France who were unable to obtain Spanish transit visas.*"[45]

Among them were Leo, Erna, and little Gerard, whose names appear on the *Serpa Pinto*'s passenger list. The ship's passengers originated from all over Europe: Marseille, Berlin, Vienna, Amsterdam, Prague, Luxemburg, Spain, and Italy. The bulletin notes as well that the Jewish immigration aid agency, HICEM, had responsibility for about three hundred and fifty of the passengers, and that the ship was scheduled to stop in the Dominican Republic, "*the first liner ever*" to sail there from a Portuguese port, where it would deliver "*between one hundred and one hundred and fifty relatives of Jewish settlers and other refugees who have obtained visas for residence in the Caribbean republic.*"

Before the war, the *Serpa Pinto* had been a luxury yacht for three hundred passengers. Now it had to transport several thousand refugees. An account of the voyage in Spanish by one of the passengers, an Italian Communist journalist named Guiseppe Garretto, was published the following year in Mexico. The book, *Serpa Pinto: Pueblos en la Tormenta* [People in the Storm], describes a nightmarish voyage, squalid and disordered, with passengers crammed into every available space and ignored by the indifferent crew, yet all hoping for a better future. The following excerpt captures the evident mood on the ship as well as illustrating Garretto's extravagant prose:

> *This disparate group of refugees has been driven by destiny to the ultimate confines of misfortune. Beyond are only madness and death. They represent all the nations of Europe and come from exile, from concentration camps and trans-Saharan labor crews. . . . Because there is no greater number of unhappy stories than in a port of flight: Casablanca. And now they are all, in that port, two steps from the boat that will deliver them to the free Americas. The emotion shines in their eyes, as if lost in a distant dream: to regain a life, to return to being people. . . .*
>
> > *This time if only. . .—shouts a happy voice.*
> > *Until we meet there. . .growls another*
> > *And a pale, skinny youth, his voice tired:*
> > *Only when we have sailed, will we rest.*

During the long and miserable voyage, the passengers tried to maintain some kind of normalcy. Garretto recounts the kindness of a passenger identified only as "Pio" who took on the job of entertaining the younger children, among them Leo's and Erna's one-and-a-half-year-old son, Gerard:

> *Pio with his "children" seems to be the master of the ship. With his crew of kids he goes everywhere, the main salon, the*

first bridge, and everywhere he garners fruits and candy for his young friends. It is quite a spectacle seeing them all together. Michou, barely a few palms in height, all belly and chubby cheeks, is tied with a double rope to Gerard, the most famous child in the entire ship. Smaller than Michou, he is always trotting along with his short bowed legs, emitting shrieks of pleasure and funny exclamations. He laughs and then looks at you with picaresque and mocking eyes. Julio watches both, inciting them to walk further by saying Ih! Ih!

Pio follows accompanied by Tita, a beautiful five-year-old with a lively intelligence, and by Pierrot, thin and a whimperer. The group strolls in a loud parade, wearing the minimal uniform of paper hats made of folded newspaper.[46]

After a month's journey via the Azores, Santo Domingo, and Cuba, the *Serpa Pinto* arrived in Mexico in December 1941. The wandering Jews and other refugees were greeted by a welcoming committee, placed in hotels in Mexico City, and provided with supplies until they had achieved a small measure of economic stability. As Leo wrote, "Not easy, *with the strange language and the new environment. But our object had been to get far away from the Nazis.*"

A month after their arrival (in January 1942), his optimism fully renewed, he described their new life in Mexico City:

Slowly we are finding our way here; little Gerard has also found a home, a lovely apartment near a large park, where he can play in the spring sunshine all day long. I spoke of our trip in my last letter; it was very expensive, more than 60,000 francs. But for now I have what I need, and when I find work that will definitely be the best. But that is yet to come. For now we are fixing up our home, that keeps me busy, and costs a lot. We do it as simply as possible, that experience teaches. Where are we finally and definitely at home? Hopefully here! . . . Though I still have interests in France, I will see to them after the war.

Erna and Leo (who began to use the name "Jack" among friends and colleagues) lived the rest of their lives in Mexico—first in Mexico City, later (after his retirement) in Guadalajara. They were happy there and prospered. He eventually got a job managing several chemical firms and later ran a pesticide factory in Irapuato, about two hundred miles northwest of the capital. Two more children arrived: Martha (named after her grandmother but always called Marthita) in 1942 and Ricardo in 1952.

Margot and Suzanne

BUT WHAT, AFTER THEIR HURRIED DEPARTURE from Germany, was the situation of the two youngest Schack sisters? There is evidence almost from the outset that things did not go smoothly for them. When they were sent to Marseille to be under the care of their brother and his new wife, both were in their early teens—a difficult age under the best of circumstances. Suzy had just turned sixteen, and Margot was thirteen. Both had been suddenly uprooted from the village life that was all they had known up to that time. The large and famously raucous city must have seemed to them an overwhelming stew of dangers and temptations. In addition, the responsibility for their care fell mainly upon their young sister-in-law. Though barely a decade older than they were, Erna was left alone with them for much of the time, with Leo initially in Paris trying to arrange exit papers for his parents, aunt, and uncle, and afterwards interned with the army.

At first, the girls' reports were happy. In a long joint letter to their sister Lina in June of 1939, Suzy describes her reaction to her *"new homeland."*

> *France is a beautiful country, the people are very good-natured and not such barbarians as they are over there in Germany. The language is very lovely, and I am glad to have the opportunity to learn it. For the moment we have mixed English-French lessons. This is how it is. We must translate the French into the English, and the German into the French. It is much easier like that, because we already know the language-teaching phrases.*

But she ends with a fatalism beyond her fifteen years: "*The Zwingenberger community is scattered to the winds. Whether we all see each other again on earth, who knows?*"

Margot, always happy to write, draws a more vivid picture of their daily lives:

> *Every morning at quarter to seven Suzy and I get up. We go downstairs and set up the business on the road. Erna taught this to us, as she doesn't want to go down with us. Once the business is down on the street, we drink coffee, wash up, go and clean the apartment. At noon we cook the meal, eat, and wash up again. We clean up the kitchen and then have our lessons, because an old teacher comes in the afternoon and teaches us English-French. In the evening the business is again brought inside. Then we eat dinner, go for a walk together or to the cinema. Saturday we may help in the business by calling out our Camembert. I call in such a way: "Allez, profitez Monsieurs, Dames, un bon Camembert à 1.75 francs." Then I sell. That I can say beautifully. Today Sunday we were in the zoological garden, and then in the coffee shop. It was very beautiful. France is a very beautiful and happy country, as much as I know so far. The people are good, and everyone may speak with one another as much as desired, and not like there, where one sometimes did not come out of the house for more than eight days out of fear that the dogs would stone him (which they really did). The sea is wonderful, and we live one street away from the old port. That is beautiful.*

Yet, as always demonstrating a wisdom and understanding unexpected in one so young, Margot does not forget those remaining in Germany: "*Now we want to see whether we can make any progress about our parents, Uncle* [Jakob], *and Aunt* [Clara]. *Dear Lina, our parents and Suzy have such a high number that they won't be able to get so fast to the U.S.A. Even if you are a citizen, because you just do not know how many people are waiting for* [entry to the U.S.] *in Stuttgart alone. But we want to hope for the best. . . . Our parents wrote this week. They are moving to Frankfurt.*" Concerned, too, about her own situation, she writes, "*I wrote our parents that they should send me my papers, so that I can go to the consulate here. Is it certain that 20,000 children can come in under the quota? That would be wonderful. Then I would soon be able to come to you?*"

But the extended family is never far from her thoughts. She urges her sister to write to their father's sister and her husband, the Schönfeldts ("*they have been very nice to us*"), and ends her "*Megillah*" (as she terms it) with criticism of their cousin Theo and his wife Carola, who "*should also write us once finally. . . . They should write to our parents in Zwingenberg. Mother already feels quite insulted because they never write her.*" Signing off with her usual extravagance, like the child she is: "*Be well and all be warmly hugged and kissed a thousand times for today from your loving Margot,*" in a postscript she remembers yet more family members, reminding her sister not to forget to write the family in St. Avold.

The long letter ends with a brief addition from Erna:

> *The children make quite good progress. Twice a week they get English-French lessons, because Margot did not want to go to school and Suzy can't do anything without language. They learn conscientiously, and, if things progress somewhat, she will take a course for hairdressers, as you wished, dear Lina. As you taught them, they always sing and perform theatricals for us."*

What Erna did not mention—and what came out only later—were the many serious conflicts between the two girls and their young and understandably overwhelmed sister-in-law. From the start, Margot was openly reluctant to go to school, and neither girl was happy about having to take orders from Erna, often about doing most of the housework. Hard feelings persisted for many years, as two of Leo's later letters imply. In one from May 1943, to my mother, he complained of her failure to respond to his letters, blaming her *"breakoff in diplomatic relations"* on *"atrocity propaganda by my dear sister Margot about what she and Suzy suffered together with us in Marseille. . . . [W]ithout thereby giving the impression to want to make any defense, I think that dear Margot, after all the time, can see with other eyes what we did for her. And for me, I will no longer talk about the childish behavior of my dear sisters Margot and Suzy."*

Two years later, in May 1945, after celebrating the war's end and expressing hope of soon hearing from those still missing, Leo again raised the subject to my mother:

> *Dear Irma, I don't understand why you never answer my cards, is it that I have done something? I don't know what. Ever since Margot came to the U.S. and told you God knows what, you have been cold to us. And nevertheless I can assure you that what dear Erna has undergone with Suzy and Margot is unimaginable, and Margot was yet a thousand times better than Suzy. I ask from where have they taken that spirit ["genie"]? Finally, it is of the past, and it is not worth the pain of revisiting.*

And in truth, during the summer and fall of 1939 Erna was in a seemingly hopeless situation: pregnant, with no source of income, and wholly responsible for the support of the two teen-aged girls. Some brief alleviation of her distress came when friends of Erna's brother Louis invited Margot to accompany them to their country house in the Vaucluse and assist with the housework. With Margot away, Erna was grateful to have one less mouth to feed.

In the three seemingly happy months Margot spent with the family Lagandanne in L'Isle-sur-la-Sorgue, a popular vacation spot on the river Sorgue, she wrote to New York only once. Yet although the place was pleasant, her letter shows persistent worry about the rest of the family:

> *It is very nice here. I often hear news about Erna and Suzy, because Madame is now in Marseille. But she will return this week. . . . From our parents, I haven't had any news for two-and-a-half months. And you? Don't worry*

about us. We are in good health, and that's the main thing . . . . Leo and Louis have left. Suzy hasn't yet found a job . . . . I embrace you with all my heart. Your sister Margot.

The main problem for those in Marseille seems to have been the shortage of food. In a late November birthday greeting to Irma, Erna spoke only vaguely about their misery:

> *Margot . . .will return next week to Marseille. . . . Sussi [sic] is always with me. Happily our health is good. Except for the terrible things I will not speak about. And yet I am happy for the moment for being able at least to spend half an hour a week with dear Leo.*

On her return to Marseille, unaware that Paul and Lina's restaurant was already defunct, Margot hinted broadly of a lack of food:

> *Since last week I am back here in Marseille. . . . How are things going with the restaurant? Yes, it's a pity that we can't eat the leftovers.*

A month later, in a mid-December letter to Lina, Erna expressed her anguish more openly:

> *I will go this week again to the American consulate for Margot; I don't know how things are going. Because it may*

be of help to you now. Unhappily nothing changes for us. And I am desperate and don't know anymore what to do. I have already written to my sister in Chile and wait to see if she can do something. Unhappily she has been there only a few months. It has been already more than three months since dear Leo left. In any case, the two little ones won't trouble you. They have all that they need and need nothing for the moment? I always have hope that our situation will change, as it is impossible that it continue like this. In any case write nothing about this to our dear parents, they have enough by themselves. I have news of them through the Swiss. Be well and I embrace you.

Margot continued to work for the Lagandannes after the return to Marseille. An undated letter, probably from mid- or late-1939 (as it speaks of Irma's imminent *accouchement*), ends abruptly: "*I am in a hurry. Madame is not feeling so well, and the soup is on the fire.*" Margot's letter (written in German, thus allowing her greater fluency) goes on to describe the current situation:

Leo is unfortunately not home yet, and Erna has many worries. Suzy still didn't find any [work], and now I am starting to believe that she will not find anything. . . . We had a very nice letter this week from Aunt Gaby. The poor thing had to leave too, and it is good that Uncle Hermann is not alive anymore to experience all that. [Hermann and Gaby's children] Margot and Arno work, and Suzanne con-

tinues to go to school there. Aunt Gaby cannot do anything now except wait. Now to the main thing. I just was at the consulate and the consul gave me a form for you, dear Lina. Whether you really have a restaurant and whether Mr. Fürst [?] really has the income stated on the affidavit. Be so good as to go directly to the notary and let it be confirmed. IN A HURRY. *Otherwise the consul said the papers are in order and I could be gone by February-March. That would be beautiful, really beautiful. Send it to me by airmail, so that I can go immediately to the consulate with it.*

Her appointment with the consulate did not materialize, however, until the following April. Two days earlier Erna had delivered baby Gerard, but Margot's focus in March 1940 was almost entirely on the upcoming interview at the American Consulate scheduled for the following week: "*I hope that everything goes well and everything will be paid by the committee.*"

By the first of May, Margot's papers were at last in order, but there was yet one more hurdle to overcome: money for the ticket. Once more she appealed to her sister Lina for help:

As you know my papers are fine now, and I could go to pick up my visa. However, dear Leo is unfortunately not able to give me such a sum of money, as he is mobilized and unfortunately cannot earn anything. If it is somehow possible for you to send me the fare, or possibly the ticket for the journey, I would be very grateful... I await your speediest reply, if possible via air mail.

What follows are detailed directions, given Margot by the "Committee" (presumably the *Committee for Aid to Refugees from Germany*) for avoiding payment, with costs then to be assumed by the agency itself:

Enclosed I transmit a copy to you, exactly as I gave it to the Committee and as the Committee told me to write it to you. You can see that they really only want to know whether you are unable to pay the journey. Do not be frightened, and just please write me immediately via airmail that you unfortunately aren't in the position to pay my journey, since the business wasn't successful, or however you want to express it. With this letter I will then go immediately to the Committee and give it to them. Then the matter is given over to Paris. Since my visa is ready to pick up, it should go now twice as fast. I have said to the Consul that you are the one who paid everything for me; it's not critical to know everything else. He already gave me a ship, which sails on the 10th of May, but I do not believe that I can go with this one, since the Committee does not act so fast. But it will surely work out with the next one. . . . Meanwhile I await your immediate answer.

Erna explained the situation further:

> As Margot already wrote you, things are going forward with her papers, and she doesn't lack any papers. Hopefully you understand what she wants to say with the letter. This is only a matter of formality, and don't let yourself be influenced. The committee pays the others also. We must only insist on it, and you too in case of inquiry. . .particularly since we know the secretary of the HICEM Marseille very well. He wants the two letters merely as a template for Paris, the one that Margot wrote to you and the response where you explain to Margot that it is impossible for you and that you are very sorry. . . . Do not write anything about the committee. Only personally to Margot. I hope you understand us. . . .

A few lines from Suzy repeat the advice: "*The quicker your answer, the sooner Margot will be with you. Do not worry about Margot. She has all her papers, and HICEM will pay. Just answer quickly.*" Nevertheless, it took almost another year before Margot was able to leave. At the end of April 1941 an exuberant letter arrived from Lisbon:

> You will be astonished to have news from me from here, but it is fortunately accurate. I came here from Marseille, where H[ICEM] is taking great care of me. I am with seven other children in a beautiful pension, and H pays every-

thing. I am planning to leave here May 9th, but I will let you know immediately as soon as I leave. Lisbon is a wonderful city, quite new and full of flowers and palms. Very clean, not like Marseille (though I nonetheless feel homesick for Marseille). I will write you again this week. . . . From here yesterday I wrote once again to our parents, after nine months. I am very glad for that and, if I have enough money, I will send something similar to Leo, because it is very, very necessary to do both.

A second letter from Lisbon, her mood somewhat dampened, followed five days later:

I unfortunately could not mail this letter yet, as I did not have the money for postage. Please excuse me for writing on such terrible paper, but I really do not have a penny to buy anything better. It pleases me very well here. H[ICEM] supplies us with meals and a place to sleep, but that's all. . . . I wrote home, but not yet to Marseille, since, as I noted above, I do not have a sou. Might dear Lina be able to send me some dollars? My shoes are totally shredded, and I have only one pair because in Marseille there is nothing to buy. Excuse me if I rush you in such a way, but I am really forced to do so. Everything is torn to pieces, and I have nobody here to ask for advice. I cannot ask the committee to buy me a pair of shoes. I will probably re-

main here for one or two more months and have really nothing more. This letter has become a complaint letter, but unfortunately I can't help it. I think that you, dear Lina, will not be angry about it, but there is terrible misery in the world. If you can send some food to Marseille and to our parents too, I would be very grateful. I would do it gladly, but I don't have the necessary means for it.

Nevertheless, on May 15th, only eleven days later, Margot was one of thirty passengers, all refugees though mostly Jews and other stateless people, who boarded the merchant ship *Ciudad de Sevilla* for the voyage to America. At the end of May, a letter from Havana brought welcome news:

We just arrived in Havana, and because I have no money to send you a telegram, I am sending you an airmail. Hopefully it will arrive there sooner than I do. We had a wonderful voyage; we were told that we would stay here for the next two days. But I have just heard that we will continue already this evening and will be in New York 3-4 days later. . . . Dear Lina, I hope that you at least are at the ship, because without a citizen I cannot get off the ship.

When the *Ciudad de Sevilla* docked in New York on June 3, 1941, Lina and my parents were at the pier to welcome their filthy, louse-ridden little sister, then three months short of sixteen.

Suzanne (Suzy)

FOR EIGHTEEN-YEAR-OLD SUZY, however, there was to be no escape. Too old to emigrate under a children's quota as Margot had done, she had been left behind in Marseille. Before they sailed, Leo and Erna had arranged for her to stay with a Swiss friend of theirs, a Frau Holz, who rented out rooms. In return for room and board, Suzy was to clean the house, walk the dog, and help out as she could.

Only a single letter of hers survives from that period of her life, when she was on her own in Marseille. In October 1941, having only then—two months after the event—received news of their mother's death, she wrote Margot:

> *The news that mother is no longer among us has made me very despondent. She should have remained with us for a long time yet, but God wanted it differently. Poor, dear father is now quite alone at home. I would so gladly do everything possible to get him out of Germany, but from here unfortunately one can do nothing. I personally would also like to come to the U.S.A., but unfortunately, I can do nothing about it because everything must be completed from over there, as everything goes through Washington. If you want to be so good as to help me do what is necessary, I would be very grateful to you. . . . If you want to write to*

me, my address is: Suzy Schack, c/o Weisser, 9 rue Grignan, Marseille B.d. Rh. I would be very happy to get news from you from time to time. I will answer immediately. This year is a very hard winter; "qu'est qu'on entend depuis longtemps, dans les quartiers de la ville, pas de savon, pas de charbon, plus des patates, pas de l'huile is a song for our time" ["what one has been hearing for a while in every quarter of the city: no more soap, no more coal, too many potatoes, no more oil!"]. *But what can one do: endure!!! Otherwise there's little new going on. In the hope of good news from you, I am for today, your Suzy.*

Her family made strenuous efforts on her behalf. Lina, especially, traveled several times to Washington to try to arrange immigration documents for her sister. Nothing, however, could be done and—until the war was over—all further connection with Suzy was lost.

After the war, safe at last in New York, Suzy refused to speak of her wartime experiences. What had happened to her from her late 1941 to the war's end in 1945 was unknown to anyone in the family until after 1995, when—at the request of their two children, Paulette and Marvin—she and her husband Otto (a survivor of seven concentration camps) gave oral testimony to an interviewer from the USC Holocaust Foundation Project established by Steven Spielberg with the goal of recording as many memories of survivors as possible. In what follows, I will quote liberally from Suzy's testimony.

From the Testimony of Suzanne Goldschmitt, née Schack, for the Shoah Foundation

In 1941 my brother, his wife, and their son (by then they had a son) managed to buy visas to go to Morocco, but everything was money then and there was not enough money for me to have the same visa. So my brother made arrangements for me to stay with a friend of theirs, a Swiss lady, who rented out several rooms in an apartment, and I stayed there to help her and walk her dog and all these things. In May 1942 the edict was passed that all foreign Jews had to register to get a récépissé [a temporary residence permit required of all foreigners applying for residence in France]. *I went to this office and this man who gave me the récépissé told me that I was on the list to be arrested the following day. That was May 30—no, it was Jeanne d'Arc Day, which is May 14.*[47] *So I went home and got whatever money I had and went to the drug store to buy sleeping pills. I took the sleeping pills; the following day I was recovering in the hospital run by French nuns. They kept me five weeks and I returned to this Swiss lady and again I had to register on August 1, and this gentleman told me again that I was on the list to be arrested the following day, deportations were rampant then. I had no more money to buy the pills, so I went to the kitchen of this lady and put the gas pipe in my mouth. And the following morning I woke up in La Concepcion* [the convent affiliated L'Hôpital de la Conception], *where they pumped out my stomach, I remember that very vividly. . . . And they kept me again five weeks and they told me they couldn't keep me, they couldn't shelter me any longer, the Germans were after them to release me.*

In response to the interviewer's question as to why she tried to commit suicide, Suzy responded simply: "*Because I knew, because I lived after all in Germany. I saw Kristallnacht and knew what they were capable of. I knew what they did to my father when he wanted to say goodbye to us.*" She continued:

> *And there was a family that came to the hospital to bring toiletries and sometimes a little bit of food, because everything was rationed at the time. And they said they would take me in. I think one of them, the wife, was Jewish, I don't think the man was, and I stayed with them on the outskirts of Marseille, not in Marseille proper, and one day my brother had a friend who later on became a leader of the Maquis, the French resistance, and he let me know if I wanted to I could pick up some food in his apartment and take it back to where I stayed. And I walked down his street and was arrested by the French police. It was a sweep, an arrest sweep, and I was taken to the Sureté. . . . That was late September 1942.*

As "Schack" is not a characteristically Jewish name, she was not identified as a Jew. However, because (as the police told her) her brother and his family had left illegally, on purchased visas, she was brought to a house of detention.

In November 1942, the Germans entered Marseille, and the deportations began. Early one day in late November, all the detainees were packed into trains, under guard of French gendarmes, and sent to Gurs, the notorious detention camp for foreign refugees.

> *We stayed in this detention home until, I think it was November 24th or so, I am not sure anymore. . . . That's when the Germans were reputed to enter Marseille. Up to then Marseille and surroundings were of course the French Free France, France Libre, and the Germans were entering Marseille that day in the morning, so we were taken to Gurs. . . . At two o'clock in the morning—they were supposed to enter Marseille at six o'clock—at two o'clock we left Marseille on a train to Gurs, and we arrived in Gurs, it was just horrendous. It was a regular train, compartments and everything, but there were so many people in one compartment.*
>
> *When I was arrested in Marseille all my belongings were in one suitcase that this Swiss lady had forwarded to the people with whom I had stayed after I was discharged from the hospital. But when I was arrested, the police asked me if I had any personal belongings that I would care for, and I said no, because I knew if they would pick up that*

suitcase they would pick up these people as well, and I did not want to betray them. So when I came to Gurs I had no personal possessions, in fact in order to get a toothbrush I sold my bread, the ration of bread that I had, because I had absolutely nothing.

One of the first established and largest of the French detention camps, Gurs opened in April 1939, more than a year before the German occupation. Located a few kilometers from the village of Gurs in the Basque country foothills of the Pyrenees, about fifty miles from the Spanish border, it became infamous for the cruelty of its conditions: overcrowding, food and water shortages, and disease (including typhus, typhoid fever, and dysentery). Many detainees died there. Initially intended for the detention of political prisoners (largely members of the International Brigade fleeing Franco's Spain), it soon became a prison camp for mostly German Jewish refugees—designated "enemy aliens"—at first for those already living in France, later for many deported from Germany. In 1942 and 1943, thousands of Jewish prisoners from Gurs were released to the Germans, who sent them first to Drancy, a transit camp in northern France, and from there to the extermination camps in the "East" (largely to Auschwitz).

Suzy described her experiences in the camp:

When we arrived in Gurs we were taken to barracks, which were located in îlots *['islets'], maybe ten barracks in* each îlot, *and were separated by barbed wire from other îlots. We were put together with people who were deported from Germany, who were deported from Baden-Württemberg, who were uprooted from their homes and were taken to Gurs in, I suppose, 1940."*

Interviewer: *"Were they Jews?*

Jews, all Jews, everyone was Jewish, uprooted, and I tried—I was very, very sick at the time and emaciated—so somebody suggested Secours Suisse [the Swiss Red Cross], *which meant I could have one meal every day, one plate of barley, and then they told me I couldn't have it anymore because I was eighteen years old, I was too old for this. But if I wanted to, I could earn my food every day by staying at night with a person who had typhoid fever in what they called a hospital. Each* îlot *had an infirmary but there was one designated building as a hospital outside of the* îlots *across from the train station. So I said sure, I would do that. So I was with this person for about four weeks, and I had a meal every day . . .of vegetables, the bread was made of sawdust, which was completely rotten after two days, and they gave us a soup dish that was made of root-type things.*

But in that hospital was an orderly who was from Spain. And he wanted to learn French and I wanted to learn Spanish. So he taught me Spanish and I taught him French and finally I said to him I really would like to go to Spain and subsequently to America because my sisters are in America. . . . "Can you help me?" And he said, "Yes, I will teach you enough Spanish so you can get along." We learned then [about] the trains, there was another camp in the southern Basque-Pyrenees, which was called Rivesaltes[48]. . . and one day, when we looked across from the hospital and saw so many trains arriving with people inside, but these people were not permitted to get off the trains. That's when we learned these people would go to the East. I don't know any more how we learned it, but we did, so I asked him if he would help me get to Spain, and he said yes, to go to Pau [just before the border]. There was another young lady, she was from Saloniki in Greece, she lived in Paris then came to Marseille, she also was deported from the detention home in Marseille to Gurs with me, and we decided we would go together to Spain. Being from Saloniki she spoke some Spanish, which was Ladino really, the Jewish Spanish and we managed to escape.

One night, it was a moonlit night, this young man escorted us, or rather he said he would meet us outside the barbed wire. So we crossed the barbed wire and all of a sudden I felt a bayonet against my chest. It was a young man who was patrolling the area, and I thought he surely would push the bayonet through, and I said to him, 'Quel âge avez-vous?' and he said he was eighteen years old, and I said, "That's just as old as I am. You're only here because you don't want to go to Germany to do forced labor." And

I talked to him to convince him that he should let me go. And finally I managed to convince him and he said, he offered a certain time, I don't know any more if it was midnight or two A.M., that he would whistle, and we should follow his whistle (this young girl and I), and he would lead us to the road that led from the camp to Pau. We did that, we escaped. I had on a dress that was completely torn to shreds because of the barbed wire that caught us. So we managed to get to the road and walked and walked, and every once in while we put our ear to the ground to hear if a car was coming to pick us up, because we always had the fear that our escape would be discovered. And when we heard cars coming we went into the ditch alongside the road, covered us with leaves, it wasn't summertime after all. Finally we got to Pau, managed to get into the railroad station into a train and we sat down. My dress was full of caked mud because of the ditch that we had been in. We cleaned ourselves off, I cleaned her and she cleaned me, and we were sort of presentable. When we sat down in that train, we see on the other side a French and a German coming in to ask for Cartes d'Identité. *So we went out onto the platform and there was a water pump, and I decided I would pump water for everybody around, and I would not be discovered. I see the German and the French gendarmes coming out and go into the next train and then into the next car. So we went back into the train and that took us to the*

French-Spanish border in Hendaye, and we wanted to walk across and that's when we were arrested by, I guess it was, the Germans. They had on brown uniforms which I learned later were from the OT, Organization Todt,[49] *they were building reinforcements along the Atlantic, and they brought us to an office where we were interrogated. I was separated from my friend, she was interrogated separately, and one of the officials said, "Denkt Sie dass sie Jüdin ist?"* ["Do you think she is a Jewess?"] *and the other one said, "Nicht mit diesen blauen augen"* ["Not with those blue eyes"]. *But I never let on that I understood what they were saying, because then they would have asked how come you speak German, and my cover would have been blown. I told them that I was born in Liège, for I learned from other people that all the archives of the town were destroyed, so they couldn't have researched me. Somebody told me that in that detention home in Marseille, and I hadn't forgotten. They shipped me then to Germany, to* travaille forcé, *forced labor, they never knew I was Jewish. And I kept a very low profile in Germany and did work in Bremen-Farge, I supposed was also reinforcement,* Organization Todt, *the same organization that built all these fortifications.*

Situated on the Weser River in northern Bremen, Bremen-Farge—the forced-labor camp where Suzy spent the remainder of the war—was part of a large industrial compound primarily dedicated to construction projects for the German Navy. Most of the workers were forced laborers—among them civilian detainees, prisoners-of-war as well as concentration camp inmates. Most worked on the construction of an underground U-boat shipyard.[50]

Suzy's descriptions of her life in the camp came largely in response to specific questions from the interviewer.

> *I was assigned to build with mortar, cement, to build these fortifications. And I always kept a very low profile, as I say I did not let on that I knew German. . . . I did not want anybody to know who I really was because you did not know if the next one would tell, you know, who I really was. You never knew. [There were] mostly women in our group but not only French, there were also Greek, Russian, and Polish. . . . A Polish woman was in charge of the group. As far as I know there were no Jews there. I was convinced I was the only one. . . . The living quarters were barracks, the food was terrible, terrible: rotten potatoes, once a day, in the evening, rotten potatoes, beans, where you could see roaches crawling, vermin crawling in it, and the day of liberation came not too soon. Sanitary conditions were terrible, terrible. . . . That one did not get dysentery or anything like that was just a wonder. Clean drinking water was very hard to obtain. I was very sick by then already, I had double pleurisy. I don't really remember all this too well.*

She told of the prisoners' being forced to rise at five in the morning for the count and lineup, lest someone escape. When asked how many days a week they worked, Suzy first said six, then seven, unable to recollect exactly (or perhaps tired at that stage of her testimony). Although some of the inmates often spoke and even sang together to keep up their morale, Suzy never joined in *"for fear of being discovered."* When asked by the interviewer if they ever heard anything about the war's progress, she replied, "*We heard rumors that the Americans came on shore in June 1944, but sometimes rumors were not true.*"

The remainder of her testimony is brief: "[We] *were liberated by the British April 24, 1945.*" Though seriously ill, she went up to the first soldier she saw and asked, in English, how to get in touch with her sister in America. She was told to talk to the Governor-General but achieved nothing. Somehow, she managed to get back to Marseille (she still did not know how) and went to the local relief organization, which sent her to a convalescent home outside the city and then to another in Lausanne, on Lake Geneva. When she heard that the atom bomb had been dropped on Japan, she was euphoric, but said she never stopped wondering what would have happened had it been dropped on Germany.

Back in Marseille, she re-encountered a friend of her brother, Otto Goldschmitt, nine years older than she was. Otto had made his way back to Marseille after having survived imprisonment in seven different camps, among them Auschwitz-Birkenau. In November 1945, Suzy and Otto were married and settled briefly in

Marseille. Suzy was unable to remember how they then subsisted.

They sailed on the *S.S. Washington* from Le Havre, arriving in New York in August 1946: *"I was expecting a baby at that time and took care of that baby."* Suzy ended her testimony with these words: *"The world has learned nothing from our experience,"* holding up as examples Cambodia, Bosnia, and Rwanda.

In his testimony, towards the end of his own vivid and gripping narrative of his experiences and remarkable survival, Otto continued and augmented Suzy's account of their reunion, decision to marry, and subsequent emigration to New York.

From the Testimony of Otto Goldschmitt for the Shoah Foundation

I met my wife the first time in the year 1939 when she came from Germany with her younger sister and [they] were accepted by her brother and his wife. Her brother Leo was one of my better friends, and naturally I met the girls there. My sister-in-law, Margot, was thirteen years old, and Suzy was fifteen years old. But that was about it, I just met her and I knew who she was. But we did not have any social connections because after all she was a young girl and I was more or less a mature man. Well, it came about that the war came between, and came 1945 and I went back to Marseille and she did too because she had nowhere else to go. And the address I knew was my uncle's former business at the Place de la République, and there I got my mail.

Well, in any case, I lived my life, I had friends which I met in the meantime, took care of me, and one day in August I was in the store and a young girl came and asked for me, probably not recognizing me. And I wasn't [working] in that store, I was just visiting. And I identified myself and she identified herself too as Suzy Schack, and she said, 'How do you do; I have regards for you.' Because one of my friends, deportees, she was in the same sanatorium as Suzy was. So we started talking to each other, and we realized that we knew each other from before the war through her brother, and we met together and talked together, and it came that I didn't have anybody living there no more and her family didn't live there no more, there was nobody to be connected with and friendly with, so I made the proposition one day, I said to Suzy, why should we not get married and take it from there and know who we are, and she looked at me, and it didn't take her long until she said 'Okay. Yes.' So that was September-October 1945. So we reported that to the camp director who was very friendly with everybody there and he said, sure, that was very nice, and we went to the temple and talked to Rabbi Salzer in Marseille [Israel Salzer, chief rabbi of Marseilles from 1929 to 1974], *and we had our friend Louis Reichenberg go with us.*

So arrangements were made, we went to city hall to make the preliminary arrangements for the marriage, and so we got married on November 24th in city hall in Marseille. But this being a Shabbos, *the wedding could not be in the temple. The temple was arranged for the next day, Sunday November 25th. And we were given a first rate ceremony, red carpet and all things, even though that Rabbi Salzer did not like my coming back. Because when I came back to Marseille, I went to his temple and while I was in his office I told him off, that he came to* Les Milles,[51] *talking and crying and all kinds of things, that he didn't have the guts to take at least one child out of it, which he didn't. He didn't do nothing; either he was scared or too lazy. There were other people who took children out of* Les Milles *and saved them from being deported, but Rabbi Salzer didn't. In any case, he had to perform the ceremony, as I said at the time, with vinegar in his mouth. Because after all he had to make a little speech and whatever. We got married on that Sunday and arrangements were made by the Jewish organization for a reception, for which I have pictures to show. It was very, very nice, especially as my two friends, Louis Reichenberg and Lilo Simpson were doing the arrangements for it. And, on the Saturday, we had also a reception at* Les Camoins, *which was a French resort, and the invited ones were the mayor of Marseille, the General of the Army from Marseille, and an elected official from the government. They were sitting next to us. As a matter of fact I have the write-up from the Marseille paper....*

Suzy's fate was unknown to her family in America until after the war, as was the fate of the rest of the family in Germany, France, and the Netherlands. Hope there was, of course, that some—perhaps miraculously all—had survived, hope articulated by Leo in an August 1944 letter to his sisters:

> *Hopefully we will very soon have news, if possible, from our dear father and Suzy as well as the* Wolfs [Clara and Jakob] *and Gaby and children, also from the Salomons* [in St. Avold]; *we did hear something about Minna's husband Sally, although it was not very good news, namely that he was deported, but so many are said to have been, it is in the realm of possibility. I was in Toulouse with Sally one day before I left France; he is a very nice fellow. It looks as if the war is beginning to come to an end; it is surely time finally to be able to receive some news and hopefully joyful news about all of those who belong to us. And also to be able to do something for them. . . ."*

Leo's hopes (and fears) were repeated the following year, in a letter from the second of May 1945, just a few days before German surrender:

> *We often hear news from dear Lina; she seems to be working hard and awaiting the return of her husband soon.*[52] *I don't believe that it can last in Europe. Just this*

instant I listened to the radio of the fall of Berlin. It will be indeed too bad if Hitler is dead, as was announced yesterday; he will have merited a greater punishment. And I hope that they will not forget to make an accounting some day. But can they ever pay for the crimes that they have committed? And now surely we will hear news of our dear father, of Suzy, of Clara and Jacob, of Aunt Gaby and her children, and Minna and hers; last of all, let us hope that the news is not too bad. Though I have very little hope after all that we have read in the newspapers about the crimes of these bandits. But it is not necessary to lose all hope.

When the war at last came to an end, there was at least some good news in word of Suzy's survival. Leo—writing in March 1946, almost a year after Germany's unconditional surrender the previous May—provides the only contemporary indication of her condition after her long incarceration:

Today we received a card from Suzy, from the Sanatorium, which affected me very much. Hopefully, hopefully, she will get healthy again. I must do everything in my power to help her. I have sent a package, and I hope that I can help her in every relationship. Hopefully all will go forward. And I hope also to see you soon in New York. Erna and I are thinking about combining a trip to New York with a business trip, once Suzy arrives. I have already requested an American visa, and perhaps we will travel as Mexicans. And I am determined to celebrate Suzy's arrival in New York. With luck, the paperwork will go smoothly, and dear Suzy will again be completely healthy.

The rest of the news, however, was devastating. Initial word of the others' fate came in the form of a letter from *Tante* Blondine Kaufman of St. Avold, the sister of *Tante* Clara's husband Jakob. In the first word in almost four years about the missing family members and written four months after the German surrender, Blondine revealed to her nieces in New York that Suzy was the sole survivor of the entire Schack and Rothensies family who had remained in Europe. My mother's screams as she read it are among my earliest and most powerful memories.

"My dear Irma and all the loved ones! I found your address via Suzy today, and I want to make immediate use of it. Unfortunately I cannot bring you any good news. I will make it short, because I am not in the mood to report all the details. I have to wait a little!" She began with the death of her son-in-law Salamon, her only child Minna's husband.

> On September 7*th*, dear Sally unfortunately died after two years of deportation. . .of general weakness, his body completely run down. Poor, good Sally was a victim of these barbarians. I am sure you can imagine how we feel, ... [his] children's entire happiness is destroyed. Liliane is 11 years old

and Georges is 3½. Poor Sally suffered badly. For five years we lived sixty kilometers from Toulouse, and there in Toulouse Sally was taken away on the street. He was in Auschwitz and had to leave there January 18 for Dachau. Under the worst conditions and deprivations he arrived in Dachau on April 27, and this was enough! The SS was always after him.

A brief, terrible summary followed, outlining what was known about the rest of the family:

Tante Gaby was shot to death, Margot and Susanne [my mother's young and gifted Saarbrücken cousins] *were burned in the gas chamber after having been abused by these barbarians. All this happened in Auschwitz-Birkenau. Of* Tante Clara *and Uncle Jakob, as well as of your father and his second wife, all traces are missing. Most probably had the same destiny as the others. About Irma's family we also know nothing. Your husband's brothers as well as their families were partially shot to death and burnt. One can never be happy again, because these events are impossible to describe in words. Later I will write more about it, but now I want to wait for mail from you. . . . For today please receive warm greetings and kisses from your Aunt Blondine.*

We now know that my grandfather, Moritz Schack, perished in Auschwitz. Clara and Jakob Wolf were among a group of 233 Jews deported from Frankfurt on September 24, 1942, and sent on a transport train, via Berlin, to Raasiku, Estonia (a small village near Talinn). On their arrival, all 1,700–1,750 passengers, except for a few young women who were chosen to be sex slaves at concentration camps in Estonia, Poland, and Germany, were immediately taken from the train station to an execution site at the nearby sand dunes at Kalevi-Liiva, in Estonia, and shot.

A few weeks later a letter from Blondine's daughter Minna added to the brief account. Though grieving about her own situation—losing her beloved husband, left alone with two young children ("*Oh Irma all the terrible things he suffered—Jewish destiny . . . . One does not want to exist anymore, so as not to know anything about this world.*")—Minna goes on to list the many dead or missing: *Aunt Gaby, like Margot and Susanne, was murdered already in 1942, but of* [her twenty-year-old son] *Arno we know nothing. Also of your Papa, Aunt Clara and Uncle Jakob it has been almost impossible to get exact news. If we want to know more, we will have to wait for people to come back and report to us.*" Other names follow, Blondine's family, some alive, some deported and missing or killed in one or another of the camps. Yet Minna ends on a slightly less despairing note, with hope a better future—"*Life is hard in France, but I believe too that this will change in a few months*"—and reminisces over better times: "*My dear Irma. I still see you in front of me, how you performed at our wedding, now twelve-and-a-half years ago and an entire life totally destroyed.*" My mother continued to correspond with both Minna and Blondine to the end of their lives.

IN THE SPRING OF 1962, WHEN I WAS twenty-two, I visited St. Avold and met Blondine, Minna, and Minna's son Georges for the first time. Minna's daughter Liliane was by that time married and living in Paris. They were wonderful and generous hosts, although my limited German and French and their lack of English somewhat impeded our conversations. Georges, just a year or so younger than I was, had learned some English in school, and he was determined to show off his American "cousin." So off we went in his little Citroën and, circling and re-circling the central square, he made certain that all his friends got a good look at me.

Blondine lived to the age of 106. My aunt Lina, on a European trip with her son and his wife in 1989 or 1990, visited her in St. Avold, when she was over 100, and reported on her astonishing mental acuity, even bringing back a video as evidence.

And what more do we know of the fates of my mother's Uncle Hermann's widow Gaby and their three children? A letter from *Tante* Clara, written from Frankfurt in September 1941, strikes an ominous note: "*Of Gaby and the children we have heard nothing more for a long time.*" Having left their home in Saarbrücken for Poitiers, where Gaby's sister lived, they were arrested in 1941 and taken to the Drancy transit camp, from where, in 1942, they were put on transports to Auschwitz-Birkenau. The Auschwitz record for Gaby, from Aug. 31, 1942, describes her cause of death as "sudden heart attack." According to the records at Yad Vashem, Gaby's "number" 23592 was "retired" on August 8, 1942, although the death certificate—of which I have a copy—lists the date as August

19, 1942. There are no explicit records of the deaths of the children: Margot, age twenty; Arno, age nineteen (his vocation was given in Auschwitz as *"fliegende handler"* or "hawker"); and Suzanne, age fifteen. Rabbi Joseph Schachter, my source at Yad Vashem, thought they might all have died in the death march, when no records were kept. The last thing heard from any of them was a note, written in blurred pencil on a scrap of paper, from the "baby" Suzanne. Thrown from a cattle car, presumably headed east into the anonymous countryside and delivered (somehow) to her Aunt Blondine in St. Avold, to whom it had been addressed, it read simply, *"Only God can help us now."*

CHAPTER 5

The Glückauf Family

Amsterdam (1933-1943)

IN 1910, MY FATHER'S FAMILY MOVED from the small city of Wanne-Eickel, their home for the past year, to the large and prosperous Ruhr Valley industrial city of Dortmund. There, over a period of years, they established several successful retail stores, some selling clothing, others household linens. However, as early as 1931 the Nazi party took strong root in Dortmund, as it did throughout the Ruhr, and there began a secret boycott of Jewish businesses. At the same time, pro-Nazi thugs began to attack Jewish businesses directly. After the Nazis assumed power in January 1933, the anti-Jewish actions of physical abuse and destruction of property of Jewish owners and employees only worsened, as occurred throughout Germany. My father's older brother Erich, in his 1976 memoir, *Begegnungen und Signale* [*Encounters and Signals*], described the continual harassment of the family brought on, at least in part, by his own Communist party affiliation.[53] In addition, Franz-Josef Schmit, in an article on the Glückauf family's history and experiences from their arrival in Wittlich to their deaths, noted the frequent house searches to which they were subjected, with all members of the family except for the youngest, Ilse, ordered to Gestapo headquarters for questioning at least three times weekly.[54]

After suffering several brutal interrogations, certain that their lives were in danger if they remained in Germany, my father and his younger brother, Werner boarded a train for Holland. Getting off at a station near the German-Dutch border, they waited until dark and stole by foot across the border, headed for Amsterdam, which already in 1933 was a haven for endangered German Jews. The day was April 19, 1933, the day before Hitler's forty-fourth birthday, which coincided with the passage of numerous anti-Jewish decrees and their widely anticipated "actions." Five months later, on September 23, their parents followed them to the Netherlands. With the interrogations continuing and their businesses all but dead, Julius and Johanna (Hanna) Glückauf, fearing further violence, decided first to close and then sell their stores at whatever price they could get and, accompanied by nineteen-year-old Ilse, join their sons in Amsterdam. Although my father was soon to leave Amsterdam to move in with his brother Erich in Saarbrücken, the rest of the family was prepared to start a new life in the Netherlands.

My father's family was part of a Jewish exodus from Germany

to Holland, France, and Belgium that began in 1933, immediately after Hitler's appointment as Chancellor, and continued into the mid-1930s. From the outset, the Dutch, both Jews and non-Jews, greeted their German brethren with ambivalence, even hostility. Dutch anti-Semitism, while muted, was nevertheless real and prevented meaningful assimilation by Dutch Jews, who were for the most part Orthodox in religion and of modest means.[55] Nor did the Netherlands welcome foreigners. In fact, they were actively opposed. Furthermore, the German Jews—generally assimilated and religiously liberal (largely Reform rather than Orthodox)—were often disdained even by their Dutch co-religionists, thought too arrogant, too affluent, and still (notwithstanding their harsh experiences) too proud of their German culture and values. Eventually a policy evolved—part governmental, part private and philanthropic—that provided some financial and other support to those in need while discouraging long-term settlement. The unfortunate result of these policies, which probably were also designed to minimize popular antagonism towards the refugees, was that most refugees received insufficient help and were left largely to their own resources. However, as noted by historian Bob Moore, other countries did no better, most of their citizens at least as unwelcoming to the influx of refugee Jews as were the Dutch.[56]

When Julius, Hanna, and Ilse arrived in Amsterdam, they had with them some furniture but little else. Hanna—always called "Mu" (for *Mutti* or Mom) by both family and friends and always exceptionally industrious—began immediately to take in boarders.

The family found a small apartment on Uithoorn Straat, in the leafy area south of the city that was to become their new home, as it became home to many of the city's newly arrived German Jews. In fact, the German Jewish settlement of the area eventually became so widespread *"that the number 24 tram was re-christened 'The Berlin Express'."*[57] That first apartment consisted of three rooms plus kitchen and bath. The entire family slept in one of the two bedrooms, renting out the other to a series of boarders, largely refugees sent by the "Committee for Special Jewish Affairs" (*Comité voor Bijzondere Joodse Belangen*) which, according to Ilse, paid "a minimal amount" for their accommodations. Funded mainly by the Dutch Jewish community, the Committee was established in 1933 to aid the increasing stream of refugees entering the Netherlands. Though engaged in some anti-Nazi propaganda, its primary function was to ease the refugees' transition between entry and emigration elsewhere. Following the German occupation, however, the Committee began to pursue a policy of cooperation with the Nazis, hoping thus to minimize Jewish persecution. It eventually was merged into a larger *Joodsche Rad* or Jewish Council, which—like similar *Judenräte* in other countries throughout occupied Europe—served as a conduit for Jewish leaders to enforce German anti-Jewish policies.

HANNA COOKED FOR THE BOARDERS, and Ilse served meals in the largest room, which had been reserved for the purpose. Other people—called "diners" to distinguish them from boarders—soon joined the group for the evening meal. Thanks to my grandmother's skill and hard work, the *pension* proved so successful that the family was soon able to move to a somewhat larger apartment, at Waalstraat 80. My parents lived there with them for a brief time after their arrival from Paris at the end of August of 1935, before renting their own apartment nearby. They continued, however, to return each evening to eat with the family, where, according to Ilse, "*they paid and were waited on like all the others.*" The late 1930s saw the Glückauf family move to a yet larger apartment in the same leafy and quiet Amsterdam-South region, on *Zuideramstelaan* 61, a long, wide boulevard (renamed *Rooseveltlaan* after the war). After the Nazi invasion, Hanna, now widowed and with few remaining boarders, moved once more, to a smaller apartment on *Merwedeplain*—the same street on which Anne Frank's family had lived before going into hiding.

Many years later, in a July 1982 letter, my aunt Ilse described daily life at the *pension* in its heyday:

> *About eight people lived in furnished rooms and were served three meals daily, and at least ten others came for the evening meal alone. Most were German refugees who were sent to our pension and financed by the Jewish Committee. There were also a few Dutch who looked for good food at a cheap price. My mother worked hard, cleaning and shopping and cooking, which she had never done before (she had always been a businesswoman); but she ad-*

justed and became a good, imaginative cook, never measured anything, mostly German specialties. And it always tasted good. I worked long hours during the day in different households: cleaning, washing, all the things maids have to do. When I came home, I helped my parents: serving dinner, helping with the dishes which was usually my father's job (I still see him sitting in front of the washbasin, washing dishes and peeling potatoes); Werner and I dried them, and I think my mother put them away.

Over the next several years, their boarders consisted of a shifting population of German Jews and a few Dutch citizens, mainly pensioners. Among the former were two couples who eventually settled in New York and whom I remember from my childhood—Walter and Trude Mendelssohn (he the grand-nephew of the great composer, and a poet and intellectual in his own right; she a flaming redhead with strong and generous sexual appetites), and Elsbeth and Herbert Gordon, who later became my parents' closest friends. Herbert too was a poet, although he became a salesman in the United States, traveling throughout the southern states selling store window decorations. Elsbeth was a tiny, mostly silent woman, whom everyone called *Mäuschen* (meaning "little mouse," which in fact she rather resembled). Werner and his wife also continued living at the boarding house, even after their marriage in 1939. Although Werner earned a small income by riding his bicycle around the neighborhood and selling miscellaneous goods, mostly to other refugees, according to his sister, "he also depended a lot on mother's care, like all of us."

Among the diners was a newly married refugee couple from Berlin, Ruth and Heinz Levitz. Ruth, who returned to Amsterdam for her last, widowed years, after many years in Los Angeles, recollected those days in a 2002 phone conversation: "*We ate there whenever we could afford the fifty cents it cost for a good dinner. Afterwards, there was always a tremendous uproar over who was going to do the dishes.*" The Dutch residents or diners included an on-again, off-again couple, Joh de Leeuw and Ester Resen (he a Christian, she a Jew), who remained steadfast friends to my grandmother until the end, as well as a shifting group of aged retirees. These (always referred to by my grandmother as "*the old ones*") received both room and board and, after the Netherlands closed its borders to German Jews, became the family's sole source of income.

The emigration to New York in 1937 of first my parents and a few months later of Ilse and her new husband, Kurt Kratz, led to a remarkable series of letters from my grandmother to her children. There are nearly a hundred letters in all, many of them long, about a third undated fragments, and all so difficult to read that I had to ask my half-sister, Lotte, in her 80s and schooled in the pseudo-Gothic script, to transcribe them. The letters chronicle the family's life in Amsterdam during the years 1938–1940, before the Nazi occupation, and then (albeit obliquely, as most were written under the censor's eye) the increasingly terrible year following the German invasion on May 10, 1940. The correspondence came to an end in October 1941, but it is through these vivid and poignant letters that I have come to know something about the grandmother I never met and others in the family. Because Hanna's letters reveal so much about those last few years of their lives, I will quote liberally from them in my effort to tell their story.

What did these letters tell me? For the first few years, most reveal Hanna's daily life of hard work but relative security, as the family, largely through her efforts, gained increasing economic stability. This reversal of the economic norm was, according to Moore, not uncommon among refugee families, with the men unable to work and the women finding some form of officially acceptable (or invisible) domestic employment. For my grandparents, however, several concurrent and obviously more distressing situations dominate the letters from mid-1938 through mid-1939.

One of these was my grandfather's illness and (after three months' hospitalization) his death. Julius, a diabetic for many years, had until 1939 been in relatively stable health, although there had been a few brief, intermittent hospitalizations. In early February 1939, however, Hanna wrote of a new, more worrisome hospitalization:

> *His condition has worsened, and his heart is somewhat weakened. He must have plenty of rest and that cannot occur here. Every little thing upsets him and his mood has been terrible. . . . We will probably also have to move from*

our apartment, as he may no longer climb stairs. For me, it's already too burdensome. . . . For a long time he hasn't helped me at all. . . .

Despite medical treatment, Julius never recovered sufficiently to return home. By late February, he was further weakened by a bout of influenza. Though he "*survived the crisis,*" neither his mood nor his underlying condition improved. Hanna described the situation in mid-March:

> *He would so much like to come home, and I would be so happy to have him. But it is very difficult because he is so weak and restless, and someone would have to care for him day and night. I am with him every day and even become nervous from that.*

Although Julius died on April 8, Hanna still wrote as if he were alive on April 13, five days after his death, no doubt reluctant to admit the truth to her children:

> *With us things no longer look good. For dear Papa it seems very bad and hopeless. Things have gone otherwise than I thought. It is very hard for me, dear children. I will try to remain strong.*

Not until a few days later did she concede the truth:

From my last lines you surely could understand that our dear father has gone from us. I never really wrote you how ill he was; nevertheless we never believed he would die so fast. It's so hard and the separation so terrible. I was still with him in the evening. Approximately half past one we were called that he had died without knowing it, on April 8 at 5 AM.

There followed yet more worrisome news. As in all her letters, Hanna refers to Erich only by his first initial, presumably fearing that the letters were not secure and that any direct mention would endanger both him and the rest of the family:

I also have a great concern about E[rich]. About three weeks ago he was stopped on the street and arrested. He had no passport and no papers and stated that he was here to visit his sick father and to attend the funeral. He stated that he had lived legally in Belgium in 1936, which is also true, and now had come from there illegally. We definitely believe that he will return to Belgium, once the information about him arrives from there. I do everything for him that I can. I am permitted to visit him once every week. It is terrible that I now have these additional sorrows.[58]

Erich

ALTHOUGH NOT YET FORTY, ERICH HAD a notable history. Having joined the German Communist youth organization shortly after the

First World War, when he was only sixteen, by 1923 he was editing Communist newspapers in Westphalia and the lower Rhine. In 1925 he married a fellow party member, Gertrud Meier, from an orthodox German Jewish family, and two years later their son, Rolf, was born. The same year, in 1927, the party sent Erich to Berlin where, in addition to his work with the parliamentary press service, he became secretary to the Communist Party faction assigned to the Reichstag. After five years in Berlin, in 1932 he was appointed chief editor of the illegal Düsseldorf communist party newspaper, *Freiheit* ["Freedom"], a position he held until the Nazis came to power in 1933. With all communists in Germany under threat of arrest following the February 1933 Reichstag fire for which they had falsely been blamed, he like others was forced to flee. His next assignment was Saarbrücken in the independent Saar Territory, where he edited the local party newspaper, *Arbeiterzeitung* ["Worker's Newspaper"] and where he first met my mother. (See Chapter 2.)

Following the Saar plebiscite in January 1935, like most other political exiles he fled to Paris, but his stay there was brief and often interrupted by party-mandated trips abroad. Always traveling under his code name "Oscar," he spent short periods in Belgium, Luxembourg, and Prague among other places. Upon the outbreak of the Spanish Civil War in 1936, he joined the International Brigade in Spain. Thus, for the past three years he had been based in Barcelona, working with the Spanish Popular Front and directing the illegal German anti-fascist radio station, *Deutscher Freiheitssender,* 29 (8) ["German Freedom Station"], traveling frequently within Spain to cover the war on various fronts.

What may have been his most important and admired broadcast occurred on the evening of November 10, 1938—the day following *Kristallnacht*—when *Deutscher Freiheitsender,* 29 (8) broadcast the following radio message to Nazi Germany. The broadcaster was Erich himself:

> *To all Germans! The Communist Party is speaking to you; it appeals to every decent German. Down with the abominable Jewish pogroms, which dishonor Germany! ... No fair-minded German can accept these Nazi atrocities. No fair-minded German can blame our Jewish fellow citizens for a rash and senseless crime that serves only fascism. The Jews are human beings like us. . . . Workers! Upstanding Germans! Turn away from these vicious pogroms! Help the persecuted and tormented Jews. . . ."*[59]

Long out of touch with his family, he at last wrote to his parents in January 1939. His mother's relief was palpable: "*Yesterday, thank God, after a long period, we again had news from E. He is fine. His address:* Redaction 'Frente Rojo' *(write 'for Oscar' on the envelope) Barcelona, Trafalgar* 14th." Within a month, with the Republicans facing total defeat by Franco's forces but to his mother's great relief, Erich wrote again. As Hanna informed Paul and Ilse, "*Today we received a few lines from E., namely from Paris. Now he is far enough away* [from the Spanish war, presumably]. *I am so glad, because I have worried tremendously about him. Thank God he always knows how to protect himself."*

Less than a week later he sent her a contact address in Sweden, in Långmora in the province of Dalarna, about two hours northwest of Stockholm. It seems likely, however, that he was not yet actually in Sweden, as barely a week later he wrote again from Brussels where—as always—he was traveling under an alias and with a false passport. At last, to his mother's great joy, he appeared unexpectedly in Amsterdam—his next assignment—having managed to cross the Dutch border illegally with the aid of Belgian party comrades. His arrest and imprisonment came on the day following his arrival. According to Erich's account of the arrest, he had gone to a cinema for an arranged meeting with the local comrade, when he was seized and arrested by two Dutch policemen.[60]

Throughout his autobiography, Erich generally presents himself as the insouciant hero of the narrative. Such is also the case in his account of his arrest, imprisonment, and release (all probably to be taken with a grain of salt): "*The hearing was short. I had no papers and said that I was a German refugee, an Anti-Fascist. They wanted to know where in Amsterdam I was living or where I had slept the previous night. I gave no information.*" When they threatened to *"put [him] on a train"* and return him to Germany, "*I answered calmly, 'If that's your decision, I can't change it, but it would then be better if you just gave me a coffin.'*"

He describes being brought into a large room, where there were twenty to twenty-five people. Most were Jews, whom the Dutch police had captured as they crossed the German border. "*They asked me who I was and from where I came. I answered, 'I am a Communist and everything else is my own business.' Then the news went from mouth to mouth, that I must be a Russian spy.*" The police searched him, and when they found the key to his Amsterdam apartment, he says that he responded: "*If you know everything, I don't have to say anything.*" His account continues with example after example of his bravado throughout his imprisonment and until his release.

Despite her grief over her husband's death, Hanna devoted all immediate effort to trying to free her son. To her continuing despair, however, he remained imprisoned through most of May. As she wrote to New York in early May: "*E. has given me considerable worry and grief. I hope that he soon can return to Belgium.*" Ten days later, she wrote again: "*With E. there is still no change. I would be so happy if he were free once again and was able to get away safely. I am trying so hard for him, but things just continue their course. Yes everything here is terrible.*"

While in prison, he managed to receive permission to attend his father's funeral, but only under the condition that his ankles be shackled to a stick so that escape was impossible. Describing the funeral in his memoir, he mourned most of all not the loss of his father but "*the sight of the eldest son, who could only laboriously and painfully advance*" because he was in ankle chains. Even in lamenting his mother's absence (she apparently had chosen to remain in her apartment), he focused on himself: *"I never saw her again. I could not give her a kiss, not even press her hand."*[61]

Not until early June was Erich finally freed and permitted to return to Belgium. In an undated fragment, probably from later June or early July, Hanna described her anxiety and subsequent relief:

I do not know if I have already written you that everything worked out so well with E. He has gotten permission to stay in Belgium and now lives freely in Brussels. I cannot tell you of all the worry and unease he has caused me here. I always imagined the most terrible things. I ran there every day to try to help him, and I've done everything possible. It is now a relief to me that everything went so well.

And then a surprise, or perhaps not a surprise given Erich's womanizing history: Notwithstanding his wife in Moscow, Erich wrote his mother of *"a dear girlfriend in Paris, whom he has also visited."* However, by late July, Erich (always on the move), wrote his mother that he was *"no longer in Paris."* She continued: *"I don't know anything definite about where he is now and wait for news. Everything happened very quickly."*

Where he was, evidently, was Norway. Together with another "comrade" and only shortly before the war's outbreak, he had been sent there by the Central Committee of the Communist Party to establish another newspaper, *Deutsche Volkzeitung* [German People's Paper]. By the end of the year, he had been joined, by his "friend" from Paris, Eva ("Evchen"); she was with him, he wrote to his mother, making him *"so happy. She runs the household and everything, of course, goes fabulously."* The newspaper, however, enjoyed only a brief existence and made little mark. As Erich recounted in a seven-page typed autobiographical manuscript, written in 1954 and found in his archives, four weeks after the Nazi invasion of Norway in April, 1940: *"I left by decision of the Norwegian party and, together with some other comrades, crossed the border to Sweden, where we were arrested by the Swedish police and interned."*[62]

The internment was at Långmora, one of fourteen Swedish internment camps established for German refugees—largely communists and Jews – although a few suspected criminals were placed there as well. There Erich remained until the end of 1940. For the next few months, he wrote from Sweden, always reassuring his mother that he was well.

By the end of 1940, thanks to the Swedish *Rote Hilfe* ("Red Help"), he was in possession of a work permit as well as a job. Throughout his internment, *Rote Hilfe*—the German affiliate of the international Communist aid organization that provided support to political prisoners worldwide—had been bringing him statistical work to do, despite his lack of prior experience in the subject. When his internment ended, he heard of, applied for, and managed to win a position with a social science institute at the University of Uppsala, north of Stockholm. Once having received the necessary residence permit, he began doing statistical research for a doctoral candidate, who was writing a thesis on *"Causes and Extent of Dis-*

eases of the Spirit in Sweden." As Erich later wrote, the knowledge of Sweden and Swedes he gained by working on that study proved invaluable afterward, as it gave him considerable insight into Swedish customs and social problems.

When that job ended, he acquired employment at a vocational school, although it is not clear in what capacity, whether as laborer or teacher. In his letters, however, he complained that the hours were long and the work hard. At last he was ordered to Stockholm to help lead the German Communist Party in Sweden and serve as a liaison to Soviet intelligence. From 1943 on, he held the position of Editor-in-Chief of the Stockholm-based German-language, antifascist magazine *Politische Information*. As soon as the war ended in 1945, he returned to Berlin.

At some point, his girlfriend Eva vanished from his life, as Hanna noted in a May 1941 letter. She had received from Erich "*a picture postcard of the Pentecost trip*" and seemed to take great pleasure in the pleasant life he described: "*He had a great time and now gets fourteen days vacation, which he is spending at the lake. The most beautiful thing he writes me is that he still likes the bachelor life very well. That's so like E.*" To the end, despite her deprivation under German occupation in Holland, with food and fuel ever scarcer, with the Jews increasingly restricted and isolated and their situation more and more dire, she continued to be genuinely supportive of Erich and always seemed proud of his good fortune. Three months later, in August, another letter again expressed joy at Erich's well being: "*From E. I had good news again. He spent fourteen days on vacation by the sea and lives very comfortably. He has also had his work permit renewed. And he still has a fine radio, even when one considers the static."*

Where, all this time, was Erich's wife? Some information was gained by Franz-Josef Schmit, who met with Erich's granddaughter, Sonja Wolfermann, then living in Halle, as well as from Erich's "Cadre File." According to Schmit, Gertrud and their young son spent the war years in the Soviet Union where, both before and during the war, she gave German lessons to Russian military personnel preparing for action in Germany.[63] According to Erich, the last time he had met with his wife until after the war, when she and their son Rolf also returned to Germany, was in May 1934, at the Hotel Lux in Moscow. The hotel was a favorite of the many exiled German party members during the mid-to-late 1930's. It was then that Stalin, becoming suspicious of the many international occupants of the hotel, began to arrest and imprison them, fearing they were spies. Most of the leading German communists who were killed in Stalin's purges were residents of Hotel Lux.

Erich and Gertrud divorced in 1947. Erich then married Edith Jordan, a lifelong party member and the daughter of a party functionary executed in Danzig [now Gdansk] in 1941. Until his death in 1977, Erich and his second wife lived comfortably in East Berlin, where they were visited several times by his sister Ilse and her husband. Although his reputation within the party was undermined by growing skepticism about the accuracy and truthfulness of his recall of events and his memoir was never given the party's official imprimatur, he was nonetheless much honored by the DDR in his later years, with a large boulevard in East Berlin given his name and a state funeral held at his death.[64]

Werner

HANNA'S LETTERS RECOUNT A HAPPIER chain of events regarding the youngest son, Werner's, courtship and marriage. Werner, described by his sister Ilse as *"very plain, unassuming, not the brightest but honest,"* was clearly a worry to his mother. Thirty years old, still living at home, and seemingly more prone to self-promoting fantasy than hard work (which, in any case, would have been difficult for him, as an immigrant, to find), he seemed destined for a life without prospects.

His engagement, in the fall of 1938, to 19-year-old Selma Mingelgrün brought his mother great joy:

> *With Werner, it seems now to be serious. We were invited to spend a few days with her parents, and tomorrow is our big reception. They are really very nice people and [she is] a fabulous girl. . . . They were originally Eastern [European] Jews, but the father has lived in Berlin since he was seventeen. Selma is slightly taller than Werner and has a good slim figure. . . . It is a fine family.*

In the letter's postscript, Selma and Werner too expressed their happiness, with Selma openly revealing her joy in the relationship: *"With Werner I get along unusually well. Do you still understand some Dutch?* Het is een schat!" ["He is a sweetheart."] Werner, no less extravagant when describing the loving family circle of parents and in-laws ended with the boast: "*I can confirm to you that I land the big prize every time.*"

The couple's great hope was that with the assistance of their American family they too could come to New York. Aware that Selma was his greatest asset for a successful emigration, Werner wrote: "*I think it best if I come over with Selma. What do you think of it? Obviously I am not coming without means. Selma is a skillful, very hard working and economical girl.*"

In early January of 1939, he wrote again of their forthcoming marriage and desire to emigrate:

> *We can report to you that next month we will most probably step into the federation of marriage. You have told us of the difficulties and possibilities over there. We were able to envision it all. As a result, we came to the following conclusion. If you want to help us to come over there, you will have fulfilled a great dream of ours. We will certainly manage it. As soon as we are married, you can initiate everything for us. You will be informed beforehand.*

To this Selma bravely added:

> *If you want to and can help us, we are not afraid of anything. In any case, I have a profession. I work with my*

father in the tailoring business and hope that once I am in America, I will find something in my field too. Otherwise, I am willing to change. I am firmly motivated to take hold of anything I am offered. . . . Perhaps we can pay you back for all your assistance and help.

Selma's diligence and willingness to work hard (even after she became ill) is a constant theme of Hanna's letters. In fact, Selma became increasingly important to her as other aspects of her life became more troubling.

The wedding, scheduled for March 9th, was to be a grand affair, as Hanna described it, with seventy-five guests and *"according to Dutch custom, both wedding and reception in a rented hall."* But although delighted with the upcoming marriage (*"It is clear that Werner is lucky, to get a girl like her"*). Hanna remained unenthusiastic about the lavish, planned celebration, especially in light of Julius' illness:

We hope that [Papa] can attend the ceremony. . .I'm not in favor of such a celebration, but the parents want it very much. If Papa cannot be there, I have no desire to go . . . . Werner has already chosen a tuxedo and top hat, on loan of course. Everything is now in great excitement. Only I am left cold. First, I'm not one for big parties, and then without Papa I have no desire. . . . I will be glad when it's all over and Werner starts his regular duties.

Plaintively, but with evident relief, she added: "*You see, dear children, that someone has now been found for Werner also.*" Although the original plan had been that Werner and Selma rent a room elsewhere and occasionally join the others for evening meals, the reality turned out to be that they lived mostly in the *pension* as, according to Hanna, "*while Selma works she has no time to cook and so must also learn.*"

With Julius's worsening illness, however, some changes in the wedding plans were required. The week before, Hanna informed the other children:

> *Thursday is the big day and Werner comes under the chuppah. It will now be celebrated in the house, but there will be about seventy people at the reception. Well, that's all right with me. I don't have much to do and will let myself be served. I was never in favor of the celebration; Werner could put the money to better use.*

And she added, showing the common German-Jewish disdain for the more religious, less-assimilated, and usually less-educated Russian and Polish Jews, "*but Eastern European Jews won't have it any other way.*"[65]

With the wedding over, Hanna delighted in her new daughter-in-law, as she wrote only a few days after the wedding: "*The young couple has now been married eight days. The wedding day was not pleasurable for me, and I was happy when everything was over. They are now with me and it is a good thing, as I am not so alone. . . . They do make a fabulous couple. Selma is really a dear girl, and I think I will get along with her very well. Next week she will begin to work.*"

Yet there followed some unexpected news: "*Selma has been sick for three weeks, and today, for the first time since the wedding, she is with her parents. On the wedding day she very much had to pull herself together.*" The subject of Selma's apparently chronic illness runs like a thread through most subsequent letters. Continually ill and losing weight, she was eventually sent to a sanatorium, where she was force-fed. Whether she was anorexic or suffered from some wasting disease is never said.

Hanna

Aside from her own daily struggles and concerns, most of my grandmother's letters reflect her worries about her absent children: my father and Ilse in Depression-ridden America; and Erich, first in Spain, later fleeing stateless from country to country in his effort to avoid deportation or arrest. In letter after letter she expressed her sorrow over the family's separation, her fears for her children's health and well-being, her longing for an eventual reunion—and her hunger for their letters. Over and over one reads the same phrases:

"*The main thing is that you are healthy and things go well.*"

"*If we all just stay healthy, we can hope to come together again.*"

"*My great hope is that we all will have our good times back and see each other again." "Just stay brave and well."*

Particularly poignant—revelatory of the current situation, wherein children emigrated and parents were left behind—is the heart-rending remark, *"Everyone says now that children have turned into letters."*

My father, especially, was a continuous source of unease to her: his health, his strength (which, according to his sister, had been of concern to his mother since his childhood), as well as his ability to find and hold a job. My mother, with her fluent English and exceptional language skills, had found a position immediately. Referred by her cousin Theo's wife, Carola, who already worked there, she was hired to do research in the Names Department of the H.W. Wilson Company, the Bronx-based publisher of bibliographical indexes like the *Reader's Guide to Periodical Literature* and the *Cumulative Book Index*. Only a short trolley ride from their apartment in Washington Heights, its offices occupied a handsome building with a distinctive lighthouse tower overlooking the Harlem River.

For Paul, on the other hand, finding a job was not easy. With little English and few transferable skills, he struggled to get work and then, as is clear from his mother's letters, to hold those jobs he found. His mother tried to encourage him: *"About you, dear Paul, I am particularly pleased that you've acquired the American tempo regarding work and have done things right. . . . Are you once again back at your old job with the brushes?"*

She was no doubt referring to an "on-again, off-again" job he held on first arriving in New York, selling shaving brushes for a German-Jewish manufacturer, Leopold Ascher, who apparently preferred hiring refugees. Paul sold brushes for Ascher again in the late 1940's. I still have one of the brushes—in fact my father's own brush. Interestingly, a few years later the young Henry Kissinger's first job was at Ascher's factory.[66] Julius, characteristically mocking the situation, had written on learning of the job, "*Mr. & Mrs. Monsieur & Miss Brush, I was very glad to hear that you now have a brush factory.*"

When his mother learned, in February 1939, that Paul, together with his sister-in-law Lina, had purchased the lease on a small luncheonette on Lafayette Street named the *Silver Star*, she was ecstatic: "*You could not bring me greater joy than when you are so brave and have such courage. I am proud that you have your energy back. It will be a lot of fun, I imagine, and Lina is really very well suited to these matters.*" With her usual good sense and practicality, and conscious, no doubt, of Paul's unhappy prior business experiences, she focused on both the risks and promise of this new undertaking:

> *You will certainly have great expenses. I suppose the money for all the utensils you need for such an operation must be borrowed and with interest. But I think if one is only 'on the post'* [auf dem Posten, a favorite expression] *one can do well and build something good. So we hope, dear children, that it really is worth your time and will succeed. Then we will pack our bags and look forward to being once*

again with you, which is still my one and only desire. Then I will see your big business, Paul, which would be lovely.

Congratulations on the new business also arrived from Irma's mother, although she was somewhat more skeptical of its success: "*For the business I can only say Mazel Tov. You are very young, and I hope you can manage to keep the operation going. You, dear Paul, are not really in the mood for it, and your head is not into it. It may be easier after some time passes, though for you, dear Lina, it's too much. I wish I could help you.*"

Hanna's optimism continued for several weeks more:

How nice to know that you are working for yourself, to be your own man. Only be careful, dear children, and work hard, then it will work out. You have in Lina such a fine partner. . . . I am already looking forward to the picture that I hope you will soon send. Now, dear Irm, you probably no longer need to cook and can go directly from work to the restaurant.

The skepticism of both mothers was confirmed when the restaurant went bankrupt after only a few weeks, although neither learned about the failure until the summer. Paul and Irma evidently were too embarrassed to spread the news. Hanna's doubts had soon arisen, as little word came from Paul. In mid-March she asked, "*Are you still so pleased with the business, dear children? I hope soon to hear from you.*" Paul's silence, however, evidently continued even as his father's health rapidly declined. After Julius's death, Paul and Irma's failure to mention the business contributed to his mother's general unease about their welfare, and she asked directly in both June and July: "*In your last letter you wrote nothing about yourselves, whether you my good Paul still have the restaurant. . . . Do you, dear Paul, have worries about the business or other things, or don't you have it anymore? For weeks you have not written. I hope nothing has happened. One thinks of all sorts of things.*"

Finally, in late June, a letter arrived from New York containing two pieces of news. The first was the admission that the restaurant had indeed failed, so that both Paul and Lina once again had been seeking employment. Hanna's response was restrained and not unsympathetic: "*For two it was surely insufficiently profitable, particularly in summer. From eating one cannot become rich, otherwise I, with all my thrift, would have gotten further.*" The second piece of news, though it evoked some mixed feelings, was more welcome: Irma was pregnant, the baby due in January. Hanna's anxiety regarding their tenuous economic situation, especially as Irma would soon have to give up her job, was mitigated by her joy in the coming grandchild: "*Perhaps it will be such that we get a replacement for dear Papa. So it is indeed in life—one comes and one goes.*"

Why did the business fail? According to my Aunt Lina, the fault was primarily my father's. As had so often happened in his employment history, his initial enthusiasm for the enterprise apparently waned quickly and he began showing up later and later, leaving most of the work to her. In addition to having paid the full $500 cost of the restaurant's lease from her savings, she simultaneously had to cook, serve the customers, and manage the ordering and the books—far too much to handle alone. Paul, she said, would turn up late in the day, usually joined by Irma. They would eat their dinner, he would perhaps help out a bit—but that was it. When the restaurant inevitably failed, the loss was considerable, even though they were able to sell its equipment to the successor to the space. That Paul's weaknesses and Irma's strengths were known even to their friends in Amsterdam is corroborated by a note the previous summer from their Dutch friend Ester Resen: "*Dear Paul and dear Irma! Hopefully you are well in every aspect! Does Paul have a job again? Is Paul still so meshugge* [mixed up, crazy] *and Irma still so good and talented?*"

DURING THEIR FIRST YEARS IN AMSTERDAM, my grandparents had been concerned primarily with establishing an economic foothold. Grateful to have escaped from Germany, they felt that they had found at least a temporary sanctuary in the Netherlands, although all but Erich saw emigration to the United States as the ultimate goal. Paul and Irma, the first to leave, were soon followed by Paul's sister, Ilse, and her husband, Kurt. Meanwhile, Hanna and her youngest son, Werner, continued to entertain the hope of following the others, as her great desire had always been that she, her husband, and Werner would be able to unite with Paul and Ilse in New York. Only after Julius' death did she acknowledge for the first time that *"Papa didn't really want to."*

With Julius' death, however, Hanna's hopes for emigration diminished drastically. Born a German citizen, as her birthplace (the town of Tuchel on the Polish-German border) had been annexed by Prussia during the first partition of Poland in 1772, she now was considered Polish, as Tuchel (now Tuchola) had been transferred to the Second Polish Republic under the terms of the 1919 Versailles Treaty. While Julius lived, Hanna, as his wife, was a German; with his death, she became a Pole, and subject to the far more restrictive United States Polish immigration quota. The result, of course, was that her emigration became almost impossible.

She understood the problem she faced: *"Now that dear Papa is no more, I must go under the Polish quota, as now Tuchel belongs to Poland."* Although she had heard a rumor that mothers of legal United States residents might be exempted from the quota, what she learned on a visit to the American Consulate in Rotterdam was that the process could still take years. A few months later, by late 1939, even that hope was dashed:

> *I had written to the consulate in R[otterdam] and asked if I might be able to come under a preferential quota, as I heard that it was possible for foreigners who live there legally to request their mother. But today I received the news that it doesn't work for mothers, only for wives and chil-*

dren. So, dear children, we have to wait to see what fate determines, and hope that yet once more and not too long from now we can be together again.

Behind this new push to emigrate was the increasingly dire situation of the Jews in Germany. From mid-1938 onward, Hanna wrote often of her fears for friends and family still there, all of whom now wanted to leave. However, as the Jews in Germany became more and more desperate, the possibilities for emigration shrank, with fewer and fewer countries granting affidavits for entry. Like its neighbors France and Belgium, the Netherlands made entry ever more difficult: closing the borders, severely limiting admission, and forcing most new immigrants (except for children, who were housed either in private homes or in institutions) into detention camps.

Hanna's letters described the situation during the summer of 1938:

There are colossally many who have already emigrated. Now everyone wants to go, if only things would go that way. Here no one gets in anymore. Toni [a friend from Cologne] *wanted to visit us last week, and then leave in fourteen days. She sat in* Emmerich [the last German town before the Dutch border] *and was not permitted to continue. We waited in vain without knowing where she was. We are waiting for further notice.... We also have with us an older cou-*

ple who do not know where to go. They have money, they struggle to get their residency permit, but they don't get it.

Money no longer helped secure escape as Julius noted in his postscript: "*What do you say now to the trouble? Things are terrible in Germany, and they get worse. Now no one need swap with a Jewish millionaire; now everyone is poor. We are doing well, and we will muddle through until our ship comes in.*"

A month later, Hanna returned to the subject of emigration:

As we read in the newspaper here, America is closed for two years; that's a terrible blow, because everyone is looking there for refuge. One really does not know what will happen. Our older couple, who have a lot of money and very much wanted to go there, have been refused for the second time. They have to be gone from here by October 3 and do not know where to go. That is the situation now for most people.

One of Julius' cousins, who lived in Berlin, did manage to pass through Amsterdam that summer on the way to Cuba, which was still granting refugee visas, although his property had been confiscated and his wife, children, and parents were forced to remain behind. "*You can imagine how much he is worrying,*" wrote Hanna. "*Yes, that is how it works now for the rich. They did not want to listen to us, and now it is too late. The amount of red tape is un-*

believable." It took two months before the cousin's wife and sons were able to leave Germany with visas for the Czech Republic. There they stayed another month, before she and the boys arrived in Amsterdam, from where they finally embarked to join their husband and father in Cuba. Only after the war ended were they able to enter the United States.

Hanna continued to express gratitude that at least two of her children were safe, notwithstanding their economic hardship. By September 1938, however, her fear for the Jews remaining in Germany as well of a possible war becomes an ongoing subject of her letters. The fear of imminent war was probably linked to the Sudetenland crisis, the first concrete sign of Hitler's plans for foreign aggression:

> *Recent days, as you know, have brought so much tension and excitement that one is always upset. What the coming time will bring one doesn't know. . . . Here it looks as if there will be no more peace. You are so well informed about everything, dear children, and you can be happy that you are there. If only there were no heavy drudgery, dear Paul. . . . By the time you receive this letter, much will have been determined. . . . Dear Irm, be glad that you're there; it is horrible to live here in Europe. Make your life as comfortable as possible. It will eventually be easier for you, my dear, only have patience that you eventually will have something better, and it will come*

slowly but surely. If one listens to what is happening in Germany and what the Jews have to endure there, we should be quite content.

As the *pension* was dependent primarily on refugee boarders, the effect of the crackdown on foreigners was immediate: "*The pension. . .is mainly empty, since no one can come any longer.*" But, as always, Hanna continued reassuring her children about her own situation:

> *With us so far everything is still all right. Up to now, we still have had boarders, mostly here for only a short time before they emigrate. To stay no longer exists as a possibility and emigration is becoming increasingly difficult. I must say that you, dear children, got out just in time. Now it would be nearly impossible. Everywhere is a disaster, everywhere is locked. How did things get that way? What do you say about the war atmosphere? Until recently, I did not expect war, despite the fact that things looked very bad. Of course, it would be better if it did not come. Yet I feel there will be no peace.*

Two families still in Germany gave her the most concern. One was her sister and her husband, Henriette (called Jettschen) and Leo Hirsch and their son George, who also had a wife and young son. The other was Irma's family—her parents and young sisters—still in

Zwingenberg. Yet for a time in 1938, emigration to America for Suzanne and Margot, both still minors, actually seemed possible: "*How beautiful that even now your sisters, dear Irm, will soon come there, then there will probably also be a way for your parents. For the children there must surely be something.* . . ." Following *Kristallnacht*, however, after November 9–10, it became almost impossible for those outside Germany to help anyone still within. Hanna described what they knew of the situation in early December 1938:

> *How glad we can all be that you and we are still safe. Everything that one hears is terrible; every day we receive the petitions and yet are unable to help. We have requested all possible relatives. But no one can get admitted here unless he is in possession of a visa and ticket that shows he will stay here only a few days. Everyone is hoping for relief, but nothing comes. For my sister, Jettchen, it's all very, very bad. Their synagogue was entirely burned down. Her husband is in the concentration camp in Oranienburg. She is now in Berlin with [her son] George, who also does not know what he should do. . . . You can only imagine the despair. And there are countless cases. For me, the thought of Jettchen is so terrible. I have written to the Minister; I hope it succeeds. She can get her husband out [of the prison camp] only when they emigrate.*

Numerous Jewish men throughout Germany were imprisoned following *Kristallnacht*, including my mother's father, who had been sent to Buchenwald. Although Hanna worked tirelessly to help her sister and brother-in-law, her efforts bore no fruit. In early January 1939, she described the current situation, and her feelings of impotence:

> *Here there is often great excitement.* [In Germany] *things are happening, I can only tell you, terrible things. Most people are affected by it. But unfortunately, we cannot help anyone. I immediately requested your sisters, dear Irm, but we have heard nothing. Nor can we do anything for your father; no one can enter here legally. The illegals are now put in camps, and I think that no more illegals will be permitted to stay except for a few days with a visa. . . . Yes, these are the conditions, and one doesn't know what to do. I also requested* Tante Jettchen; *they were totally burned out and her husband was in the camp,* [though] *happily is now out. They no longer know where they should go and have nothing. But we still have not heard.*

She tried to help Irma's family by inviting them to "visit," hoping by that means to get them permanently out of Germany:

> *From your mother, dear Irm, we got news this morning that* [your father] *cannot come to visit here, he was back home. I had in fact requested the children because here it was said that children can come in, probably some have already*

come, but everything takes so long. Your mother thinks that your father is doing all right. But no one is allowed to come on visits any longer. Over there [in America] *they think it's all so easy. Unless you're risking your lives to get over the border 'on the black'* [i.e. illegally], *no one gets in here. I will write to him to come when he can, as he would be in good hands with us. Unfortunately, we cannot do more.*

Things only worsened as 1939 progressed. That February, although Werner, rather confidently (if naively) expressed his optimism ("*Until now, everything is still in the butter* [i.e., "going splendidly," always his favorite phrase]. *We live in such an island of peace*"), his mother did not conceal her worries about the current situation:

From D[eutschland] *one hears only suffering and misery. I have requested that* Tante Jettchen *and Uncle Leo come to us; perhaps they may succeed in getting here. I had to specify everything to the police. One must help people as one can. Besides the relatives, we also have a letter of request from* [friends] *from Frankfurt. . . . Refugee men have all been interned in a camp. Sp*[ain] *is completely devastated, and we have no idea where E*[rich] *is. It looks like there will be war, and here will probably be no peace until everything is destroyed. Unfortunately, we cannot change anything. I'm just glad that you got away in time.*

Though in the midst of her own difficulties, with Julius near death and Werner's wedding imminent, she worried greatly about Irma's family in Zwingenberg On February 19, 1939, she wrote Paul and Irma, apparently unaware that Margot and Suzy were already in France:

> *I think so often of your last words, my boy: 'Why are you crying, Mutti? If things go badly for us, we'll come; if all goes well, you come.'. . . I know dear Irm that you want most that I do something for the children* [i.e., Margot and Suzy]. *I did start something but never heard back. There are probably so many more children, though little ones. What will happen to the many thousands? I will write again to your parents so that they also try from there. But they must be doing things too. How about France?*

A few days later she wrote again, lamenting her helplessness, but having now learned that Margot and Suzy were safely with their brother in Marseille:

> *That your children, dear Irm, have gotten out, I am very pleased to hear; now we must also find some way for your parents. . .I feel terrible, dear Irm, that I can do nothing for your parents. It is impossible, since one hardly can do anything for next of kin, parents, etc. I was called to the police already four weeks ago for Tante Jettchen, and everything*

was recorded, but I have not heard since. They are doing so very badly, and she fears that her husband will soon be arrested again. One is not able to do anything about it. Can't your parents go to France at least temporarily? I would have loved so much help the children.

Her sister's fate was soon confirmed. Yet there remained some hope for others:

> Now, through Tante Jettchen, [I have heard] that their emigration is cut off. It is so terrible: they have lived so long with that hope and do not know where to turn. But I have done everything I could. One is just powerless. It's all so terribly sad there.... I have already written to Ilse about [American] affidavits for Werner and Selma. Now Kurt's parents are coming here before they have affidavits. There is also a chance for them to get away. His father has spent many weeks in a concentration camp.

Among the lucky few who did manage to escape to safety was Hanna's nephew George Hirsch, who with his wife and young son received affidavits for Shanghai and sailed on July 1. After the war, George and his family settled in Israel.

By July 1939, the situation was worse, as Hanna wrote despondently: "*From D[eutschland] one hears nothing good.... Tante Jettchen is very sick in a hospital in Berlin.... Who knows if war will come soon, it's all now so tense again with Danzig."* Her letter ends with a brief note that Irma's parents have moved to Frankfurt

One event alone brightened the otherwise gloomy summer. In July, Ilse arrived for a few weeks' visit, bearing gifts and briefly dissipating the gloom. The visit brought joy to her mother, whose greatest sorrow was always the separation from her children. Those few weeks, however, passed all too quickly. (Hanna afterward described the visit as *"like a dream."*) Ilse sailed back to New York in late August, just a few days before Hitler invaded Poland and war became inevitable.

For those in the Netherlands, the war was frightening but still distant: *"Yes,"* Hanna wrote, *"it has changed considerably in this time. For us it's still as quiet as in peacetime, and hopefully it will stay that way. One must wait, as one cannot change anything. . . . Let us hope that we remain spared from everything directly. But one is anxious about what will happen."* Yet the imminent onset of war seemed, paradoxically, to offer some hope for the Jews still in Germany as well as for her own future:

> *About your family, dear Irm, you needn't worry. Now the J[ews] will be left in peace, as there are greater things for others to think about. It is certainly a shame that they are not yet out. I am only imagining, unfortunately, but it is just an idea of mine that things could now go faster with my number, because no one can get out of Poland any longer. What do you think about that?*

But despite the surface calm, uncertainty prevailed into October: "*For us it is all peaceful, thank God. Let us hope that it remains so. What is to come now is unknown. One cannot count on peace, it all looks so sad. But we cannot change things and must accept what is. Now the whole world is in upheaval.*"

My birth, in mid-January 1940, brought "*joy in the dark days.*" Four days after, thanking them for informing her so quickly, the new grandmother wrote to the new parents:

> *So the little lady has arrived. I'm so glad, and happy tears wet this paper. I have waited day and night for this news. I see you my boy standing wonderingly in front of the bed. How much I too want to be there.... How happy you must be, dear Irm; you have wanted this for so long. I think back how happy I also was, and I can picture everything. So, my children, the best for you and the sweet little creature. I would hope that for me, too, this happiness is destined: to press my dear little grandchild to my heart.*

That wish, of course, was never granted: she never met either of her two grandchildren: neither Erich's son Rolf, then six years old and living with his mother in Moscow, nor me in New York.

And darker times ensued. Hanna deplored the uncertainty:

> *One cannot now predict anything at all. That is the case everywhere. We can do nothing about it and must wait*

patiently for what the future brings. There probably has not been such a cold winter for 100 years, and the snow is also quite high. Our cold apartment is also not so pleasant, [although] *my room is okay if I heat in a disciplined way. But even that will pass.*

More worrisome was the reality that there were now too few boarders to cover the expenses of the large apartment: "*I no longer have many people. There are no more retirees. . . . For a few weeks I have had a 75-year-old lady via the Committee for eight and a half guilders. The large room I have rented to a couple. Not ideal, as these are now the whole of my pensioners.*" The dearth of pensioners and the problems that caused was still the subject in mid-March:

For us things are very quiet. Hardly an occupied chair to see in the evening. No more pensioners are coming. We intend to take another, small, apartment. I was with the Committee lawyer, and he will make a request to the Minister, because Werner's benefits are bound here to this house and in special cases the Minister may authorize a change. If Werner can retain his benefits, we will move. The apartment is too large and too high up and impractical.

Yet even with her own difficulties, she did not forget Irma's parents, now in the ghetto in Frankfurt: "*I sent your parents coffee, dear Irm, and asked what they wished for. They answered me: Butter, she wrote she had enough of. They want some good fat and cheese. I'll send them something soon. It's a pity that they did not get away, but unfortunately that fate is shared by so many."* She soon sent another package, although she feared this might be the last:

> *I sent your parents coffee and butter; I want to send something more often. There are now all sorts of requirements when one wants to help. No end is in sight of this misery, and one can say nothing. I have just heard that it is now forbidden to send food to D[eutschland], so today I quickly packed and mailed a package for your parents, dear Irm: cheese, fat, coffee, milk, and some little snacks. They will be glad. I also sent something to my sister. It must indeed be terrible there, but your parents seem to have butter, because they do not want that. It's good that they are still together.*

Hanna Glückauf's letters of 1940 initially focus primarily on two subjects: her new granddaughter and her longing to come to New York to see and help care for *"our sweet Joan"* as she often referred to me. In March, Selma, never well, evidently suffered a miscarriage that even she herself saw as a mixed misfortune: "*Oh, it is perhaps better than if a baby had come. Everything is so uncertain for the moment; we do not know how things will continue for us.*"

Yet things seemed to lighten up a bit in early April, as Hanna wrote:

> *I have now rented the big room and to a single woman of eighty-two years. I get seventy guilders, very nice. A nephew, who has a factory here, faithfully provides for her. But as you can imagine, she is rather old-maidish and will probably eventually display all kinds of annoying characteristics. But as long as it lasts, it is good to have. I got them through a recommendation, because otherwise there are no pensioners. I no longer drive myself so crazy. Otherwise, I feel quite well, thank God, and everyone says I look well. . . . Selle feels well again and is working again diligently. Werner also earns quite a bit. Everything costs, of course.*

There follows some detailed grandmotherly advice about caring for my parents' *"sweet little doll"*:

> *If I could just watch her grow up and occasionally cuddle and kiss her, as I did with you my Paul. — But, dear Irm, don't make yourself so nervous. I did that too, but afterwards you always think it wasn't necessary. Yes, here too one starts with cod liver oil and an early dinner. You need not be so anxious, dear Irm, and just feed Joan properly. Selma's sister-in-law also has a little girl, and at first she was afraid that the child would starve. Now she is five*

months old and eats like a grown-up. Two slices of bread mashed with milk, then a plate of vegetables: spinach, carrots, etc. I've seen it, just fabulous. . . . I always think of our sweet Joan. But you, dear Irm, can surely make it correctly. — Whenever I get a letter from you, she is already four weeks older and when I write, the same. Time flies so fast, and when I come she will be running toward me. Of that, of course, I should not think at all. Now we want to remain calm and firm. That she sleeps through the night is very fine indeed. Yes, my dear boy, now you see how much work and effort children are but, as you write, one's great love of the children makes it all worthwhile. You always wanted a child, Irma, and I know you're now happy. It's good that you didn't take her out in the cold. It was such a terrible winter. Now little Joan is probably taken for a walk daily.

I can only surmise how my mother (never one to accept advice gracefully) received her distant mother-in-law's program of infant nurturing practices.

ALTHOUGH THREE OF THE FOUR GLÜCKAUF CHILDREN were now safely in exile, the situation of the Jews in Holland rapidly worsened. On May 10, 1940, Germany invaded France and the Low Countries, and the German occupation of the Netherlands began. Judging by my grandmother's correspondence, the occupation initially brought few changes. Two weeks after the invasion, Hanna sent a postcard to New York to reassure the family "*that we are all doing well and are healthy. I only wish to come to you quickly. If it were possible, I would telegraph to you even now. So have no worries my dear children, it is all right.*"

A second postcard, the first to bear the censor's mark that marks all subsequent correspondence, followed three weeks later, and is somewhat more guarded: "*For a time we have heard nothing from each other, and a lot has happened in the meantime. But the main thing is that we all are healthy now, as the telegram said. I was so happy that I could send you news so quickly. Just keep your heads high, dear children, it will all be well.*" Subsequent letters lament the frequent failure of the postal service and often open with a complaint that she is receiving no mail from New York. In August, after months of erratic mail, she hit on the solution—that they all use Erich, in neutral Sweden, as a conduit for their letters: "*I will write to E. today asking him to write to you. You can then reply to him immediately, because I do believe that from there it goes out more quickly. I write to you regularly every week, but I do not know whether you receive my letters.*" Once more she reassured them: "*Thank God that things are well for us and we are all healthy. . . . Everything goes here as usual, and I'm coping well with everything.*"

The letters of the next several months—most addressed to Ilse and Kurt (with frequent complaints that she heard all too seldom from my parents) and all showing the censor's mark—consist largely of news of daily life. Hanna writes of Werner's continuing unemployment, Selma's characteristic diligence, and the routine of what she referred to as her "retirement home"—and (always) about her visions of her beloved Joan's development and her longing to see the *kleinen Liebling*. Werner's brief postscripts, too, suggest that things are going well and life continues normally: *"I can only say dass noch alles in Butter bei uns ist"* [i.e., everything is still "in the butter"]. *All week we go to bed early, occasionally we are also more daring. Saturdays we pay a visit or vice versa and Sunday evenings we often go to the Café Victoria and drink our pale glasses."*

And, surprisingly, notwithstanding the German occupation, everything did seem to be going well at first. As Moore testifies, there were remarkably few changes during the occupation's early months, initial German policy being to maintain an appearance of normalcy and forestall opposition.[67] Nonetheless, there was no doubt that all of the Netherlands' estimated 140,000 Jews (about 14,500 of whom were German or Austrian refugees) had great reason to fear the future. German refugees felt particularly vulnerable. Although they had escaped Hitler's persecutions once, they were still considered "enemy aliens" by the Dutch and felt themselves to be entirely without social and political support. Many Jews—both Dutch and foreign—tried to emigrate. For most, however, escape proved impossible: there were few, if any, functioning procedures for emigration and, more critically, for most there was nowhere to go. Few Jews had the financial means and influence to get out themselves, let alone bring their families with them. Suicides increased dramatically, especially among the German Jews. Among them were several prominent Jewish politicians. According to Moore:

> *The Jewish cemeteries contain a disproportionate number of headstones dated 15 May or soon afterwards. Graves often contained whole families, and not just individuals. [A.J.] Herzberg speaks of simple, ordinary, middle-class people drinking tea, eating biscuits and calmly discussing how to save their children from the Nazi menace by killing them on the grounds that it was better that they should do it than Hitler.*[68]

In the course of 1940, the initial military government was replaced by a civilian government, directly under the Reich, that assumed control of the Dutch Civil Service. Mirroring almost exactly what had occurred within Germany, the occupying Nazi government formulated and gradually instituted official anti-Jewish policies of *"identifying, marginalising, and finally isolating the Jews."*[69] By the fall of 1940, restrictions on employment began to appear. First came the exclusion of Jewish employees from education, public office, and business—all with the compliance of the Dutch High Court. By mid-October, despite some unavailing protests by the Dutch Reformed Church and various university and *lycée* faculties, an "Aryan attestation" (a proof of "Aryan" origin) became a requirement for civil service positions: a single Jewish grandparent and membership in a Jewish community was sufficient to require dismissal. Towards the end of 1940, *Jews Not Welcome* signs appeared in restaurant and café windows. By January 1941, Jews were no longer permitted in cinemas, libraries, and concert halls; nor could Mendelssohn be performed. Jews could no longer employ non-Jews as servants, leading to Hanna's difficult search for a Jewish housemaid to help her care for the few remaining boarders. By February 1941, Jewish students were more-or-less banned from the universities, permitted to sit for examinations only with special permission from the head of the Department of Education. An unintended, although welcome, benefit of these "exclusions" was that unemployed Jews (Werner presumably among them) were prohibited from being drafted into the labor contingents sent to Germany and thus, ironically, were the only ones to continue receiving government aid.

In late February 1941, roundups and deportations began, centered on the traditional Jewish neighborhood surrounding the synagogue in central Amsterdam, which the Germans—with the assistance of the Dutch police—were hoping to turn into a *de facto* ghetto. A raid on the Jewish quarter led to the arrest of 600 men, who were sent first to Buchenwald, then to Mauthausen. None survived.[70] Although the brutality of this attack evoked resistance in the form of a Communist and Social-Democrat led general strike, the impact of the protest was minimal. Mostly it served as a reminder to the Germans to operate more discreetly.

All along, despite lack of a coherent German policy regarding what was to be done about the Jews of the Netherlands, there was a continuing effort to encourage them to believe that emigration was still possible. Under orders of Reinhard Heydrich, chief of the Reich's main security office in Berlin (and thus head of both the Gestapo and the criminal police), a *Central Office for Jewish Emigration* was established in Amsterdam early in 1941, despite the fact that—given the few opportunities for emigration by that time—the only actual goal could be mass deportation. Nevertheless, the office managed by various deceptive initiatives to persuade the Jewish Council that real possibilities still existed, although its main role, behind the scenes, was to prepare for the Jews' deportation. In August 1941, any doubt that "emigration" meant "deportation to the east" was eliminated in a document linking the two, with the earlier-used word "*Auswanderung*" ("emigration") replaced by "*Aussiedlung*" ("resettlement").[71] The following year, Heydrich served as chairman of the Wannsee Conference that formulated the "Final Solution" of exterminating all Jews remaining in Europe.

The year and a half between February 1941 and July 1942 (when the actual deportations began) had seen the systematic isolation and exclusion of all Jews in the Netherlands. Legislation was introduced only piecemeal, whether, as Moore puts it, to "*keep the Jewish community guessing about German intentions, or mere sadism on the part of those involved*" Over the course of the first six months of 1941, most Jewish newspapers were shut down, Jews were forbidden to own radios and were ordered to turn them in, various Jewish professionals (among them doctors, lawyers, and pharmacists) could no longer serve non-Jews, orchestras were "Aryanized," and Jews could no longer swim in public pools. By the summer, large-scale arrests began, with the victims again sent to Mauthausen. Resistance was met with violent retaliation and further deportations. The Jewish Council's policy of cooperation resulted only in greater restrictions. By late summer and early autumn of 1941, all Jewish assets (both money and property) had to be registered at a bank, formerly Jewish but now German. Jewish children were banned from the public schools. Forbidden for Jews signs appeared "*in parks, zoos, hotels, cafes, guest houses, theatres, cabaret and concert halls, libraries and reading rooms.*" Traveling became impossible without permission, and Jews were prohibited from visiting holiday resorts. Jews lost most economic rights, including their pension protections and the protection against arbitrary dismissal. In September, all German Jews were required to register for emigration with the *Central Office for Jewish Emigration*, a direct result of Hitler's explicit demand that the first deportees from the Netherlands should be its German refugees. Though they had to fill out thirty different forms, no one had yet received an exit visa by late November. In addition, it was now decided that the rapidly growing number of unemployed Jews would be eligible to be sent to labor camps after all. Though many were initially declared physically unfit by Dutch physicians (two Jewish doctors among them) and others failed to turn up at the station, those who passed were sent during the worst time of that cold winter to the eastern Netherlands, replacing Dutch labor contingents sent home because of the harsh weather. From winter onward, thousands of Jewish men were sent to the labor camps, living on more limited rations and working for lower pay than Dutch workers.

Even more devastatingly, in early 1942 the Germans began sending all non-Dutch Jews to the concentration camp at Westerbork in the northeast Netherlands, the first step towards deportation to the east. Simultaneously, largely because Westerbork even at its most crowded was too small to hold all the Jews in the Netherlands, the Germans rounded up all the Dutch Jews they could from the provinces, confiscated their property, and relocated them to central Amsterdam, where they were crammed into the apartments of the unwilling Amsterdam Jewish residents. Moreover, in January, all Jews were required to have their identity papers stamped, initially with "J" (for *Jood*) or, for the offspring of mixed marriages, "B" (for *bastaart*), though the latter was shortly replaced by "G" (for *gemengd* or "mixed"). By the end of March 1942, all sections of the Nurnberg laws were declared applicable to the Netherlands. The main effect was to prohibit marriage and sexual relations between Jews and others. Jews betrothed to Christians were ordered to report to the Security Police (SIPO). Of those who complied, the women were immediately sent to Ravensbrück, the men to Mauthausen; all perished. At the end of April, it became mandatory for all Jews to wear the yellow star, making it easier to implement their exclusion from public places. As Moore concludes, "*The isolation of Jews in the Netherlands was all but complete by the summer of 1942.*"

Hanna's silence about these events is a striking though understandable response to the Nazi occupiers' censorship of all mail. During the first months of the occupation, from late May to August 1940, there are only two letters. In both, she laments only the infrequency or absence of mail from her children, although once the process was implemented of posting letters first to Erich via neutral Sweden rather than directly between United States and the Netherlands, she soon began to receive more mail. Generally, in her early letters after the occupation began, she tried to reassure her children that things were not as bad as they may have been imagining, reassurances echoed by Werner in his occasional postscripts. In the spring of 1940, she was still able to write: "*With us things are still quite good, we lack nothing. . . . I, thank God, feel very well, look good, and I have no difficulty doing the things I must do. Today for dinner we have eaten a fine chicken. We lack nothing.*"

A dramatic change in October 1940 was the family's sudden move to a smaller apartment. As always, my grandmother described the change as a matter of choice:

> *You'll probably wonder why we're moving so quickly. There is nothing going on here in this cold shack. If I have only few people now I can get through. I have really no more desire to feed people for these few cents. Also, the fact that Ester has moved out, that we hadn't expected. But I took these matters seriously and immediately rented another apartment. So [the new address is] Merwedeplain 10, four rooms with central heating. I think we can move already by the middle of next month.*

In early November, she wrote again:

What do you say to my quick decision, to take such a nice apartment? I think I have made the right decision. Things will be easier and more enjoyable for me. There is nothing more here. Now we will have something small but nice. I will have only one room to rent, yes there are only four. All the old commotion will be done with.

As she explained, the benefits were obvious: the ground floor rather than the first (hence no more stairs), a lovely garden outside, and but one set of tenants to care for. Yet according to Ilse and Kurt, the move had been forced, and the larger apartment in which they had been living was taken over by a Nazi official.

Though her letters always emphasized the warmth of the new apartment and the beauty and peace of her beloved "*Tuin*" (always using the Dutch word for "beautiful garden"), there are hints throughout the summer and fall of 1940 of increasing restrictions: "*In our garden, it is still nice; I no longer go to the one in the city. You know that I always prefer to remain in our neighborhood. . . . Soon one will be able to meet everyone on a bench.*" Even their financial situation seemed bearable as late as September 1940: "*Selle still has a lot to do and Werner also earns something. If things continue this way, we will be satisfied.*" In fact, in the same letter she mentions that "*I am once again writing a poem,*" this time in honor of the upcoming birthday of their Dutch friend Joh.

Food became increasingly scarce. By February 1941 a chicken dinner was only a wistful dream. Reading Ilse's account of her birthday celebration (in late January), Hanna only responded: "*The chicken, dear children, I would so much love to have, and everything else you describe also sounds so lovely. Now we must wait and see how things develop.*" And their isolation was evident, although Hanna tried to make it seem voluntary: "*We are always at home; the evenings bring visits from the family in our little garden.*" (July 12); "*I have a lot of acquaintances, but still go to no one. The evenings are getting dark so early, and then it is still best at home.*" (October 1) She does not mention the general curfew that had been imposed in February 1941 after days of anti-Nazi strikes and riots that made arrest likely for anyone on the street after dark.[72]

As always she tried to put a positive spin on her remarks:

> *In the last week we have had fabulous summer weather. Sitting on the bench in the sun I also have some time to relax. At noon I lie down often in our garden for an hour and envelop myself in blankets. One must enjoy life as it comes, one does not know how everything will turn out. One cannot change anything and everything must go according to Fate.*

A belief that emigration was still possible continued to bolster her hopes that she (and perhaps Werner and Selma too) might yet be able to join the others in New York. As a result, as late as the spring and summer of 1941, she continued her efforts to obtain an affidavit from the American consulate in Rotterdam. Her letters to New York from May to August 1941 illustrate the difficulties faced by anyone still hoping to emigrate.

In a May 1941 letter to Ilse and Kurt, Hanna described the bureaucratic morass she was encountering, caused partly by confusion as to the number of affidavits requested:

> *So now time is our concern. As yet nothing has been achieved. The misconception that the affidavits should be for us three is probably not yet cleared up, in spite of the fact that Ester* [their friend Ester Resen, who knew English] *has written about it. Today I received another report from the R*[otterdam] *consulate. They are also of the view that the matter is based on an error, because the affidavit for me alone must be sufficient. I must now return again tomorrow to all the correspondence from R. and the Committee and then take the matter immediately in hand. It probably will take a while for me before things are that far. Nor can I get the papers from Tuchel* [i.e., verifying her birth], *so this must come from Berlin. . . . You have completed it now for me and hopefully the papers will come quickly now. I do not know now how long everything may take, and who knows what will be. So, dear children, we must wait patiently and let everything go on as usual. We are still well cared for and will be satisfied if things stay that way.*

The process, however, proved hopeless. Whether the reason for failure was honest confusion about the number of affidavits she had requested or the American consulate's bureaucratic blindness or even deliberate obfuscation, no affidavits were forthcoming. Instead, there was only a frustrating series of refusals and requests for further documentation. Yet she persisted: *"Now that I have done everything so deliberately and Ester again read the letter from the consul, she is sure that it must necessarily be based on an error, as the consul also wrote in his letter about me and the family. So Ester has again today written to the consul to clarify the matter. I will now wait for the answer and give you the news."*

The following week's letter describes yet further difficulties and illustrates the unlikelihood of escape for Jews remaining in the German-occupied Netherlands:

My beloved children! I will quickly write you a few lines, because I have something I must discuss with you. As I wrote in my last letter, the consul has not accepted the affidavits as sufficient. Well, we thought that was based on an error, since the letter was addressed to Werner and we were still both registered. We have written immediately that the affidavit in question was just for me alone. Then I received the enclosed letter in reply, which I send on to you at the local consul's request. . . . At the Committee they told me you might send me a supplementary affidavit, as the letter shows that it is not enough (not even for me alone). I do not know now what can be done about it, my dear children. It will of course drag out everything, but there is nothing to be done about that. It is probably always the case that everything doesn't go as one hopes. I would have liked to go to the consul myself, but I would have needed extra permission [to travel]. *I am enclosing the letter so that you can see for yourselves.*

What we can do now, dear children, I do not know. I received my birth certificate, but the dates do not quite agree. In those days they were probably not so accurate. I really have to hear what I can do. In any case, my good children, we will wait patiently. For the time being, we can still be content. Our garden is now so wonderful and Selle lies outside all day and I as well whenever I have time. I'm just sorry, my dears, that I cause you so much effort and expense. But it will work out in the end. That is always the main thing, to get the papers in order. Others wait for years, too. Things just don't go so fast.

By August, she was forced to acknowledge, even to her children, that emigration was no longer likely:

Yes, we were hoping that I could soon come to you, but nothing came of it. I had also never expected that it could come so quickly. We just have to hope on, however fate determines. *We always hope for better times soon, but who knows when. I'm always glad that things go well for you children. We have to be content whatever happens.*

Hanna's final letter to New York, with greetings from Werner and Selma, was written on October 1, 1941. She described her sixty-first birthday celebration in proud detail, but she no longer mentioned emigration.

DURING THE YEARS OF OCCUPATION, HOW were they living, and what were they living on? In 1941, Hanna expressed relief that they now had a couple of elderly tenants with small appetites as well as a diner or two who provided at least some income. How she managed to feed at least half a dozen people, given the food shortages in the Netherlands, is a question. Though she did not belabor the issue (and how could she, given the inevitable censorship), her letters make clear that food was both scarce and limited in nature. In August, she described their customary menu, one benefit of which was, as she announced, a decrease in her high blood pressure: "*We now eat quite a lot of fish, which here is good and fresh, also there are now enough vegetables and salad. I chop a lot of raw carrots* [she always used the Dutch word 'wortelsches'], *very healthful. In recent days we could not go into the garden. I prefer going nowhere else and shop only in the morning.*"

In October, she noted that Joh, their good Dutch friend, continued to join them for his main meal: "*Things taste best to him here. We still have enough to eat to satisfaction. One only must not be so demanding. Tonight we will have fried plaice with potato salad, soup before, and then apple compote.*"

In only one (undated) letter, probably written late in 1941, does she seem somewhat discouraged: "*Now I have to cook a difficult and big dinner: cauliflower soup ('without')*" [i.e., presumably without cauliflower], "*carrots, marrowfat peas with rice, potato, and salad. Why so much salad you will ask—for the vitamins. But quite a spread of food for everyone's taste.*"

Selma's ongoing illness and constant weight loss remained a continuing topic, though its cause was never made clear. It had been of concern from the time of her marriage to Werner, but in late 1940 and early 1941 things seemed to come to a crisis. In early December of 1940, Hanna had discussed her concerns:

> *Selle has been a few days at home as she has something of a cold. The doctor now thinks that they should undertake a treatment to fatten her up, as she is too thin. She's gotten even thinner. I wanted* [her to go for treatment] *a year ago, because the time was probably better. Well, we will do our best here. She will probably also get injections, which are intended to help fatten her up. It is the case with all her siblings, because they never got enough to eat. But she will probably continue to work. Tomorrow the doctor comes to give the instructions. It should soon be the case that she is eating more.*

Selma's further decline was undoubtedly related to both the stress of their situation and their poor diet. Initially she was ordered to stay home for four weeks to *"fatten up."* By the spring of 1941, still seriously underweight, she was given *"extra allocations."* Whatever the nature of Selma's disease, by mid-July the medical authorities felt it grave enough that they insisted that she enter the Jewish convalescent home at Hilversum, fifteen miles southeast of Amsterdam, where she was expected to remain for several months. There Werner visited her twice weekly, writing in early October that *"she has gained seven pounds"* and might be released in another four weeks.

One additional letter, undated but written sometime in the fall of 1941, provides something of a coda to this rich but painful correspondence. On August 9, 1941, at the age of fifty-six, Martha Schack—Irma's mother—had died in Frankfurt of tuberculosis, her death evidently abetted by self-induced starvation. In offering condolences, Hanna opened a rare window into her own thoughts and fears during those dark days:

> *My beloved children! I have known for quite a while that your dear mother, Irma, has been freed from her suffering. Although the pain for you children is of course great, yet you must always say to yourselves that she no longer sees all the dangers and suffering and has found peace and rest. Surely she was too young, but unfortunately we are not asked. She was a great hero like all mothers are more or less,*

and she will live on as a model with and within you. . . .

I've also seen and been through so much and such awful times, and we are still nowhere near the end. Life is not at all so beautiful, but what helps is that we carry on and are patient. Yes, my dear Paul, it would certainly be nice if we could have met again when it seemed possible. But you need not reproach yourself about it, my boy, for everything looked different then. We must, dear children, take it as it comes and hope for the best. It is all Fate and, if it is determined for us, we will certainly be together again. In this thought, we must remain strong. Up to now, things are still going pretty well for us, and we muddle through. One cannot predict the future. I am glad that you are well taken care of, and I wish that Wernlein could be there too and visit you. . . . Soon I will bake my plaice and dinner will begin. Life goes on and we have to go with it. I hope, dear children, that everything still goes well.

This letter—my paternal grandmother's condolences on my maternal grandmother's death – are probably the last words she wrote to America. With war between the United States and Germany declared in December 1941, postal service between occupied Europe and the United States ceased. However, Hanna was able to maintain contact with her son Erich in neutral Sweden almost to the end. In his memoir, Erich cites in full (and prints a photographic copy of) her last letter to him, dated November 12, 1942:

> My beloved Erich! Just when I had mailed the letter to you, I received news from you, which always makes me happy. Yes, I am happy when I get good news from you, my boy, it is a comfort to me. Now it has gotten really cold and dark. The time passes quickly, even though it is sorrowful and troubled. Nevertheless I don't have much new to tell you, you know everything that's going on. One does not know how long the misery will last. Though it looks so different at the moment, we hope, my good E., that all will still go well and we will see each other again. If one just stays strong enough, one can survive everything. I have unfortunately been through too much. But people are very strong. I embrace and kiss you, Your loving mother.

What we know about Hanna Glückauf's final months derives entirely from Selma's family, two letters probably written to Erich, and then (presumably) sent by him to Paul and Ilse in New York. The first, dated December 18, 1942—only a month after Hanna's final letter to Erich—came from Rachel Mingelgrün, Selma's mother. Though the letter is cautious and vague, its news is not surprising to anyone who has read Hanna's last letter to Erich:

> Dear Hr. Glückauf, on behalf of your mother, I want to answer your letter of 12-5-42. Unfortunately, your mother's health has recently become worse. All the different events that occurred recently, particularly since the departure of Werner

and Selma, have destroyed your mother's resilience. For so long she kept things up bravely, but because she was alone so much and had a lot of time to brood, her health is very much strained. I have been very busy trying to create order here; in particular I have been trying to get rid of all the tenants, which unfortunately nowadays is very difficult.

Your mother is under treatment by a specialist. The only thing your mother needs is good care and rest. As much as possible I am trying to be with her. Although her condition is not yet alarming, I thought it my duty to inform you about your mother. I will continue to keep you up to date as long as your mother cannot write to you herself. You can also write me at my new address, if you want to know anything else.

Although no details are provided about exactly what had occurred, it seems that Werner and Selma were probably among the many arrested in the August 1942 raids on Amsterdam South. Mrs. Mingelgrün's "new address," Biesboschstraat 21, lies just a block from the Glückauf apartment on Merwedeplein, within the Jewish ghetto established by the Germans.

The second letter is yet harder to bear. Dated two months later, February 2, 1943, and written by Selma's older brother, Simon, it makes clear the rapidity with which Hanna's plight—as well as that of his own family and of Holland's Jewish population in general—had worsened and the dire circumstances in which they now found themselves.

Dear Hr. Glückauf: I received your letter of February 7. I am pleased that I still have the opportunity to answer you. Of my parents I only know so far that they are in a labor camp in Holland. Up to now, I have not received any written news from them. To this day we haven't heard anything from Werner and Selma, nor from my remaining brothers and sisters, and it will probably remain that way.

Unfortunately I cannot report to you any good news about your mother. I believe that Fräulein Resen [Ester] already wrote you concerning her. If this should not be the case, then I will take on the unpleasant function myself now, since it was the express desire of the physician to indicate, if possible, to one of the closest relatives, your mother's true condition. You can trust me that writing all this to you is very hard for me, but you are the only one whom I can contact.

Already more than two months ago your mother, in an unsupervised moment, tried to take her life by hanging herself. The loneliness and constant weeping and suffering probably drove her to do it. My mother found her unconscious in the attic, and a doctor who was called sent her to a hospital. This may sound harsh, but it would surely have been better for your mother if my mother had not found her so fast, because due to the strangulation a brain hemorrhage occurred, whereby her general status even worsened, so that she had to be delivered into an institution for the mentally disabled. She has already been in "A." for over two weeks, and I will give you the exact address at the end, in case you can possibly use it. The physician found that there is unfortunately little hope for improvement.

I spoke also with Mrs. Polak [presumably a friend]. *She intends to visit your mother. Unfortunately it is not possible for me, because she* [i.e., Hanna] *is not in Amsterdam. I also wrote you about the little package* [presumably something Erich wanted to send from Sweden either to his mother or Simon]. *I would not recommend sending anything, because I do not know what the future will bring. Anyhow you will be kept abreast of events, even if I am no longer in a position to do it.*

With cordial greetings.

S[imon, born Siegmund] *Mingelgrün*

Those are the last known words from or about the members of my father's family who remained in Amsterdam after the German occupation. According to German records, Werner and Selma were both killed in Auschwitz in 1942: he was thirty-three, she twenty-three. Selma's brother Arno died in Auschwitz, age twenty, on August 19th of the same year. Selma's parents, Rachel and David Mingelgrün, died in Auschwitz, both on the same day, September 24, 1943 (presumably the day they arrived): she was fifty-five, he fifty-six. Simon's wife and not quite two-year-old daughter were killed in Auschwitz on the same day six months later (March 6, 1944), following a lengthy imprisonment in Westerbork. Simon himself died in July of the same year, somewhere in central Europe. What happened to the rest of the Mingelgrün brothers and sisters is unknown.

My grandmother, Hanna, too, was lost in the pages of history; of her ultimate fate there exists no record. The institution referred to by Simon as "A." might be Amersfoort, the site of both a Jewish sponsored psychiatric hospital called "Sun and Shield" and a concentration camp, but it more likely refers to the large Jewish psychiatric hospital, *Het Appeldoornse Bos*, which held the largest number of Jewish patients and lay just outside the city of Apeldoorn in the eastern Netherlands.

Although Simon seems unaware of the situation, Hanna was probably already dead. Moore described what occurred at *Het Appeldoornse Bos* on January 21-22, 1943:

> [T]he *German police ransacked the building and horribly beat and maltreated many of the (defenseless) inmates. . . . The deportees were thrown into lorries and transported to the cordoned-off station. The same 'horrible and bestial behavior' befell the children who were also taken to the station and loaded on to the cattle-wagons. The train with the patients and fifty nurses was sent directly to Auschwitz where nearly all were gassed immediately on arrival and none of the remainder survived the war.*[73]

If Hanna was a patient at Het Appeldoorne Bos, she most likely was deported after the January 21, 1943 raid and, like most other

Dutch Jews, was murdered in Auschwitz or Sobibor if she survived the cattle car ride to Poland. Sobibor was purely an extermination camp and was the deportation site for most Dutch Jews. Because most were deported either there or to the extermination camps at Auschwitz, the survival rate of Dutch Jews was far lower than that of the Jews of any other Western European country.[74]

Erich, in his 1976 memoir, gives a wildly inaccurate account of his mother's end. Whether the reason lies in Erich's failure to remember the actual contents of the Mingelgrün letters, of which he must have been the recipient and which he had forwarded to New York more than thirty years earlier, or (perhaps more likely) from an impulse to dramatize and politicize his own history, is impossible to know. This is his account, which he claims he learned from a letter written by a Dutch woman who had been a long-time diner at his mother's table (not, as was the case of his mother's actual fate, from his brother's wife's brother):

> One morning there appeared in Mother's small home, just as she was preparing dinner, a troop of Gestapo people. In a commanding tone they cried to Mother: "Where is your son Erich?" Mother answered..."I have no idea." At that the Gestapo threatened and said they would beat her; she responded full of hate and pride: "A mother does not betray her son, even when she knows where he is.' At that the Gestapo did what they had said. A "short process." Mother was hanged in her kitchen.

He writes of later trying to find his mother's grave and to learn the fate of the Dutch woman, but to no avail. Evidently this was not the book's only inaccuracy. Shortly following its publication, the book lost the Communist party imprimatur and was withdrawn from sale in the DDR. The reason given was "*shortcomings, inaccuracies, and inconsistencies,*" deriving from objections raised by several long-time party members.[76] Erich argued with the Politburo in his book's defense, but to no avail. His death two weeks later was no doubt related to distress over his rejection by the party.

As for my grandmother, Hanna Glückauf *née* Rehfeld, her memory lives through her words only. I conclude with a poem that she—the grandmother I never met—wrote me on the occasion of my first birthday. Here follow my grandmother's witty, rhyming couplets and my literal English translation, which does far too little justice to the original:

> On the 18th of January, 1941:
> den Eltern zur Freude,
> der Oma zum Glück,
> legt unser Liebling heute sein erstes Jahr zurück—
> Ich hab jetzt etwas Neues zu verrichten
> und für dich, kleinster Liebling, ein paar Verse zu dichten.
> Du bist noch so klein und wirst's nicht erfahren,
> doch lesen wirst du's mal in späteren Jahren.
> Nun ist ein Jahr schon vergangen,

wo du geschenkt uns dein Leben,
Eine grosser Freud konnt's für uns gar nicht geben.
Dein Papa schrieb mir: "und kostet's noch so viel Geld,
dafür hab'n wir das schönste Baby der ganzen Welt!"
Wie stolz bin ich erst, wenn ich so etwas hör,
dazu sähst du mir änlich, was will ich noch mehr?
Werde gross nun und stark, mein Joanlein,
das Schönste auf Erden soll beschieden dir sein!
Stets lachend wie jetzt sollst durchs Leben du gehn
und alle Lieben sol'ln nur Freud' bei dir sehn.
Auch wir werrdenn feiern den Tag deiner Ehr',
mit Kaffee und Kuchen und sonst alles mehr.
Ich stell' in mein Zimmer ein paar Blumen auf's Tischchen,
darunter dein Bild mit dem süssen Gesichtchen,
träum' von der Zukunft und schönern Tagen,
der Zeit, wo ich dich auf'm Arm werde tragen.
Wenn ich dich herze mit dir spiele und singe
und du fragst mich so verschiedene Dinge.
Ich backe mit dir eine richtigen Kuchen
und warte nicht bis uns der Bäcker gerufen.
Ich spiele auch "Talerchen" auf dein'm Händschen,
Mit Küken, Kälbchen und mit Schwänzchen.
Du freust dich und lachst und — was hör ich denn da?
du rufst wie einst dein Papa: "Ich Oma, noch ma."
Nur das O, das hat sich dazu geschlichen
und sehr viele Jahre sind seitdem verstrichen —

JOAN GLUCKAUF HAAHR

Doch wie gern denkt man noch oft zurück
an die Sorgen, die Freuden und an das Glück!
Du kommst auch gern mal zu mir ins Bett;
denn bei der Oma ist's immer nett;
die kan so viel' Geschichten erzählen,
du wolltest, sie würden kein Ende nehmen,
vom Hänsel, Gretl, vom Knusperhäuschen,
du lauscht und sitzt still genau wie ein Mäuschen.

Wir feiern deine Geburtstag mit allen Verwanten,
mit Papa und Mama, mit Onkeln und Tanten,
Ich in der Mitt', klein Joan auf'm Schoss,
nichts gibt's mehr zu wünschen, die Freude ist gross.
Ich denke: "Wie schön, nun bist du dort,
was du so lang gewünscht...und brauchst nicht mehr fort."—

Der Traum ist zu Ende, ich werde wach
und denke ein Weilchen darüber nach.
Leider ist's ein Traum nur gewesen
und ihr könnt es auf Papier nun lesen.
Doch ich weiss, es wird in Erfüllung mal gehn
und wir werd'n uns in Freuden wiedersehn. . . .
Jetzt feiert nur tüchtig, ich hör' es so gern,
und—denkt an die Oma in weiter Fern!

For the joy of the parents,
for the grandmother's joy,
our darling has just completed her first year of life.
I have something new to make now,
and for you, my little sweetheart, I want to compose some verses.
You are still very young and you won't know about it,
but you will read it in later years.

Now a year is already over,
a year in which you gave us the gift of your life,
and for us there is no greater joy than that.
Your Papa once wrote to me: "And even if it costs a lot of money,
still we have the most beautiful baby in the entire world!"
How proud I always am when I hear such a thing,
that you look like me, what more can I wish for?
Grow big now and strong, my little Joan,
the most beautiful things of the Earth shall be yours!
Go through your life always laughing, like now,
and all your loved ones shall only see joy in you.
We too will celebrate this day in your honor,
with coffee and cake and many more treats.

I am putting a few flowers on the table in my room,
among them a picture of you, with your sweet face,
and dream of a future with better days,
a time when I will hold you in my arms.

JOAN GLUCKAUF HAAHR

When I will cherish you with games and songs,
and you will ask me so many different things.
Together we will bake a real cake,
and will not wait until the baker comes.

I will play "Talerchen"[77] on your little hand,
With chicken, calf, and with tail.

You are happy and you laugh, and what do I hear then?
You call me, just as your Papa once did: "Do it again, Oma...."
Only the "O" managed to slip in,
and many years have passed since then....

But how gladly one thinks of the past,
the sorrows, the joys and the happiness!

You also love to join me in my bed,
because with Oma it's always so nice.
She knows so many stories to tell,
and you wish they would never end.
About Hansel, Gretel, and the Gingerbread House,
you listen and sit in silence, just like a little mouse.
We celebrate your birthday with all our family,
with Papa and Mama, with uncles and aunts,
I in the middle, little Joan on my lap,
there is nothing more to wish for, the joy is enormous.

I think: "How beautiful, that you are now there,
what you so long wished for ... and you will never have to leave."
The dream is over, I am awake,
And I think about it for a little while.

Unfortunately, it was just a dream,
And you can now read it on this paper.
But I know that someday it will turn into reality
and we will meet once again with joy.

Now celebrate well, I want to hear all about it.
And think about your Oma so far away.)

Part 3
Immigrants and Exiles

CHAPTER 6

The Early Years

> *"What's interesting about the Yekke [the German Jews]: How long did they live in Germany? Until they were twenty, twenty-five, or thirty. Then they lived in Israel for fifty years. Still, their hearts stayed in the first twenty years they spent in Germany."*
>
> —*The Flat.*[78]

Sometime in the late 1850s, during the tumultuous years following the 1848 uprisings in Europe and nearly a century before my parents and their siblings arrived in America, my great-great-uncle David Rothensies (1838–1913), the eldest brother of my maternal great-grandfather, Aron, fled the German military draft and sailed to New York. Soon abandoning the city for more rural precincts upstate, he eventually settled in Delaware County and was joined a few years later by his youngest brother, Joseph (1848–1918). The two brothers—always referred to in our family as "the uncles Rothensies"—married two American Protestant sisters, Ida and Matilda (Tillie) Russell, both probably considerably younger than they were. A photo of David's home in Walton, New York, taken around the turn of the twentieth century, shows a modest frame and stucco house—two stories plus an attic and a large front porch—that uncannily resembles my house in the Bronx, built in 1927.

We know little about Joseph's life. David, however, became a prominent Delaware County merchant and cigar manufacturer, and the historical record shows a remarkably successful assimilation. An article in *A Biographical Review of the Leading Citizens of Delaware County* (1895) describes David's trajectory from dry goods peddler and commercial traveler to prosperous manufacturer and village postmaster. Their families were church members, but there is no evidence that either brother ever formally converted to Christianity, although David evidently contributed money to several local Protestant churches, and an obituary for Joseph's young son, Aron (c. 1913), refers to a Congregational Church funeral. David's own funeral however, although conducted by a minister, was held in his brother's home rather than in a church, suggesting that he may not have converted.

My grandmother's sister Betty Rothensies—headstrong, independent, and, according to my mother, too much for her family to handle—chose to leave Zwingenberg at the age of nineteen to work in the households of her American uncles. The only family member of her generation to emigrate, she sailed from Hamburg on the ship *Normannia*, arriving at Ellis Island on October 24, 1896. Although the plan had been that she serve as a housemaid for both uncles and their families, the domestic service arrangement did not last very long. A servant's life in rural New York was evidently not much to her liking, and Bessie (as she began to call herself, deeming Betty too old-fashioned and "old-country") soon took off for New York City. There she acquired a position as a corset fitter at McCreery's, one of the new, luxury department stores on increasingly mercantile Fourteenth Street. For a time, she lived at the Clara de Hirsch home for German Jewish homeless working girls, on far uptown East 63rd Street, but she eventually was able to rent her own small apartment. She once showed me photos of the New York of her youth: carriages, low-scale three- or four-story buildings, ladies with parasols, bustles, and elaborate hats—Edith Wharton's New York.

On her own, without a dowry and with no family to look out for her, marriage seemed an unlikely prospect. It was not until the 1930s, when she was nearing fifty, that she finally did marry a slightly older man, Sigmund Steiner, whom she met through other members of the German-Jewish community. I have vague recollections of Uncle Sigmund, who died in 1943, as a mild, good-natured, and rather feeble figure, sitting in his corner and leaning on his cane, his head nodding, either smiling vacantly or making slow, confident pronouncements in response to which my mother and aunts tried to avoid one another's eyes.

As a child I looked forward to visiting Aunt Bessie's apartment on Davidson Avenue in the Fordham section of the Bronx, first boarding the trolley on Amsterdam Avenue, then transferring to the University Avenue bus at 181st Street. Though small and dark, the apartment's five rooms seemed full of treasures: an Aunt Jemima string saver on a kitchen wall, the string to be pulled through the smiling, red lips of the turbaned, black face; the two plush settees with their ornately carved cherry wood frames—one burgundy, the other green—in the living room, or parlor (the Victorian word somehow more apt); the clock on the breakfront, a glass dome on a golden base, with a horizontal pendulum like a seesaw moving back and forth. An ancient doll sprawled loosely on one of the settees—its plaster head with painted hair, its stuffed body decked in a worn pink ruffled dress—offering a rare if musty breath of childhood among the antiques, although its play value was nil, and I remember usually discarding it impatiently soon after picking it up. Best of all, unquestionably, was the pile of movie fan magazines on the side table, an art form that I first encountered there. At the time, it didn't seem strange at all that my elderly and somewhat intimidating great aunt, by then in her seventies, entertained herself with the Hollywood gossip that was just beginning to interest me.

Throughout her life Aunt Bessie remained a powerful force in our family. Her requests were few, as I now realize, but no one ever refused them. One expectation was that we visit on her birthday, joining a group of about twenty-or-so acquaintances and elderly distant cousins, whose importance was determined—at least in part—by how long they or their families had lived in America. A few were lucky enough to have been born there. One cousin, born during the great New York blizzard of 1888, was actually named Blizzard. Professions, too, or I should rather say education, loomed large, with the few with college educations—largely retired teachers—laying claim to the highest status. How could we tell? They patronized us, or at least we felt they did: my mother and aunts, whose educations had been disrupted or abandoned and who clung to a fragile subsistence in those early post-war years.

Aunt Bessie was also a fixture on our birthdays. In fact, she was the star of all festivities because she always brought the cake: a magnificent confection from the famed Sutter's Bakery on the Grand Concourse. The cake was always the same and always delicious: vanilla cake layers covered with mocha butter cream (not too sweet), with an apricot filling. *Happy Birthday* and the celebrant's name discreetly decorated the top, inscribed in green and pink butter cream and encircled by butter cream rosettes. It was, of course, Aunt Bessie's responsibility to cut the cake, which she did with great precision, first excising a central circular piece, then slicing the surrounding "donut" into the penuriously thin slices that to this day we call "Aunt Bessie slices." She also customarily gave an additional birthday gift of three dollars. To everyone's amusement, my little brother on his third birthday asked her if, when he turned six, the three dollars would also become six.

I suppose she was something of a martinet. Because, to children, all adults are odd and often threatening, I didn't realize until much later how much she terrorized my mother and aunts. Two incidents come to mind.

The first was her visit to my Aunt Lina's country house, a tiny two-room bungalow in the hills overlooking Lake Hopatcong, New Jersey. The houses on the lake were large and imposing, those in the hills (like my aunt's) cramped and close together. When Aunt Bessie was scheduled to visit, not only my aunt but also all the neighbors did major housecleaning, even to the extent of cleaning out drawers and closets, as Aunt Bessie never hesitated to open anyone's closed doors or drawers for inspection. Not that she did or said anything about whatever it was she may have discovered, but the thought of her even silent disapproval was enough to intimidate everyone on the street.

The second occurred when my mother was newly widowed and at her most agoraphobic. I must have been about twelve. While at my friend Mary Ann's one Sunday morning, I received a panicked phone call from my mother that Aunt Bessie was coming and that, as a result, she herself was leaving. I must come home, she said, watch my little brother, and serve as hostess. So I did, of course, angry, puzzled, and with a prepared lie: my mother, I said (as usual protecting her from criticism, though I was always ready to criticize her myself), had been called away by the sudden illness of an acquaintance. Whether or not Aunt Bessie bought the excuse I never knew, but she graciously accepted the tea and cookies I offered her. After she left, my mother—apparently lurking somewhere nearby—returned home, taking for granted, as she always did, the rescue from an undesirable or frightening situation.

After Aunt Bessie broke her hip in the revolving door of a midtown restaurant, she grew considerably less formidable. In fact, she seldom left the nursing facility that then became her home, although she happily played a leader's role among her fellow residents. But we dutifully visited, my mother and her sisters, a couple of times a month, with families in tow. Too dutifully: there was too much duty and not enough real affection in those visits, something I think we all regretted later when we realized what a game old bird she really was. Aunt Bessie, like the other residents lucid and mobile enough to do so, would sit at the entrance awaiting visitors, disappointed when there were none but ready to find occupation elsewhere. She never complained. Once when my mother, my husband, Jorn, and I joined her and a few of her aged companions on a bench in the corridor, one of us sighed and said, "We're all getting there," to which Aunt Bessie quickly replied, "Some of us are already there." She had a sense of humor to the end, which came peacefully in the nursing home after a brief bout with pneumonia—a disease she had always referred to as "the old people's friend."

Two additional ambitious immigrant ancestors forged successful lives in early twentieth-century America. One was a second cousin of my grandmother, Julius Roten (his name shortened from Rothensies), the son of a brother of my mother's great-grandfather, Loeb Rothensies. Born in 1888, he left Germany for New York in 1912, at the age of twenty-four and, joining the chemical petroleum business of a distant family acquaintance, achieved millionaire status. The other was my mother's cousin Theodore (Theo) Gruen, son of her mother's eldest sister Lina Grünebaum, who left Zwingenberg in the 1920's and—like a number of other immigrant German Jews—became wealthy in the scrap metal business.

JOAN GLUCKAUF HAAHR

UNLIKE THEIR PREDECESSORS, VOLUNTARY IMMIGRANTS all, my parents and other members of their generation—the refugees of the 1930s—were reluctant exiles. Moreover, most were ambivalent about this new American homeland. Even as the United States evoked gratitude, admiration, and patriotic attachment, both for offering a safe harbor and for its vitality and variety, it also often seemed crude and cutthroat when compared with the sophisticated and free-spirited Weimar culture of their youth. Undeniably thankful to have escaped Hitler's genocidal crusade, they nonetheless lamented the loss of a way of life that had promised so much before the Nazis came to power. And while the end of the war brought great joy with word of Suzy's seemingly miraculous survival and Lina's husband's safe return from the Italian Front, it also brought the devasating news that almost everyone else in the family was dead. How news of Suzy's survival first reached them I do not know, but in June 1945, Lina received a letter from Leo's brother-in-law Louis, in Marseille that no one had yet heard directly from her, although he seemed aware that she was alive:

> *I inquired here, but without success, because Madame Hotz, who had charge of Suzy after Leo's departure went to Switzerland, and I was looking for her address, finally asking around but no one has seen her after Gurs and all those who were at Gurs were deported long before the Liberation. I am sorry to bring you this sad news, but everyone*

who could saved 'their skin,' because, believe me, it was very difficult to escape those bandits. They did not stop until there remained very few Jews in Europe. . . . I count on Suzy's returning to Marseille as soon as she is released, as all must return to their former home, and I promise you a telegram without delay as soon as possible.

As we know, Suzy did return to Marseille after her release and convalescence, met and married Otto, and eventually both immigrated to America.

THAT THE FIVE SCHACK SIBLINGS HAD SURVIVED when so many had perished was cause for gratitude. But of the rest of what had been a large extended family only a handful survived the war: my father's Communist older brother, Erich, and his cousin George, who had fled with his wife and son to Shanghai; an uncle and cousin of my mother's who had emigrated to Argentina; my father's half-cousins, also in Argentina, and a couple of distant cousins in the United States; and one or two distant cousins in England. So, in addition to the difficulties of their new lives in America, all of them—though some more and some less—were haunted by feelings of loss and what is referred to as survivors' guilt.

In my mother's case the pain must surely have been augmented by the arrival of a letter that, years after her death, I found among her many documents. From the American-appointed mayor of Zwingenberg, it was written just one month after Blondine's terrible missive. How Ludwig Mütz had discovered that my mother was alive is not known, although presumably it was through U.S. military channels. It is clear that he had no idea of her actual location or the fact that she was married and had children:

> Zwingenberg, 10-24-1945
> Dear Fräulein Schack,
>
> It made me very happy today to receive a sign of life from you. How are your parents and where did you end up? What are your other siblings doing? Hopefully you will soon come to Zwingenberg. We have survived the war in good shape. Our son Ludwig is not back yet. . . . You would not even know me anymore. I am the son-in-law of the deaf-mute seamstress who from time to time worked for your family. Now I have been installed here as mayor by the Americans. A difficult office now in shambles. Let us soon hear something from you.
> Kind regards
> Ludwig Mütz

What can my mother's response have been to such a letter? Unaware that Mütz himself, as a communist, had suffered numerous arrests and imprisonments, she was no doubt enraged by his failure to acknowledge what every Zwingenberg citizen must have known about the deportation of the village's Jews, the theft of their property, and their probable fates. Knowing my mother, I doubt the letter was answered. From Fritz Kilthau, the unofficial historian of Zwingenberg's Jewish past, I learned that Ludwig Mütz was still alive in 2014 but was too feeble to respond to questions.

While the post-war years brought to these refugees from Hitler some measure of peace and security, they could not forget. For despite the many rumors and the lack of news during wartime, no one had anticipated a catastrophe of such magnitude. Nor is it unfair to say that with the exception of Lina (increasingly Americanized, now calling herself "Len" and blessed with an inextinguishably cheerful temperament) and the ever-optimistic Leo in Mexico City, these young adults—only in their twenties and early thirties when the war ended—seemed prematurely old. Like survivors of a shipwreck or a plague, they carried out their daily routines, but it was as if the cumulative losses had sapped their energy and killed their aspirations for a brighter future. What remained vital for most of them were the memories, reflected in their efforts to recreate what they could of the old culture in their new lives.

MY PARENTS ARRIVED IN NEW YORK on June 1, 1937, in the midst of a record heat wave—the temperature almost 100 degrees—and a seemingly endless economic depression. They spent the first few days with Lina, who had sailed to New York two years earlier, but they soon rented their own apartment, one of the several virtually identical apartments in Northern Manhattan—most "walk-ups" of several flights, with two rooms, kitchen, and bath—that circumscribed their early years. In those days, when so-called "concessions" of rent-free months were routinely awarded to new tenants, it paid to move whenever the lease was up or the painter due. When my father's sister Ilse and her husband arrived in New York from Amsterdam later that summer, the four shared an apartment for a few weeks. That, however, did not work out. My father was stubborn and proud, my uncle Kurt pompous and self-righteous. Despite the efforts of my mother and aunt to keep the peace, the two men could not suppress their dislike of each other, and the arrangement soon ended.

During my second year, my parents moved to the lobby-floor apartment on Audubon Avenue in which I spent my childhood. As children, we heard rumors that, when first built, the building had been elegant and graced with a doorman and an awning—those New York City marks of distinction. Remnants of its original grandeur remained in the large marble foyers and the elegant courtyard with its encircling colonnade of carved granite pillars bridged by horizontal ledges that my friends and I often "rode" as if they were horses.

My father, whose English was never very fluent, began what was to be a long series of relatively short-lived jobs, all low paying (at the outset $7–8 weekly), all insecure. My mother was more fortunate: with her linguistic and secretarial skills—as well as the intervention of her cousin Theo's wife, Carola, who already worked there—she obtained a position in the "Names Department" of the H.W. Wilson Company, the publisher of several indispensable library indexes, where for twelve dollars a week she sat eight hours a day checking the accuracy of bibliographical references in German, French, Italian, Spanish, or English.

I suppose their lives were not too hard during those first childless years. Although there were money worries, they were young, had their family and friends, and New York was, in the late 1930's, a vital and exciting place to be, free for the most part from those dangers which would come later. People speak of the LaGuardia years of 1934 to 1945 as a time when the city "worked," when its mayor (the jovial if hard-nosed Fiorello) seemed to mirror in his brash conviviality what was best in the city and its people.

Their northern Manhattan neighborhood of Washington Heights was defined by two elevated cliffs, each overlooking one of the two rivers—the Hudson to the west and the Harlem to the east—each bordered by a series of parks and divided by the "canyon" of Broadway. The area was called (not entirely facetiously) "The Fourth Reich" or "Frankfurt on the Hudson," as it was home to many of the resettled German Jews fortunate enough to have escaped in time to avoid arrest and deportation. "*When did you get out?*" was asked of every new acquaintance. Differing in countless ways, urban and rural, educated and uneducated, these refugees for the most part shared a nostalgia for the German life they had lost. Painfully aware of the incongruity of such an intense longing for the land of their persecutors, they nevertheless indulged it: strolling on Sunday afternoons among the immaculate flowerbeds overlooking the Hudson in Fort Tryon Park that reminded them of the parks they had known in Frankfurt or Berlin or Düsseldorf; meeting their friends at the Hungarian-owned Nash's *Konditorei* on Dyckman Street for Sunday afternoon coffee and cakes—the *Schwetchekuche, Sachertorte, Othellotorte, Éclairs,* and *Strudel* like those they remembered from home; and reading the *Aufbau*—the newspaper based on its Berlin original, written in German, and founded by refugees for refugees—as well as their New York paper of choice. Following the war, it was to the *Aufbau* that many eagerly turned each week to read the lists of those who had perished in the camps, searching for those they knew. Often, it was the first notice they received.

Entertainment meant radio and—above all—movies. In those days and throughout my childhood, there were seven movie theaters in our immediate neighborhood: two second-run movie "palaces," two third-run houses, one fourth-run house, and an art film theater (*The Heights*), where at the age of twelve I saw my first foreign film: the unforgettable *The Miracle*, in which Anna Magnani plays an ignorant peasant girl raped by a drifter whom she envisions as St. Joseph. My father was a regular at all of them, but especially *The Heights*, where he could follow the exciting trends in post-war European films. No activity, in his estimation, surpassed going to the movies. After we children arrived, making it impossible for my parents to go out anymore as a couple, as they could not afford babysitters, he was not averse to disappearing into one or another theater for a few hours during an evening or on his day off, unapologetically returning home to weather my mother's furious reception.

He also loved playing cards, especially the popular German game *Skat*, for which he met weekly with two émigré friends, all three smoking non-stop as they concentrated intensely on their game. Later he succumbed to the frenzy surrounding the introduction of canasta.

After my birth in 1940 (the baby they couldn't afford, in the opinion of many members of the family, including my father's mother), my mother resigned from the Wilson Company, and without her salary things got harder. Not that we ever went hungry. Despite wartime rationing, food—our typical German diet of meat, potatoes, and vegetables—always seemed plentiful. Nor did we lack treats. I remember my father's regular early Sunday morning excursions to one of several local bakeries, and his return home with a bag of fresh rolls, a "small sour rye bread sliced," and a cake (usually a marble pound cake or whipped cream covered apple or chocolate cream pie) for our essential Sunday afternoon *Kaffee und Kuchen*.

My father, Paul, was a small, slight man, no more than 5'4", with fine, light brown hair, combed straight back without a part, the hairline slowly receding to reveal ever larger temples. A cigarette (Philip Morris—unfiltered, of course, even after filters were introduced) invariably dangled from either his lips or his fingertips, and he held the cigarette between fore- and middle finger in the European manner thought slightly effeminate by Americans. His small stature belied his considerable stubbornness and pride, both of which emerged in his characteristic resistance to both my mother and his employers.

As we saw earlier (Chapter 5), employment for him remained hard to find and to retain. The various jobs that came his way were always insecure and usually short-lived, sometimes because the job was only temporary, sometimes because the low-status, low-paying jobs he was forced to take, combined with his stubborn temperament and less-than-fluent English, too often made him a tactless and resentful subordinate. There was the job selling shaving brushes on commission for Leopold Ascher, during which, small and slight as he was, he had to carry the heavy sample case from drugstore to drugstore. The Lafayette Street restaurant he and Lina tried to manage failed quickly. In the mid-1940s, together with his old friend from Amsterdam, Herbert Gordon, he ran a newsstand in the Times Square subway station and, in the late 1940s, another in the St. George Hotel in Brooklyn Heights. The last provided me with an unforgettable memory. Having taken the long subway ride to Brooklyn to pay a rare visit to my father at work one Saturday afternoon, my mother, brother, and I saw a wholly naked woman ambling nonchalantly through the hotel's lobby. Eyes popping, my four-year-old brother and I watched as the police came, wrapped her in a blanket, and led her gently away.

The uncertainty caused by my father's frequent unemployment brought on endless arguments between him and my mother. The unexpected sound of his key in the door in the middle of the day would cause my mother to turn pale as she anticipated another period of unemployment and no income. He would make excuses: the work was unsuitable, his boss unreasonable; his boss had no respect for him, he had no choice but to quit, and so on. Whatever the reason, the result was the same: a difficult search for another job, often less lucrative than the previous one. And my mother, first ashen-faced, then accusatory, berating him—he standing silent until the moment that he walked out the door, always cigarette in hand, returning late in the evening when her anger had turned to despair and he was able (in his incomparably gentle way) to comfort her and to assure her that things would turn out for the best. Eventually my father took on a series of menial shipping clerk positions, none of which seemed to last very long.

Understandably, my parents fought constantly about money. Notwithstanding his own expenditures for the cigarettes he chain-smoked and the movies to which he was addicted, he was stingy with my mother, praising her for bargains, for cut corners, for penny savings, and berating her if he felt that she had "wasted" money on anything he deemed frivolous. Once my mother saw a pair of red dress shoes on sale at the local department store and bought them on a whim. My father reacted furiously and, as a result, my mother—enraged and humiliated—never wore them. Nonetheless, the shoes sat on a shelf high in the closet, a memento of her persistent grudge, until I finally threw them out when she moved from Washington Heights to Riverdale many years after his death.

Yet he was a kind and wonderful father. When asked that question children love to ask each other: "Who do you love more? Your mother or your father?" I was the only one of my friends hard put to answer. The others all responded easily, "My mother, of course," but I wasn't so sure. For while their fathers were often gruff and intimidating—uninterested in or annoyed by our play, sometimes frighteningly loud or even occasionally drunk—my father was always quiet, gentle, sober. If my mother, with her far better English, was the one who always read to me, it was my father who played not just with me but also with my friends, something none of the other fathers did with their daughters. He painstakingly hand-sewed clothes for my dolls, which though ill-fitting and crude, nevertheless gave them a wardrobe they otherwise would not have had. Demonstrating the drawing skills that I have inherited, he bought me a set of pastels and taught me how to use them. Together we drew in my scrapbook faces that strangely (I recognized later) sometimes presaged my own face as an adult.

Of course, I now understand that my parents' anger toward each other most likely stemmed not only from their ever-present economic worries but also from their continuing fear about the fate of those left behind as well as guilt over their own escapes. For after 1940, the news from Europe had taken a darker turn. Letters from their parents and my mother's brother Leo described the increasingly untenable situations in Germany, Holland, and France. Margot's arrival in New York, in June 1941, and Leo's family's immigration to Mexico later that year eased a few concerns. But with all news from Europe stopped, with only silence from my mother's parents. aunt and uncle in Frankfurt, my father's mother and brother and his wife in Amsterdam, and eighteen-year-old Suzy, alone in Marseille, what must they have been feeling? And after the war, when they finally learned the terrible reality, Irma's depression and Paul's escapism seem more understandable.

In addition, the war itself brought tension and uncertainty for them as it did for all Americans. There were, for example, the blackouts (or more accurately "dim-outs"), with my mother incongruously (and totally out of character) elected to serve as air-raid warden for our floor, her responsibility each evening consisting of a walk around the building to check that no lights from the five apartments were visible from outside. At the sound of the warning sirens, my parents and I would enter our front hall closet, so large that it seemed a small, windowless room. With ceiling-high shelves on three sides, and a pull-string ceiling light, there was room enough for a card table and four chairs. In "the dark closet" (as we called it), we could enclose ourselves safely, no light escaping, and play games until the all-clear signal sounded. For me, then a preschooler, this was great fun. And the closet was a wonder: throughout our childhood, when my brother and I played hide and seek, it was the best place to hide, its piles of household discards and old clothes providing perfect cover.

Other things I remember from the war: the ration books and the shortages of sugar and coffee; streets without traffic, safe enough for even the smallest child to play without fear of accidents; the slow return of the automobile as late as 1948—sturdy, powerful machines like my Uncle Kurt's green Hudson—and the way the cars, trucks, and buses took over those streets again. I remember my parents' low voices when they discussed politics, their determination to avoid any public disclosure of their fears, and later—in the growing anti-Communist climate of the late 1940s—their leftist sympathies and connections, especially with my father's brother Erich (from whom no one had heard since the end of the war) presumably living somewhere behind the Iron Curtain.

Among friends and neighbors, I always felt a bit of an outcast. Not only did my parents speak German at home (although, once I was introduced to English on the street, I refused to answer to German or speak it, announcing to my parents that "*German hurts my mouth*") but through a strange hereditary quirk of fate, I looked Asian, seemingly having inherited the epicanthic fold of that long-ago purported Tatar ancestor, the peddler who was said to have accompanied Napoleon's defeated armies back from Russia. Thus, during the war, I would occasionally be taunted by other children in the playground with cries of "Hey, Jap! Why doncha go back where ya came from?"

During my first year or two, my mother—driven by the urgent need for money—returned to her job at the Wilson Company, hiring two successive nannies, both German-Jewish refugees, to take care of me. I remember little but the name of middle-aged "*Tante*" Irene. But Viola, who came when I was about a year and a half old, was young and beautiful and—I was always told—loved me as if I were her own child. Following her move with her husband to Los Angeles in 1942, she maintained an intermittent correspondence with us for many years, though often, in her letters, she complained of my mother's failure to reply.

I have nearly twenty of her warm and affectionate letters, the early ones in German, the later in English, most addressed to my mother, but a few sent directly to me. The last letter she wrote us, dated January 1952 when she was in her early thirties, was a condolence letter following my father's death. Shortly after, notwithstanding her marriage, the two small daughters whom she obviously adored, and the survival and proximity in Los Angeles of most of her immediate family—mother, sister, and grandmother—she committed suicide.

Two excerpts from her post-war letters may shed some light on that otherwise hard to fathom act. The first was written shortly after the end of the war, on the first day of September 1945:

> *In the meantime, the war has come to an end and even though we have all the best reasons for rejoicing too much has happened to us and the human race to feel any cause for real celebrating. The way they carry on here and judging by the Hearst press and other politicians and reactionary men we are just bound to get into another war—atom bomb or no atom bomb—and this one we are certain not to survive. Maybe it is just as well. There is no hope for the human race—they are hopelessly greedy and selfish and mean.*

The second was from early 1946:

> Yes...one could really enjoy one's life out here in warm and ever-sunny California, if it weren't for the gloomy-looking world around us. It is terrible how much ignorance, bigotry, and greediness exists in the world.... How can people want to drag us into another war right after one as terrible as the just finished one?
>
> I was terribly shocked to hear about the tragic fate of yours and your husband's family. We too lost everybody who was still left behind in Germany. Aunts, uncles, and cousins, and also a little one-year-old niece of mine. One will be able to forget these things at times, but we will never be able to get over it.

After Viola left, I was old enough to be placed in a small private nursery school, also run by German Jews. Aunt Lilly's Kindergarten served the surrounding refugee community, and the teachers and most of the children switched easily between English and German. However, that, too, did not last more than a year. Although I was otherwise thriving there, I was constantly catching colds, and my mother, with no alternative childcare options readily available, withdrew me from the school and decided to stay home permanently to care for me.

Among my earliest memories:

My parents, aunts, and uncles gathered around a dining table, underneath which I—an uncooperative three-year-old—had tried to escape from their demand that I recite the *Pledge of Allegiance*. Eventually I was pinned down and forced to perform my trick, affirming both what they saw as my precocity and their own American patriotism.

FDR's death on April 12, 1945, probably the first time I was aware of my mother's tears, as she listened to the NBC Radio's correspondent, Morgan Bailey, mournfully announce the news.

VJ day, August 14, 1945: After a wondrous day at Rye Playland with Aunt Lina and a couple of my "Italian" cousins (her husband Fred's niece and nephew), my pleasure only slightly diminished by my having vomited from the top of the Ferris wheel upon all those below, we returned to Fred's sister Josephine's apartment, heard the wonderful news that the war was over, and—our highly anticipated homemade ravioli dinner forgotten – climbed to the roof of their six-story building near Pelham Parkway to join millions of city celebrants in throwing roll after roll of unspooled toilet paper into the streets.

And I remember the tears, more and more of them, when the first letters from Europe arrived with news of what had befallen those left behind.

My brother, Peter, was born on February 16, 1945. I was five. During my mother's ten-day stay in the hospital (the standard requirement in those days), Aunt Lina came to help out. The memory of a "game" we played has stayed with me: As we both stood beside the kitchen sink, Lina washed the seemingly endless parade of cockroaches down the drain over and over and then —using the toilet plunger—made them rise again, repeatedly exclaiming (to my great delight) *"Elevator going down! Elevator going up!"* Many years later, she told me that my father (always ungenerous with money) had tried to charge her for the cost of her stay.

After Peter's birth there was no longer any talk of my mother's returning to work, partly because of her worsening depression, whose onset she later dated to this time, and partly because she was convinced that Peter was more fragile than most babies and thus in need of special care. Because of this concern, although I had already begun to attend public kindergarten in September, she withdrew me from school to prevent my bringing any dangerous germs into our home. Whenever we approached the new baby, we had to put on surgical masks. And I, imitating my mother, invariably checked his breathing while he slept, always with the momentary terror that it might have stopped. But Peter was an alert and cheerful baby, and in truth I was totally in love with him from the moment he arrived. With his curly red hair, inherited from our maternal grandmother, fair (and later very freckled) skin, and small, soft body, he was as different in appearance from me (dark haired, olive skinned, heavy-boned, and tall) as imaginable. We shared the apartment's sole bedroom—our parents' double bed was in the living room—and our few, well-worn toys were stored in the bottom drawer of the second-hand dresser whose two upper drawers held our few clothes. As Peter grew older, we played endlessly at home, our games interrupted only by my time at school and with friends. It soon became clear that Peter was extraordinarily intelligent, not only learning everything with astonishing rapidity but able to remember it all as well. After he learned to read, he memorized all the battles of the Civil War (one of his great passions), and when he grew a little older and became a devoted New York Yankees fan, he was able to rattle off from memory all the statistics in the *Baseball Encyclopedia* that became his bible. His was also a quirky and independent way of thinking. Twice during his early elementary school years, our mother was asked to come into the school to speak with the teacher. The first time, when he was in first grade, it was because he had filled in all the "O"s in his penmanship exercise with smiley faces (this was long before they became ubiquitous) and refused to redo the assignment; the second occurred during a school assembly when, refusing to pledge allegiance to the flag, he was sent to the principal's office.

Small, skinny, and awkward, looking rather like a cuter Howdy Doody with heavy eyeglasses, he had only a few friends, most of them the more bookish children in his class. Sports, aside from the statistics, held little interest for him. Most of the children in our building treated him rather like an intellectual mascot and ready source of information, enjoying his performances and not hesitating to ask him to explain things they didn't understand. Two of the boys, however, became his friends. One was a large and ungainly only child who lived with his parents in the "walk-in" apartment south of the building's main entrance. Jeffrey was, if anything, even less comfortable with other people than my brother, and though he often struggled in school and seemed not to share any of Peter's real interests, the two, luckily, seemed to get on. The other was my best friend Terry's brother Frankie. Nine months younger than my brother, Frankie nevertheless was a natural leader, and his open respect and affection for Peter (whom he called "The Brain") resulted in his protecting him from teasing or violence by the rougher boys in the neighborhood.

There were many children in our building. In the afternoons and evenings after school once the weather got mild enough and all day during vacations, Terry and I played jacks on the front stoop while, in the street, the boys played stickball or "*Caw Caw Ring-O-Leevio*," seizing hats, gloves, books, or other small objects from any child within reach and tossing them endlessly among themselves while repeatedly shouting out the mysterious phrase. In the evenings, our figures increasingly obscured in the diminishing twilight, girls and boys played together, sidewalk games of stealth and skill like "*Red Light, Green Light*" or the handball game we called "*Chinese*" with the pink "s*paldeens*" (rubber balls manufactured by the Spalding factory), whose appearance in the candy stores was the first real sign of spring. As many as four or five children would take turns hitting the ball against the building's wall trying to score points, the sidewalk squares demarcating our spaces like a tennis net, until an irate tenant or the building's superintendent would chase us away.

Our building offered a rich variety of hiding places for "*Hide and Seek*" or "*Cops and Robbers*": behind the granite courtyard pillars, in the hallways, under the stairwells (the first floor stairwell forever memorable as the spot where a boy named Freddy once ate his own feces on a dare), or in the basement, a warren of winding corridors and mysterious, locked rooms, its dirty, whitewashed walls dampened by the water that oozed continually from overhead pipes and its concrete floor blackened by many years' soot buildup from the coal furnace. Although supposedly off limits, except for the warped metal garbage cans lining its entrance and the laundry room in the rear, the basement lured us with its mixture of the mundane and the forbidden. When we hid there, there was always a little thrill of fear deriving from our uncertainty as to whether we would be accosted by the "super," the "seeker" (the "cop" of the game), or some mysterious spectral inhabitant of those nether regions.

Lina ("Len")

THROUGHOUT MY CHILDHOOD, OUR SOCIAL CIRCLE consisted primarily of my aunts and their husbands, our grandmother's sister Aunt Bessie, and a few German-Jewish friends. My mother's three sisters—Lina, Margot, and Suzy—played the largest role. In my early years, especially during the war, we saw Lina often. With her fiancé, Fred Scarano, serving in Italy as a technician with what was then called the Army Air Force, she spent many of her evenings and weekends with us. Always fun-loving and with an impressive ability to tell jokes well (something that continued to the end of her long life), Lina was also the person who had largely been responsible for Margot's escape from France.

On the other hand, her own immigration to the United States, in 1935, had largely been a matter of accident and luck. Living in Paris, where she had followed her brother Leo, she served as a nanny to two young children from a wealthy family and was so fluent in French that—as she told me—everyone was always surprised that she herself was not French. However, when the time came to renew her residence permit at *"the Prefecture on an island in the middle of the Seine,"* the renewal was refused. And although a United States visa had been acquired for her by her American relatives—Aunt Bessie, Cousin Theo, and the wealthy Julius Roten— the French would not allow her to pick it up in Paris, forcing her (notwithstanding the obvious danger) to return to Germany and collect it at a stipulated office in Stuttgart. So, she returned home to Zwingenberg—her last visit—and anxiously boarded the train to Stuttgart, about a hundred miles to the south.

On arriving she made her way to the office. Then occurred something strange and fortunate that she spoke of often in her later years: While she was waiting in the office, a group of young Nazi women, all government clerks and wearing the police uniform of black skirts and white blouses, began singing and otherwise letting off steam. Coincidentally, Lina was similarly dressed in black and white. ("I had no clothes; that was what I had.") A group of Nazi officers in uniform entered and began shouting at the clerks for slacking off; unintimidated and giggling, the young women kept singing. One of the officers then peered at Len and asked the others, "Is she with you?"

"Yes," they replied, "she is."

"And that's how those young Nazi women saved my life," Lina always ended the story. "Pure dumb luck!" Affidavits in hand, she paid 320 Marks for a berth on the ship *Hamburg* sailing to New York.

Young as she was, not yet twenty when she arrived, Lina took on the responsibility of trying to rescue the rest of her family. Though her own funds were meager—she had arrived at the height of the Depression and jobs were hard to find – she nonetheless sent money home to her parents and sisters as long as she could, while pursuing the affidavits essential to their immigration. It was largely her energy and persistence that resulted in all three of her sisters eventually settling in New York.

During one of Fred's home leaves, he and Lina married on July 3, 1944. Once he returned from Europe and was discharged from the army, they rented an apartment in the neighborhood called Inwood in Northern Manhattan, on Hillside Avenue: a pleasant street curving up from Broadway and across from Fort Tryon Park, about a half hour's downhill walk from where we lived up on "the Heights." In December 1946, their son Robert was born, the first of our New York cousins, followed one month later, in February 1947, by Suzy and Otto's daughter, Paulette, and, in May, by Margot and Henri's daughter Linda. Eventually Lina obtained apartments in her building for both younger sisters and their families, so for several years during my childhood visiting one aunt and her family always meant going from apartment to apartment and visiting all three.

JOAN GLUCKAUF HAAHR

Margot

MARGOT ARRIVED AT NEW YORK HARBOR in June 1941 on the *Ciudad de Sevilla*, a Spanish merchant ship that had sailed a three-week long, circuitous path from Lisbon through the U-boat plagued Atlantic. She was then not quite sixteen, alone among the sailors and the thirty other passengers, all Jews and political refugees who, despite uncertainty and seasickness, undoubtedly blessed their good fortune in having escaped a continent at war. On the ship she fell in love with a boy about her age, most likely a member of the crew, and when they landed in New York she disembarked with great reluctance, having hoped to follow him to Santo Domingo. She arrived in New York with few possessions beyond the clothes on her back—filthy, louse-ridden, and with a strong affection for sailors.

My mother, my father (still a stranger to her), and Lina met her at the pier. On reaching our apartment, the first thing they did was remove her clothes and scrub her, my kind and conscientious father meticulously picking the lice out of her hair and crushing them with his fingers. Lina washed the worn and dirt-encrusted clothes in the kitchen sink; Paul took them up to the roof to hang out to dry, neglecting (whether accidentally or intentionally) to attach them to the lines with clothespins, so that to no one's sorrow they blew away.

How did Margot react to all this unaccustomed concern? In truth, not very well. Although the three years in Marseille had been spent under the ostensible care of her brother and his wife, she had felt more tolerated than loved by them, and escaped when she could to enjoy the freedoms of that colorful port city. Still suspicious and angry in New York, she similarly resented all attempts to restrict her freedom. Though they tried sending her to school, she soon stopped attending. Not having attended school regularly since early childhood, she had no desire to submit to high school discipline. Moreover, although fluent in German and French, she spoke English awkwardly, and—in those days, long before bilingual classes made the integration of non-native speakers more routine—she was often treated as an outcast, left to sit alone and unattended. After a brief period she simply declared that she would not go back. A photo of her taken sometime before the War's end shows a skinny young woman, her heavily painted lips in a big smile, her right arm wrapped around a tree. She half sits on one of those tubular wrought-iron fences then used to enclose parks and other grassy places. Belying the youthful face are the clothes: skin-tight dress with a white flounce emerging from her cleavage, glamorous large-brimmed hat, white platform sandals. Sometime before this she had—in the fashion of the day—shaved off her eyebrows, and the painted lines that thereafter replaced the eyebrows that never grew back show clearly in the photo. She seems proud of herself, the tawdry imitation of current fashion apparently fulfilling her dreams of beauty and glamour.

When the war ended and peacetime commerce once more resumed, she took to frequenting the piers where the merchant ships from Belgium and France docked in New York harbor. Accompanied by a girlfriend or two, she would greet the disembarking sailors and, striding off together arm-in-arm, they would spend the evening together. One of these, Henri Adam, a coarsely handsome Belgian merchant sailor with craggy features and reddish-blond hair, was ready to abandon life at sea and jump ship in New York, and they soon began living together. When Margot was twenty-two and pregnant, they eloped to Elkton, Maryland (then the Gretna Green of the East Coast), where wedding licenses were granted on demand and the ceremony performed by a conveniently situated Justice of the Peace. Her sisters reacted with ambivalence, somewhat dismayed at her uncertain prospects yet, with their husbands, relieved that Margot was no longer their sole responsibility. The baby, my cousin Linda, was born just three months after the wedding and had Henri's red-blond hair and blue eyes.

They moved into a brownstone apartment in the West Seventies. In those days, just after the war, most of the brownstones on Manhattan's West Side—once townhouses for the newly affluent commercial classes, as the city expanded northward—had been broken up into cheap housing for the poor, each formerly majestic, high-ceilinged room now a tiny apartment with combination living- and bedroom, kitchenette, and bath. Although Henri was a gifted artist, creating striking pastel portraits from photographs (one of me as bright-eyed three-year old hangs in our hallway), he worked as a waiter in a series of French restaurants while Margot stayed home with the baby. The early years of malnutrition had destroyed her teeth, and she had them all extracted. "That way," she said, "I'll never have to worry about them again." Without teeth, she suddenly looked far older than her twenty-three years, the curved, penciled eyebrows (like an upside-down smile or the frown on a "happy face") giving an incongruously quizzical look to her too-thin face with its rouged, concave cheeks.

As I reconstruct that period of her life, I see her taking the baby out in the carriage to Central Park just a couple of blocks to the east and sitting for a while on a wooden slat bench beside a path, watching the roller skaters, the cyclists, and the strollers, some casual, some determined. Usually she sits alone, lighting one cigarette after another and impatiently discarding it when finished, probably shunning the occasional friendly overtures of other mothers, who quickly discover that she does not welcome their company. Sometimes one of her sisters undertakes the forty-five-minute subway ride downtown and joins her on the bench, the young cousins playing together in the sandbox while their mothers talk.

It may have been around this time that Margot started drinking. She was no stranger to wine, of course, having spent years in France where wine is a casual accompaniment to everyday life and regularly served even to children. But now she began to drink seriously—and often alone. Concerned about her sister's increasing isolation, Lina persuaded Margot and Henri to move uptown to join her in the building on Hillside Avenue.

They decorated their new apartment in what in the early 1950's seemed to my friends and me the latest style: sleek blond furniture (for us it made no difference that it was laminate, not wood) with nubby earth-toned cushions; beige carpeting; a Formica covered kitchen table with leatherette-upholstered chairs. Henri was the best cook I knew—and we were a family of good cooks. A waiter in a series of elegant and expensive bistros, where he went each afternoon wearing a black tie and tuxedo, his experience in the restaurant business had given him a sophisticated and subtle knowledge of food. When Uncle Henri prepared the meal, we knew we were in for a treat: shrimp-stuffed tomatoes (the cold shrimp in a rich dressing of *crème fraiche* and herbs); homemade *pommes frites*, deep-fried to a luscious, golden crispness; perfectly broiled filet mignon or herbed lamb chops. Dessert was usually a homemade tart.

And they danced. To the sultry and evocative songs of Edith Piaf or Yves Montand, they spun around the room cheek-to-cheek, Margot's eyes closed (a dreamy smile on her face), Henri a strong and forceful leader, both gliding gracefully from corner to corner of the apartment, while my friends and I would watch amazed and a bit embarrassed. None of our parents did anything like this: always staid, even stodgy, their most exciting entertainment was an occasional visit to a restaurant (or in the case of my parents, the opera). This, in contrast, was almost like the movies.

Suzy

SUZY AND OTTO ARRIVED IN NEW YORK from France in August 1946. Following their marriage in Marseille in November 1945 and through the combined efforts of Lina and Otto's brothers in New York, they had been able to obtain United States visas, although the process took longer than they had anticipated. In his Shoah Foundation testimony, Otto described their frustration with the Hebrew Immigrant Aid Society (HIAS), which was responsible for distributing the visas and arranging passage.

From the Testimony of Otto Goldschmitt for the Shoah Foundation

HIAS *dragged it along and dragged it along, we didn't get no passage, we didn't get no transportation, didn't get no visa. And I went to the HIAS office in Marseille one day, very aggravated, because you have to realize that I was not in a very good mood after things happened, and told them to send the money back to my brother, I don't want to have anything to do with them no more, because they were unable to book me transportation. Which they did, and through my friend, he was at the time working for the American OZ* [the Zionist Organization of America?] *and for the Distribution* [Joint Distribution Committee], *he took us to the consulate in Marseille, and within two days we had the visa.*

Now to get the passage, we had to book some kind of transportation, and he arranged that also for us through another employee. Well, we were supposed to leave Paris at the end of July with a certain ship. We left Marseille, we went to Paris to get the tickets: there were no tickets. The one who was supposed to book the passage had put the money in his pocket and disappeared. Now we were stranded in Paris, and that was the end of July '46. And there too we went to Jewish organizations and they didn't help us. As a matter of fact, there are two organizations that I don't want to hear about, and I don't want to mention their names. Because I got very aggravated, they just as much as throwing us out of the office in Paris. Well I got in touch with my brothers with a telegram, they sent the money, and we were able to book passage immediately on the SS Washington, which was converted to a passenger ship. And we got that passage and we came here to New York on the 14th or 13th of August.

At first they lived with Otto's childless oldest brother and his wife, but they soon acquired a furnished room in another of the old brownstones on the West Side, not far from Margot and Henri. However, with Suzy pregnant—the baby expected in January—it was essential to find an apartment, which they did—on Beck Street in the Southeast Bronx, even then a depressed and dangerous area. A memorable incident occurred around 1950: Suzy had visited her sisters at Hillside Avenue, and Lina had given her a heavy metal pot with a long handle. Walking home alone from the bus, Suzy was accosted by a mugger, who demanded her purse. Without even thinking, as if on instinct, she slammed him on the head with the pot as hard as she could. And then she ran, triumphant in her victory. Before long, however, Suzy, Otto, and their baby daughter Paulette also moved to Hillside Avenue. With all three of my mother's sisters and their families so close by (each family now with two children), frequent visits were a matter of course, though the situation changed somewhat after Lina and Fred bought a small Cape Cod-style house beside the railroad tracks in Fairlawn, New Jersey, and they began their lives as suburbanites.

Ilse

ANOTHER AUNT LIVED MUCH CLOSER TO US, my father's sister Ilse, who shared a studio apartment with her husband just a short block away. Our relationship with them was more complicated than with my mother's family. My father and Ilse's husband, Kurt, continued to dislike each other intensely, disagreeing about almost everything, so we seldom got together as a family. Nonetheless, I looked forward to their occasional visits. For one thing, Kurt worked for the Tootsie Roll Company (then located in Hoboken, New Jersey), where he had risen to the position of chief traffic manager, overseeing delivery of the candy nationwide. What that meant was that whenever they came we received a large box filled with Tootsie Roll products: small Tootsie rolls (the one- or two-cent size), large Tootsie Rolls (the five-cent size), and a multitude of red, orange, yellow, purple, and brown Tootsie Pops, their exteriors hard candy in various flavors and their interiors a delectable ball of Tootsie fudge. In addition, childless double earners as they were, they always gave me my best gifts. It was from them I received my only pair of ice skates, my tennis racket, and even (for my wedding) the Corningware pots and Farberware rotisserie that I continue to use more than fifty years later.

As children, my friend Terry and I delighted in visiting their small apartment in the doorman building where they lived. I am certain that their feelings were more mixed, as our favorite time to visit was early Sunday mornings, when we often woke them from sleep. Nonetheless, they always greeted us cheerfully, invited us to join them for breakfast, and then Uncle Kurt would—to our delight—wiggle his ears (he was a master!) and bounce us up and down on his knees. That he was a pompous and officious man whom my father disliked intensely, I not only knew from my parents but also could observe for myself, so I seldom mentioned these visits at home. But Ilse and Kurt obviously enjoyed us children and we (Terry and I) understood that and enjoyed their attention in return.

After my father's death, Ilse and Kurt moved to New Jersey, and all contact between them and my mother ceased for many years. Only when I was in college did I receive a letter from them pleading for a response, and I answered, visiting them when I was in New York on college breaks and finally telling my mother that I thought it was time to re-establish a relationship. And so we did, uneasily but cordially. They even drove to Binghamton for my college graduation. But in 1965 Tootsie Roll closed its Hoboken headquarters and relocated to Chicago. Ilse and Kurt moved with the company and, when Kurt—notwithstanding his long devotion to his employer—was soon laid off as new management took over, they moved yet further west, ultimately settling in San Diego. And thus our contact, except for occasional visits, ceased entirely until many years later when Ilse and Kurt were old and my mother was dead.

FAR MORE FREQUENT WERE VISITS with my parents' old friends from the Amsterdam boarding house, the Gordons, Herbert and Elsbeth (still called Mäuschen for her small size and resemblance to a small mouse). Years later Herbert provided the guarantees for my Danish husband's immigration to the U.S. and became godfather (a titular accolade only) to our first-born, Paul.

We spent almost every Sunday afternoon in their company, whether enjoying *Kaffee und Kuchen* at one of our apartments or *Nash's Konditorei* on Dyckman Street, or—in good weather—meeting in Fort Tryon Park for leisurely walks (the *Spaziergänge* of German tradition) along the long, flower-bordered paths. Among the earliest of our acquaintances to have a car, the Gordons generously took us along with them on weekend excursions, especially after my father's death, when my mother, Peter, and I were able to squeeze into the car's rear seat. In those days, before the construction of the Tappan Zee Bridge, Rockland and Orange counties, northwest of the city, were rural and undeveloped, and it was possible to experience a real country jaunt after a one- or two-hour drive. One place we spent a few weekends—a favorite of theirs—was a small, inexpensive guest farm in Walker Valley, run by German refugees, about eighty-five miles north of us. I still remember the enormous farm breakfasts, the large wooden table laden with homemade jams, large vats of homemade cottage cheese, fresh baked breads, and eggs in any form we wanted. To Peter and me, with little experience beyond the city's borders, it was a magical place.

Sometimes at the Gordons' home we encountered other old friends of my parents from the Amsterdam days, among them Walter and Trude Mendelssohn. In Berlin a writer and poet of cabaret lyrics, Walter continued to write German poetry in New York, although for a sadly diminished audience. Nonetheless, one came to expect from him amusing and clever birthday cards and—for those who could understand his witty German, which by and large remained his only fluent language—an ongoing stream of notable remarks. Trude remained as she always had been: bright red-haired, fiery, also witty, and unstoppably promiscuous. People always referred to her as "hot stuff."

Two other refugee couples completed this small social circle of my parents' life in New York. Hannah Lehman was a sister of my uncle Leo's wife Erna; Max was her husband. A heavy-set, slow-moving man, with an enormous leonine head topped by a mane of red hair, he was a semi-invalid because of an ongoing heart condition. They were unique among our close acquaintances in being religious and keeping a kosher household. As a child, I always loved visiting them because Max worked for the publishers of *Archie* comics. Their apartment seemed to have an endless supply of comic books, and I invariably returned home with a large stack of my own.

I don't know where my parents became acquainted with another couple, Eddy and Hedy Futran, possibly also in Amsterdam. Eddy was Jewish, Hedy was Gentile but from a family of Communists. Both were blond and beautiful, Hedy especially the very picture of Hitler's Aryan ideal. Eddy was a jazz accordionist, who played at the Metropole on Times Square, and I realized only much later how good he must have been to have been a regular part of that famous jazz scene. Active and athletic, they were avid skiers—something rare in those days and completely unknown in our circle. We became accustomed to their annual Christmas photo, their beautiful, blond family standing proudly on skis, with at least one adult or child inevitably in a cast and on crutches. Hedy and Eddy bore the air of true lovers; when Eddy died of cancer when he was not yet forty, Hedy, left alone with three young children, mourned for the rest of her life.

My parents and most of their family and friends seemed, as much as possible, to want to live as if they had never left Europe. But theirs were very private lives, and it was clear that all were reluctant to be taken note of by the larger society. All displayed anxiety, even fear, of being sought out for any reason (after all, no reason, in their experience, could bode well), and they tried as much as possible not to draw attention – to speak in low voices when outside, to avoid confrontations of any sort, never to complain or (as it was often phrased) "look for trouble." The expectation was that trouble would inevitably find them, and even when they became American citizens (which all did as soon as possible, having been made stateless by Germany), they never lost their awareness of the uncertainty of political assurances.

For my parents and my father's sister Ilse and her husband, the McCarthy era witch hunts of the late 1940s and early 1950s of anyone named (by anyone) as a leftist or "Red" created special anxieties. Their brother, Erich, was by then a high functionary in the East German government, Deputy Chairman of the Mecklenburg Communist party, with a name unusual enough that it could easily be recognized. Although none of them had had any contact with Erich since his time in Sweden during the war, given the anti-Communist hysteria of the time they were all fearful of being, in some way, associated with him. "*Keep quiet! Don't draw attention to yourself! Don't make waves!*" was the code we lived by in those years, and to some extent it governed my parents' lives and those of most of their acquaintances until their deaths. Having experienced political betrayal once, they had no confidence that it could not happen again—so they kept their mouths shut in public. My father read the left-wing newspaper *PM* until it closed down after having been sold in 1948, they voted as they wished—usually Democratic, occasionally for the American Labor Party candidates—and they argued about politics and social issues in private and among themselves.

CHAPTER 7

The Later Years

AFTER PETER'S BIRTH AND THE DEVASTATING REVELATIONS after the war, my mother's ability to cope, always fragile, disintegrated further. I can now see from her perspective the seemingly endless poverty and isolation with no end in sight, although I deeply resented at the time what I saw as her failure to be the warm and loving mother I longed for. Her depression increased, though no one seemed to recognize or acknowledge it. To most of her family she appeared only a "difficult" person, unwilling to accept her responsibilities. And she was difficult: increasingly agoraphobic, she left the house as little as possible, mainly to visit her several doctors in a search for some physiological diagnosis of heart or stomach ailment to explain her numerous "symptoms." Her sisters openly spoke of her as spoiled and too complaining.

Nor was I any more sympathetic. Seeking adult attention and

support from surrogates like teachers or neighbors, I encouraged my mother to focus on my brother, who, five years younger than I, was more tractable and obedient than I had ever been. When she concentrated on Peter, she didn't think so much about me, which suited me just fine.

Our confrontations had begun long before my adolescence. I was no more than three or four when, refusing to pick up a doll from the floor at her command, I watched her furiously snatch it up and smash it onto the floor, the plaster head shattering into many fragments. Shrieking my hatred of her, I rejected her pained apology. I suppose I got another doll soon afterward, but, in fact, I don't remember any other dolls until some years later, when I received, as a departure gift from the free Masonic Camp I attended for two weeks, a beautiful Effanbee doll I named Patsy.

The years went by. My parents quarreled frequently—about money and my father's erratic employment, or his frequent solitary excursions to the movies, or the time spent playing card games with his friends, or about friends who dropped in at what were, to my mother, inopportune times (although there were seldom opportune times).

And then, a month before his forty-sixth birthday, my father died. There had been signs of a problem in some acute leg pains during the past few months, but Dr. Freudenberger, our elderly family physician, had reassured my father that there was nothing to worry about. But on December 15, 1951, while riding the subway home from his current job as a shipping clerk, he suffered what turned out to be a fatal heart attack. Weak and vomiting, he staggered onto the One Hundred and Sixty-Eighth Street Station platform, conscious that Columbia Presbyterian Hospital was a mere elevator ride above. But he collapsed on the platform and, covered in vomit, was (to his great humiliation, as he told my mother when she later visited him at the hospital) assumed by the police to be drunk. Only in the emergency room was he finally diagnosed with an "acute coronary thrombosis." In those days, however, there was little to be done for what now is successfully treated by angioplasty or, at worst, open heart surgery followed by a few days' hospital stay and medication. He was placed in an oxygen tent, while we and the doctors watched and waited.

One week later he was dead. To his funeral I wore the green Girl Scout uniform he had given me a few weeks before as an early Christmas present. Like many New York Jews in those days, we celebrated Christmas with a present or two. Hannukah was definitely considered a lesser holiday. Because gifts were precious in our family, the purchase of the expensive uniform with all its accessories—the yellow scarf-tie with its trefoil insignia at each end, the beret, belt, and purse—had surprised and moved me. Nevertheless, I was unable to cry at the funeral. Not until reaching middle age was I able to grieve over his premature loss, my feelings at the time (feelings, as I later learned, not uncommon among adolescents) more of shame at being singled out by having a parent die than of grief.

Suddenly and unexpectedly, my mother found herself a widow

with two young children, ages eleven and six, and—in what came as a total shock to everyone—another baby on the way. To support the remaining family, besides the small Social Security Survivors' Pension, there was only a $5,000 insurance policy that my father, at Cousin Theo's insistence, had reluctantly agreed to take out a few months earlier and that proved clearly to be a bad deal for Metropolitan Life. The unexpected baby was something I learned about only after my mother miscarried about a week or so after my father's death, in the midst of the Christmas holidays. While going to visit my father at the hospital one day, she had fallen on the icy sidewalk, not at all aware that she was pregnant. A few days after my father's funeral, Peter and I were taken to our aunts on Hillside Avenue, where I learned from the fragments of whispers around me of the reason for my mother's sudden hospitalization. Everyone regarded the miscarriage as a blessing. Later, when I was older, my mother and I spoke openly about it, although she would sometimes wonder aloud what "that child" would have been like and how our lives would have been different had it lived.

After my father's death, soon to enter my teens with all the attendant baggage of burgeoning adolescence, I was disdainful of what I viewed as her hysterical responses to my moves toward independence. I tended to react to her concerns with hostility, resenting that she was too fearful about my independence to let me do as my friends did. To me it seemed that whatever moves I made towards even slight autonomy evoked a negative response, her constant litany being: "Don't do that, it's too dangerous." As a result,

I told her less and less as I roamed the neighborhood with my friends whose mothers never seemed to worry about them so long as they were home at the appointed time.

From the outset, my mother had been good at finding and attacking my weak spots. When, in adolescence, I felt my most unattractive, she snarled at me during one of our many verbal confrontations, "You think you're so beautiful, always looking in the mirror. Well, you're not. You're ugly." And then, of course, she apologized. To the end of her life, my response to her attacks was usually silence. I could not fight "dirty" the way she could. Nor did she usually remember the things she had said. When she was old and needed my assistance with most aspects of daily life, she would sometimes say, as if to comfort me, "Oh, you know that I say things I don't mean. Just don't pay attention." And I would try to forget, knowing that she was right, that her angry words didn't mean anything—to her. And I usually did forget the words but remembered the anger, both hers and mine.

The year following my father's death, when I was twelve, she, returned for a brief period to work again at the Wilson Company, as the Social Security pension was barely enough to cover the rent, let alone our other needs. Peter and I necessarily became latchkey children, something we both enjoyed, although now, after having raised my own children, I can better understand her anxiety about seven-year-old Peter's roaming the neighborhood without supervision. But her working career did not last; her anxiety and depression increased until one morning she simply refused to get out of bed. For months she stayed in the apartment, getting up only to use the bathroom or to cook; through it all she continued cooking and serving us dinner, although I did much of the shopping as well as laundry and housekeeping, and took care of my little brother. Among her papers, after her death, I discovered an "illness narrative" she wrote in the early 1960s about her memories of that period:

> *In August 1953, I started to work in a company where I had worked when we first came here on a part-time basis. However, I became very ill with a severe depression in December 1954 and was home for 6 months. Where I had had difficulties before that in being with people, I could not stand to see anyone anymore. When one of my sisters came to the house, I barricaded myself in the bedroom. I only went out once a week to see [a psychiatrist] in Medical Center. I walked back and forth because I felt very sick when I was forced to use bus or subway. I was extremely agitated and could not sit for one minute. Even while I was with the doctor, I walked up and down.*

What amazes me now, looking back at all this after so many years, is that no one intervened to offer help. Here we were, a young widow and two young children, with very little money, desperately trying to survive—and my aunts and uncles, and whoever else of friends and family were looking on, did absolutely nothing.

Or maybe not nothing, maybe their few, feeble efforts at assistance were rejected. But what we needed was someone forceful enough to step in. I suppose they all had too many worries themselves to muster that force.

Brief salvation arrived from an unexpected direction. All three of us came down with the Asian flu during one of those sweeping periodic epidemics. The mother of one of my school friends, aware of our pitiable situation and after making several unavailing pleas to Jewish agencies, called Catholic Charities, which responded immediately. When the doorbell rang, there stood not Mary Poppins but someone almost as welcome, Sister Peter, who would live with us for the next week or so, nursing us, shopping, cooking, cleaning, and otherwise setting our disordered household to rights. No work was too demeaning for her. With her black veil hiding her hair and a starched white wimple covering her forehead, she was a nun (in those days before Vatican II) of the old-fashioned sort. But she did not hesitate to roll up the sleeves of her long black habit and scrub the toilet. She would coax my mother to eat some chicken soup she had made, and would talk to me for hours about her life in the convent and her work, all the while busily scrubbing the kitchen counters or cutting up vegetables or mending the torn socks she found in the "mending bag" in the closet. I learned from her that nuns could take any saints' names they wanted, male or female; hence her name and that of her superior, Mother Joseph, who came periodically to supervise. Never a word about religion, about our not being Catholic, although we saw her often with missal or rosary in hand, mouthing silent prayers. It was impossible to determine her age; to my child's eyes, she could have been anywhere from twenty-five to sixty, although her vigor suggested the former more than the latter. She proved a stalwart friend for that brief time, and although we never saw her again after she left, I have a warm spot in my heart for nuns to this day. From that time, we always gave a bit to Catholic Charities, even when we had little to give.

Lotte

A FEW WEEKS AFTER MY FATHER'S DEATH, following my twelfth birthday, my mother told me the astonishing news that I had a half-sister in Germany. Neither my father's early marriage nor Lotte, the daughter who had sprung from that brief union with Elsa Oestreicher, had even been whispered of in my presence. At first I was shocked and disturbed by the news that I was not, as I had taken for granted, my father's only daughter. But soon I began to welcome it; after all, I had always wanted a sister, and now one had miraculously appeared. And her appearance was indeed miraculous.

According to my mother's account, my father had left Mannheim soon after Hitler came to power in 1933, three years after his divorce from Elsa, and returned to his family in Dortmund. Lotte, many years later, told me of his persecution because of his mixed marriage and the article in *Der Stürmer* that had followed his departure from Mannheim. [See Chapter 5] With no further contact, she was unaware of what happened afterward, how he and his brother Werner had soon fled to Amsterdam to escape Dortmund's virulent anti-Semitism as well as the police harassment drawn by his brother Erich's Communist activism, and how—later that same year—their parents and sister had joined them. Regarding the fate of his former wife and their daughter, my father's (and my mother's) assumption had always been that, given the increasing persecution of the Jews, Elsa had no doubt concealed Lotte's half-Jewish parentage, married a Nazi, and put her former life behind her.

The truth, however, turned out to be surprisingly different. Elsa had indeed remarried (although not to a Nazi), become pregnant soon after, and had died in childbirth already in 1935, at the age of twenty-three. With no interest from her stepfather in raising a child not his own, Lotte was taken in by her maternal grandmother. No effort was made to conceal Lotte's Jewish paternity: in such a small town as the Mannheim suburb of Käferthal, where they lived, that would have been impossible. The grandmother (always called "*Die Oma*") was, however, a strong and fierce woman, much respected in the community, and through force of will she evidently was able to protect her granddaughter until the war's end. Lotte has told me that every day, as the Allies were drawing closer, she and her grandmother prayed for an Allied victory, hoping against hope that the Americans would arrive before Lotte (now almost eighteen) was arrested and imprisoned. And so it happened: The Americans came and she survived.

But the strangest part of the story is yet to come. Lotte barely remembered her father—our father—although the two or three photographs in her possession served as a reminder, and she studied them intently throughout her childhood. She had no idea whether he had survived, nor, of course, did she imagine that he had another family. And although she was eventually prohibited from attending school, her grandmother arranged some private tutoring for her. Among other skills, she was encouraged to learn English, as her grandparents assumed that she would, when it was possible, emigrate to England or America. After the war ended, she was, thanks to her fluent English, hired by the German Restitution Office to receive and process the applications for restitution now pouring in from former German Jews who, forced into exile, had lost all their prior assets. And lo and behold: on one of the applications, filed by the American descendants of Julius and Hanna Glückauf from Dortmund, she saw her own name listed among the descendants. As she later told me, she almost fainted. The claim had been filed by my father's sister Ilse and her husband, together with my mother, in my name and Peter's. At the last minute, my mother had—over her sister- and brother-in-law's strong objections—added Lotte Glückauf's name to the list of descendants, more out of curiosity and a bit of mischief than because she thought anything would come of it. In fact, the main benefit from the claim turned out to be Lotte herself, not any material compensation, as Julius and Hanna had voluntarily disposed of most of their property (albeit at great loss) when they fled Germany in 1933.

Lotte wrote immediately to both my mother and Ilse, her letters causing great excitement. We discovered that she still lived in Mannheim with her young daughter, Petra. She was separated from her husband, who—we later learned—had revealed his homosexuality shortly after their marriage, eventually moving to Berlin to live with his long-time boyfriend. From then on our contact was constant, first with letters back and forth, later with visits to each other's homes, and—with the coming of the Internet—frequent interchange of emails and photos. Lotte, having outlived three husbands, died in April 2019, at the age of ninety-two. Some years earlier, she had moved from Mannheim to the small Bavarian city of Marktheidenfeld to be near her daughter, granddaughter, and great-grandchildren. Though we seldom met, we remained close for the rest of her life, and when we met (as we did for the last time in the summer of 2018), we felt that we were indeed sisters—with Lotte, in fact, resembling our common father more than I do.

THAT I WAS RESPONSIBLE FOR MOST of the housecleaning during those years of my early teens was not as strange as it sounds; my closest friends, Terry and Mary Ann, had similar responsibilities. Saturday mornings were allotted to these chores, which we all had learned to perform effectively in our required home-economics class. There girls were taught to scrub bathrooms and kitchens, to dust and to polish. My friends and I would start by establishing a rough timetable by phone; the routine was that after we had finished we could go to the movies. Then we would each tune into the *Top 40 hits* on the radio to listen to "Sh-Boom, Sh-Boom" and

Earth Angel—these were the early years of rock-and-roll—as well as more traditional favorites by Patti Page, Perry Como, Rosemary Clooney, and Nat King Cole.

Sharing my friends' interests, the only difference being my obsessive reading of as many books as I was able to carry home from the library, I was happily heading on the same path as theirs, to take the commercial track at our local public high school and become a secretary—one of four career options then considered possible for young women of our circle: nurse, teacher, secretary, or beautician. For what, most parents felt, was the purpose of educating girls, who would just go on to marry and have children? My friends were my models, my support, my constant companions, and, given the lack of guidance from home, whom else should I follow? So when, in eighth grade, we were called on to declare our high school choices, I did as they did, signing up for the commercial courses at George Washington High School, a few blocks north of where we lived.

Almost at once, however, came a call from the principal's office: Mr. Gross wanted to see me. What had I done wrong, I wondered, as I ran down the two flights to his office on the main floor. Anxiously I entered. He wasted no time getting to the point: "*You*," he said brusquely, "are not taking a commercial course. I have placed you in the Honors Program." And that was that. With those few words my future was altered. I have often thought of him with gratitude, of how lucky I was that someone was looking out for me, as I have contemplated the many children for whom the chips fall as they may. For me there followed a year at George

Washington, three years at New York's specialized High School of Music and Art, four years at Harpur College (now Binghamton University but then only a few years old), a year as a Fulbright Scholar at the University of Copenhagen (where I met my husband), an M.A. and Ph.D. from Harvard, followed by a rewarding academic career. And I owe it all to Mr. Gross—short, plump, and bald—an elderly man with a gruff manner and strong Brooklyn accent, who was paying attention to the children under his care and took his job seriously.

Lina (Len)

OF THE FOUR SCHACK SISTERS, IT WAS LINA (now calling herself Len) who adapted best to American life, perhaps because she was the only one to marry an American, a circumstance that helped pave the way for a smoother assimilation. But her easy assumption of American manners was also emblematic of her flexible temperament and innate sociability. Gregarious and fun-loving, Len made friends readily, charming them with her often off-color jokes and easy accommodation to local customs, wherever she was living. Her husband, Fred, was the youngest of four children of a traditional Italian-Catholic family; only the two youngest were born in America. Raised largely by his oldest sister, Josephine, who retained many of the traditional ways (not least as a cook of spectacularly good southern Italian food), he shocked them all when
he married this Jewish refugee from Germany.

The first in our family to own a car (a sturdy Dumont), Len and Fred took advantage of the G.I. bill to purchase a tiny bungalow in the Hopatcong Hills in then rural Sussex County, New Jersey. There their growing family spent summers, with Fred commuting back and forth by train on weekends. A few years later, they became true suburbanites, buying a small, older house beside the railroad tracks in Fairlawn, New Jersey. Originally just a single-story Cape Cod, Fred had dormers put in so that (according to my cousin Linda) "there were two decent-sized bedrooms upstairs that one could actually stand up in." A few years later they moved again, this time to a larger colonial (or what Aunt Len called a "bastard colonial" because it was new, not old) in one of the many new developments springing up all over Bergen County to house the growing number of suburbanites.

To the rest of us, it seemed that Len and Fred had "made it" as no one else in the family had done. While most of us still lived in our one-bedroom city apartments, they now were experiencing the kind of suburban life that was being promoted nationwide as Modern America and that we increasingly saw illustrated in the popular magazines and TV shows of the time. To visit their house in Hillsdale, which we did often, was to enter a new and different world, seemingly freer and more expansive than our own urban setting of tightly packed apartment houses and sparse greenery. That their house, which seemed when they purchased it to overlook a broad and uninterrupted expanse of woods, within months had its view disturbed by the construction of a large supermarket just below was of course disappointing, but nonetheless we were in awe of the way in which their life resembled what we had come to see as quintessentially American.

Of course, we knew that the reality was somewhat different from the *Ozzie and Harriet* world depicted on our TVs. Their marriage reflected the usual disagreements and quarrels, often due to Fred's perpetual tardiness, which was both a family irritant and a joke. After his death long afterward from the lung cancer brought on by his many years of heavy smoking, Len—irrepressible even in old age—always referred to him with a laugh as "my late husband," never failing to add, "And he was *always* late." Their eldest child, Bobby, was an obsessive collector of wild animals: birds, rodents, and especially snakes, which drove his family to distraction. Shouts of "Help me! The boa constrictor is loose somewhere in the house," were not uncommon, and Len and Fred often were called on to drive Bobby to some nearby woods so that he could return newly healed animals to the wild. Bobby never lost that love for animals. Even after he married, several snake terraria occupied the living room of the rent-controlled Soho loft in which he lived with his wife, Ann, and at his death (he was the first of my cousins to die, of lung cancer, like his father), Ann, who had always been supportive of his hobby, had to figure out what to do with them. Len and Fred's two younger children, Claire (ten years my junior) and Michael (born three years later), were young enough that during my teen years I often babysat for them.

Now more than ever Len and Fred hosted the rest of the family. There were barbecues in the summer, although the grilled meat—for which Fred, as the male of the house, was of course responsible—was invariably not yet done hours after the guests' arrival. They also traditionally hosted our Thanksgiving dinner, although the turkey was always late and Fred often needed to be found, so that by the time the large, extended family sat at the table we were all ravenous with hunger.

Nonetheless, that we felt ourselves a family bound by traditions and community was due in large part to Len and Fred's hospitality. No one else—not my mother, not Suzy and Otto, not Margot and Henri, not Aunt Bessie—had either the space or the will to host large family gatherings. My mother, reclusive after my father's death, almost never invited any guests at all to our small and dreary apartment, although we occasionally visited Suzy and Otto, usually for one of the Jewish holidays. Dinner invitations to Margot and Henri's were infrequent but welcome, especially if Henri cooked one of his French specialties, although to Margot always fell the responsibility for double frying the marvelous *pommes frites.*

When Len, Fred, and their youngest son Michael moved to San Diego in the early 1960s (their oldest son was married by then and their daughter in college), our family lost whatever cohesiveness it had had. Of course, all the children were growing up and going their own way, but thereafter the siblings met only infrequently, dependent for their rare get-togethers on visits to New York from Len and Fred from California or Leo and Erna from Mexico.

Margot

By the early 1950s Margot was drinking ever more heavily, increasingly neglecting her household and, less forgivably, her two children—Linda, born in 1947, and Steven, another redhead, in 1949. Nonetheless, I loved her dearly, as did my mother. Generous to a fault and fun-loving (especially when she had had a little too much to drink), she could, notwithstanding her drinking, always be counted on to be there when needed—the only one of my aunts on whom we could rely under all circumstances. And she welcomed my teenaged friends, too, as if we were her peers, inviting us, when we dropped in unannounced to her apartment, to sit around the table and schmooze and—depending what she was then drinking—to join her for a glass of vermouth on ice or a beer. Her vodka preference began later.

After their marriage, her husband Henri, who had always been handy with tools, opened a woodworking/cabinet-making shop in Hoboken, but that soon failed, and he returned to the restaurant business, where he could always find a job as a waiter or *maître d'* in one of the numerous French bistros that then sprinkled the Theater District north and west of Times Square. Somewhere along the way, however, his behavior became noticeably odder. The first thing that led family members to whisper among themselves was when he turned the small coat closet in the foyer into what he called his "office," removing the clothing bars and making a desk from a shelf supported on two brackets, on which he set a small typewriter. Henri's ambition was to write erotic French novels, and to this end he established a reference library, crammed in on the shelves he hung above the desk—French and English paperbacks, their lurid covers showing screaming half-naked girls fleeing in terror from the violent grasp of male attackers. Since he worked evenings, he had most of the day to write, and we all got used to the sound of the typewriter's clacking away behind the closed closet door. That he didn't suffocate was a miracle, for there was no ventilation beyond what entered from the small gap where the door met the floor. He stayed in there for hours, emerging only when he had to—to use the bathroom, to eat, or to leave for work.

Both Henri and Margot had quick tempers, and their fights—about money, about their dissatisfaction with their situation, each attacking the other for his or her failures—got worse. One day, Margot called in a locksmith to change the lock on the front door. When Henri arrived home from work that night, he found most of his clothes dumped in the hallway outside the front door. Although he tried to get in, banging loudly on the door and shouting, the late hour and the angry neighbors, who opened their doors to see what the commotion was about, caused him to retire in furious defeat. What occupied Margot while all this was going on is not hard to imagine: She most likely sat in her kitchen, a bottle of vermouth in front of her, smoking cigarette after cigarette, and deliberately ignoring the tumult outside.

He returned a few days later to get the rest of his possessions and, while there, tried to persuade her to let him move back in, but she was adamant. With the children in school all day, Margot took a job as a waitress at Leo's, a busy and popular luncheonette on Eighty-Sixth Street, just off Lexington Avenue. She worked the lunch shift, made good money in tips, and was able to get home not long after the children returned from school. And, for a while, the drinking moderated, probably at least in part because she was occupied during the day and so tired at night that she fell into bed soon after dinner. So now it was mainly on weekends that she could be found with the bottle in front of her at the kitchen table. A stint in rehab led to a period of sobriety, but eventually she began to drink again, continuing a cycle that lasted almost until her death.

Strangely enough, though, we were less content when she was sober than we probably should have been, for, like many alcoholics, she was most entertaining and affectionate when drunk. When sober, she became close-mouthed and suspicious, sometimes even angry and bitter—mechanically taking the subway to work, trudging uncomplainingly back and forth between the restaurant's kitchen and the tables she waited on, taciturn, seldom smiling except to her favorite "regulars," returning home exhausted, avoiding even those closest to her.

All this was hardest, of course, on her children. Toward them, she tended to extremes: sometimes smothering them with affection, sometimes ignoring them as if they hardly existed. With Margot, there seemed to be no middle ground. What made all this even harder for the children was its unpredictability. Coming home from school each afternoon to an empty house, they would sit in front of the television, squabbling and uneasy, until she finally appeared. Sometimes all smiles, she would gather them in her too thin arms and clutch them to her as if she never wanted to let them go. Squirming and ill at ease, they would endure her fervid, discomfiting kisses partly out of desire for the affection so often withheld, partly in terror of her desperate hunger and passion. These, they knew, were good days. On these days, they would eat together, like a real family, their mother having roasted a chicken—baked potatoes and a salad on the side—or some other meal they liked.

But these evenings were more exception than rule. More often she came home tired, silently letting herself into the apartment, grunting at the children, slapping down in front of them a hot dog and some potato salad and coleslaw purchased from a neighborhood deli (on these evenings, she herself never seemed to eat) and withdrawing into her own private world. What she thought as she sat alone in the dark, who can guess? The children ate in similar silence, frightened, their eyes barely meeting, anxious to finish and return to the television, its canned laughter and artificial applause a barrier against misery. Sometimes, if they accidentally got in her way, her hand would swing out—as if on its own volition –and they would find a cheek red and smarting from the casual smack. On those nights, they went to bed without protest—although they often lay awake, unable to sleep, the unnatural silence within the apartment magnifying the sound of every toilet flush or car horn.

Margot stayed sober for two or three years and then started drinking heavily again, how or under what circumstances no one really knew. But we gradually became aware of her increased cheerfulness and conviviality. Once again she came to family gatherings, clearly enjoying the large group, unlike the past couple of years when she had wanted us only singly if at all. At home, she spent most of her time—once more—at the kitchen table, a rapidly emptying bottle of vodka in front of her, drinking until she passed out on her bed or, if she couldn't make it all the way to the next room, on the floor. Miraculously, she continued going faithfully to work each day, not drinking until she came home, although she changed to the breakfast and lunch shift so that she could be home earlier. When the children came in from school, they sometimes found her half-drunk in the kitchen, sometimes already unconscious. Now no one took care of the house or regularly prepared meals.

Our few family gatherings became increasingly uncomfortable. She would arrive already drunk—cheerful, a bit raucous, husky-voiced and expansive—and would get more and more drunk—first belligerent, then lachrymose, as the day progressed—and would eventually have to be half-carried home and put to bed by one of her brothers-in-law or nephews. She was a perfect illustration of the paradigmatic "five stages of drunkenness": verbose, jocose, bellicose, morose, comatose. "*What to do about Margot?*" became the topic most discussed among us.

Two incidents from those days have stayed in my mind. Both, interestingly, occurred in restaurants, seemingly the atmosphere that sparked her most outrageous behavior. By this time, my own household was in trouble, my father dead and my mother depressed and agoraphobic. My brother and I returned from school each day to a funereal apartment—the room-darkening shades drawn and our mother in bed with the covers over her head. Margot was one of the brightest spots in our gloomy lives. We looked forward to her visits, which even managed to cheer up our mother. Somehow, our still-young aunt was more relaxed with us than with her own children, perhaps because what she did for us sprang from feelings of generosity, not responsibility.

On the first day I am thinking of, Margot had shown up at our door late in the afternoon with our cousins. "*C'mon kids,*" she said as soon as she came in, "*Let's go out to eat at the deli, for a change.*" We looked eagerly at our mother to see if she would agree. Although at her sister's plea she had risen from her bed, she refused to go out, but had no objections to our going.

Dave's, our favorite deli, was a mere block away on St. Nicholas Avenue, a very paradise of traditional deli treats. The pastrami and corned beef, deep red and edged with a slight layer of fat, were served warm and moist on fresh, seeded rye. The homemade French fries were thick cut and double-fried, crisp on the outside, soft within. The pickles—fished from a deep, brine-filled barrel—were what we called "green," lightly dilled, with only the raw edge taken off the cucumber. Even the mustard had its own special color and taste—a deeper gold and more redolent of vinegar and spices than our usual supermarket Gulden's.

We entered and sat at one of the large tables at the back of the restaurant. Margot was jovial and loquacious, asking the waiter for a beer as soon as we were seated. As we ate—happily stuffing ourselves—we barely noticed that the beer kept coming. Nor did we really see that Margot's conversation with the waiter was getting more and more indecorous and that she was having a harder and harder time sitting straight in her chair. Finally it was time to pay. Margot looked at the check, smiled, and pulled out a hundred-dollar bill. "Keep the change," she waved majestically to the astonished waiter and quickly herded us out, deliberately ignoring our dumbfounded (and embarrassed) stares. For the bill had come to no more than twenty dollars (a large enough sum in those pre-inflation days), and she had given what amounted to a 500-percent tip. But it was a grand gesture from a waitress who knew what it meant to scrounge for tips, and she never (as far as I knew) regretted it, even when she missed the money when her own bills came due. My mother, when I told her, was understandably horrified.

The second incident occurred some years later. Uncle Leo and his wife, now prosperous and successful Mexican citizens, were paying one of their infrequent visits to New York. On impulse, Margot invited the whole family—sisters, cousins, nieces and nephews and their spouses (by then several of us were married)—to the popular French bistro *Les Pyrenees*, on Fifty-Second Street, to celebrate the rare reunion. A party of nearly twenty people, we sat squeezed closely together at long tables, enjoying the good food and cheerful company. At first, only those closest to her noticed Margot's increasing inebriation. Soon it was evident to all. She staggered from table to table, draping her arms around her brothers-in-law' and nephews' shoulders, loudly declaring her affection. She turned her attentions to the *maître'd*, and—her arms encircling his neck—ignoring his evident discomfiture, tried to persuade him to dance. Within a short time, she had to be taken home by one of her nephews. Leo, the guest of honor, ended up paying the bill—apparently happy to do so and refusing all offers to share the costs. But the incident left the rest of us embarrassed, unhappy, and yet more wary about letting ourselves depend on Margot's good intentions.

Upon his return to Mexico, Leo wrote to my mother:

> *Regarding Margot I wrote her a very serious letter; maybe she says once more 'shit' and throws it in the basket. Maybe she starts thinking? The only one who could help could be her husband, but I have the feeling that he helps to get her under the earth. Both will claim all the time that they are big enough to handle their own business, and that nobody should mind. Even trying to put her in some correctional* [sic] *needs the approval of her husband. So maybe the best is to help with good words, show her the way. I think that her liver damage is not* definitif, *that she can still recover, at least this is my hope, as I am not a doctor. . . . What else can I suggest? Of course, I will do* [what is] *necessary to have her sent all the medicine she needs at my expense. Talk to her when she is sober.*

Imagine our surprise when, a few years later, she and Henri moved back together. None of us knew exactly when, but suddenly he was there, a bit more subdued than in earlier years and showing an unexpected devotion to his wife. What was also evident was that some conditions had been set prior to the reconciliation, some sacrifices made to marital harmony: Margot once again stopped drinking, and Henri was no longer writing porn. Unable to work due to his serious emphysema—he had smoked heavily all his life—he collected a small disability pension. We never knew whether it was pity that led to her change of heart, or loneliness, or simply submission to the inevitable: in all those years of separation, there had, to our knowledge, been no other man in her life.

They moved to a new apartment in a well-maintained complex overlooking the Hudson River in Yonkers, and, while Margot—now the chief breadwinner—went off each morning on the train to work, Henri stayed home, taking care of the household and puttering around, sometimes in his darkroom, sometimes doing carpentry, lining the walls of the apartment with built-in storage spaces, or repainting. A new topic of contention arose between them: the extravagance of his purchases. With each new hobby came a load of new and usually expensive equipment. As his interest in each hobby faded, the supplies joined their predecessors in the closet.

During this period, we didn't hear from them very often, and we saw them even less. Holidays, perhaps—Thanksgiving or Christmas—or birthdays, but for the most part we all went our individual ways. As far as I can recall, we never visited their apartment. When we saw them it was usually a brief visit at our apartment or occasionally at a restaurant. What precipitated a change was the increasing severity of Henri's emphysema. Margot's phone calls telling us that Henri was in the hospital became more frequent. His doctors recommended that he move to Denver, to enter the Jewish Hospital for Respiratory Diseases, which he did for a time, but eventually, heeding his pulmonologists' advice that he permanently leave New York for a drier and milder climate, he decided to move to San Diego where Len and Fred were already living. Within a few days he found a trailer park in El Cajon and purchased a small trailer and immediately began to outfit it with built-ins, as if it were a small, trim ship.

At first, Margot remained behind, having no desire to relocate. For several months she lived alone in the Yonkers apartment, taking the train each day to work the lunchtime shift at the restaurant on Eighty-Sixth Street. At some point she had begun drinking again—whether before or after Henri left we never knew. One of the first signs was an increased volubility. Whereas sober she was quiet and withdrawn, drunk she became gregarious, phoning her sisters several times a day and holding them to the telephone with long, repetitive monologues. And she became more sociable; after Henri's departure, she often dropped by in the evenings to sit and talk, leaving only when it became clear to her that everyone else was ready for bed. Nor, when she got home—as we became gradually aware—did she sleep, but sat up with her bottle most of the night, occasionally laying her head on the table for a cat nap, and somehow, miraculously, sobering up enough to go to work again in the morning.

All this time, Henri was urging her to join him, and finally she agreed, making arrangements to relocate. But of course she was, by this time, incapable of seeing to the logistics of moving. On the morning of the move, my husband and I, in what was our first and only visit to her apartment, found her sitting bewildered at her table, half-packed cartons around her. Strewn on the bed were boxes of jewelry—the "*hocking stuff*" (as she always called it) that she had collected through the years, much of it undoubtedly stolen (*hot*, as she would say), purchased from venders who came into the restaurant offering their goods. Some of the boxes had fallen open, the gold necklaces, bracelets, rings, and pins spilling carelessly onto the bed. Quickly scooping up the jewelry before the moving men arrived and packing it all into a large handbag, we set ourselves to take care of the rest of the mess. That it all got done—that the movers were able to load the truck that day—is a testimony to our dogged efforts. We even got her to the plane on time.

Selling the trailer in advance of her arrival, Henri had rented an apartment in one of those ubiquitous southern California garden apartment complexes built around a small pool. Unlike her sister Len, however, who had adapted from the start, Margot responded ambivalently to California life, liking the climate but hating the isolation. Never one for devoting herself to housework, she was nevertheless unable to take a job because of her lack of mobility. She had never learned to drive. Her instincts were urban—she had thrived on New York's frenzy—and the quiet orderliness of San Diego, its manicured parks and pedestrian-free streets, bored her.

This could have been a happy time for her. After all, she was not uncomfortable, Henri (less ill than he had been, although the attacks persisted) was devoted to her, her daughter Linda, who had moved to San Diego with two young sons, lived nearby, and soon her son, Steve—discharged from the Navy and now working for the telephone company—arranged a transfer so that he could join them. But the years of heavy smoking and drinking had taken their toll. A few months after her arrival, she began complaining of pains in her chest and back. The doctors discovered advanced lung cancer; with shocking lack of tact, they told her the fatal diagnosis at once, without any effort to cushion the blow. Her response was more rage than sorrow—rage at the doctors, whose cruel frankness she never forgave, as much as at the circumstances.

Others told me of her pain and bitterness. The cause of the former was clearly the cancer itself, apparently immune to radiation or chemotherapy. The reasons for the latter were more complex, and I'm not sure I can unravel them all. Of course, under treatment, she could not drink, although she continued smoking to the end ("*Why not?*" she would ask. "*It's got me already.*") And sobriety had always made her more aloof. But beyond that, the illness seemed to create precisely the kind of situation she—in her life-long pride and self-reliance—most dreaded. Weak and dependent, she shrank from the pitying attentions of others. She became touchy and irritable, angry when others wanted to help, resentful of what she interpreted as patronizing behavior, accepting only Henri's ministrations (although, too weak to do much for herself, she had little choice). Her siblings tried to help: my mother and Suzy flew from New York to visit, as did Leo from Mexico, and Len, of course, was with her often, but their efforts, made awkward and uncertain by sorrow were coolly rejected. When she died in 1978, at the age of fifty-three, Henri had her ashes placed within an ornate and imposing marble mausoleum, the kind of ostentatious interment she would surely have mocked. That she was the youngest of her siblings, that she was the most loved, made her death especially painful to us all. After Margot's death, Henri went back to living in a trailer. Until the end of his life, he would go each week to lay a single lily beside the "drawer" containing her remains.

Leo

THE REAL OUTLIER WAS, OF COURSE, Leo in Mexico City. From the start he had been determined to build a comfortable new life for his growing family. Blessed, like his sister Lina, with an easygoing temperament and effortless sociability, he (like Lina) adapted to changed circumstances in a way that proved impossible for the others. Fortunate enough to gain entry into the burgeoning chemical business, which in Mexico at the time largely meant pesticides, he rose to top positions in a series of firms, eventually achieving the presidency of the Mexican pesticide manufacturers association. Although his success evolved slowly and not without setbacks, succeed he did, enough to provide a comfortable life for his wife and family and to educate their three children at good international schools. Called "Jack" by all his friends and colleagues, he rapidly became as fluent in Spanish as he was in French, German, and English (a remarkable linguistic facility inherited by all his children) and easily adopted the ways of his new, Latin environment.

Nor did he ever lose his passion for soccer. While still young and agile, he played with several amateur clubs and coached in his spare time. After his knees gave out and he gave up playing, his involvement with the game continued. He became president of the *Tribunal de Penas* of the Mexican Football Association (the committee that determined penalties in official games), and served for a time in FIFA (*Fédération Internationale de Football Association*), the international governing body of the world's most popular sport.

During the 1970 World Cup, he was appointed coordinator of referees in Guadalajara. He faithfully attended every World Cup until old age made traveling impossible. Throughout his life he often returned to Europe, partly to visit his wife's extended family in France and England, partly to reestablish contact with old friends in Germany, among them those who had hustled him out of Zwingenberg in advance of the SS on that long-ago night in 1933. Through his soccer connections, too, he made many new friends, including the Social Democratic Prime Minister, Willy Brandt, with whom he exchanged visits in Germany and Mexico.

After his retirement, he and Erna moved from Mexico City to Guadalajara, where they lived until their deaths. Only at the very end of his life, after Erna's death (when she was eighty-one and he eighty-two), did his life-long optimism seem to vanish. Lonely—

with two of his three children and most of his grandchildren living abroad and his hearing and heart both failing him—Leo's last few letters reflect little of the *joie de vivre* that had carried him through the many difficult years:

> *Since my dear Erna left me alone, surely against her will last year, I have been unable to do anything,"* he wrote to me (in English) a year after her death. *"Surely, sixty-two years of friendship and fifty-seven of happy marriage cannot be easily overcome.... All* [children and grandchildren] *are very kind to me, but my life has drastically changed.... Now more than ever I feel how much I loved this great woman.* "Durch Dick un Dünn is sie mit mir gegangen, niemals hat see geklagt!" he wrote me shortly after her death in 1995. ["Through thick and thin she was my companion; never did she complain."] Leo outlived his wife by less than three years.

Suzy

WHEN I THINK OF MY AUNT SUZY, I think of her silence. Unlike her generally voluble siblings, she seldom spoke more than a few words except to her husband and children, even during the most heated family conversations. Some of this reticence may have been due to shyness, some traceable to her forced silence during her long imprisonment in Nazi Germany, some to her somewhat self-conscious English and her refusal to speak German. Of all my aunts, I felt that I knew Suzy least. That many years later I was the person with her when she died, her hand clutching mine for comfort, seems a strange turn of fate. My husband and I had gone to visit her as she lay in her apartment bedroom attended by a hospice nurse—something we did all too seldom. Her long battle against colon cancer was nearing an end. She was too weak to do more than smile wanly, but it was clear that she welcomed our visit. As I held her hand, she drifted into sleep, her final sleep. That may have been our closest moment.

She never mentioned the years spent in forced labor at the Bremen-Fargen works in Germany, where, for almost four years she seldom spoke to others to avoid revealing her true identity. Only late in life, at the urging of her children, did she recount to the interviewer from the Holocaust Foundation the events of the years following her abandonment in Marseille and arrest by the Occupation police. [See Chapter 4]. We all knew that awful things had happened to Suzy and Otto—the numbers branded on his arm attested to his concentration camp imprisonment—but we also knew we were never to mention those things to them. Even their children knew nothing of their parents' experiences until they gave their formal testimonies. Otto was generally garrulous, but he never spoke of the past—only of his current jobs, of politics (where he stood far to the right of most of us), of his family in New York.

Instead Suzy devoted herself almost obsessively to housekeeping—cleaning and scrubbing, accumulating gadget after gadget, and *chotchke* after *chotchke* to place on the tables and shelves in their cluttered kitchen and living room. Her home responsibilities occupied all her time. Though she herself was a vegetarian, she cooked robust and hearty meat meals for Otto, who demanded meat for dinner each night. Overstrict with their daughter, who was often reprimanded for supposed misbehavior, she and Otto were more indulgent with their son, who (as the rest of the family often said) "got away with everything." She never visited our apartment, or if she did it was too seldom for me to recall, although we were often invited to theirs for our family's usual truncated *Seder* and extensive Passover dinner, always introduced by Suzy's delicious, traditional sweet and sour carp, with its thick, raisin-filled sauce—the German-Jewish variant of Eastern Europe's gefilte fish. The carp's innumerable tiny bones had to be carefully removed, then placed on a special silver fishbone dish elegantly attached to each china plate. The meal always ended with Suzy's excellent *Matzo Charlotte with White Wine Sauce*, another holiday specialty remembered from "home."

Irma

MY MOTHER HAD SUFFERED MANY BLOWS throughout her life, but the greatest blow came on the Friday before Labor Day weekend of 1960. That morning she had received a call from her sister Len, who invited her and Peter to join her family at a recreational lake in New Jersey for a picnic and a day of swimming. My mother's instinct, as always, was to refuse, but after some persuasion she reluctantly agreed. I was in lower Manhattan at work, the last week of my summer office job before I was to return to college for my senior year. Late in the afternoon I received a phone call from my Uncle Henri, something that had never happened before. No one ever called me at the office, least of all Henri, with whom I seldom spoke! He was coming to pick me up. *There had been an accident. My brother had drowned. My brother was dead.* There followed a nightmarish subway ride to the George Washington Bridge Terminal, where we caught a bus to New Jersey.

My aunt's house was filled with her friends and neighbors, my mother doubled over in shock in one corner, and others gathered around her. Someone told me what had happened. The lake had been crowded, and the lifeguards, having taken their lunch break all together, were huddled in a corner joking among themselves and inattentive to what was going on around them. My mother watched my brother swim out—*too far, too far*—and tried calling, but he was unable to hear, and her voice faded into in the general tumult. And suddenly she no longer saw him. She began to scream, but no one paid attention except her sister, who kept telling her she must be mistaken, that Peter was surely somewhere around. By the time the lifeguards appeared, it was too late. Using their megaphones, they ordered all swimmers out of the water. When they dredged the lake they found my brother's body on the bottom, near the opposite shore.

A funeral had to be arranged. My aunt, who was a member of the Ethical Culture Society (a humanistic non-theistic community that fulfilled some of the roles of synagogue or church), phoned Howard Radetz, their group's "leader," and he agreed to preside at the funeral. So arrangements were made, by whom I never knew. The burial plot beside my father at Cedar Park Cemetery in Paramus, New Jersey, purchased by my mother for herself at the time of his death, became my brother's final resting place as well. Unlike my father's funeral, which hardly had an impact on me, I went through Peter's in a complete daze, and in truth I remember nothing of it. Barely conscious of what was happening, silent and numb, I was as if in a trance, throughout the week, as mourners came to my aunt's house bringing food and sympathy.

Everyone's focus was on my mother. Unstable as she had been for so long, no one knew how she would react now. Of course she was medicated and showed little understanding of what was going on, clearly unable to grasp the terrible truth although she kept moaning and lamenting "*He's dead. He's dead.*" But a day or two after the funeral, at the recommendation of Howard Radetz (who, like others, was afraid she might take her own life if left alone), my mother was admitted as an in-patient to the New York State Psychiatric Institute at Columbia. She remained there for a year—half the time in a locked ward, later able to come and go as she wished—and I returned to Binghamton to complete my remaining year of college.

I think what saved her, even more than the medications and therapy, was John Kennedy's presidential campaign, in which she became deeply and enthusiastically invested. What saved me were my friends and my immersion in schoolwork, especially the labor of researching and writing my honors thesis on *Beowulf* and the escape it permitted into the world of early medieval Britain.

As the year progressed, newly conscious that I also had to escape somehow from my mother's dependency, now more pronounced than ever, I applied for (and received) a Fulbright Grant to the University of Copenhagen. There I met my husband, Jorn Haahr, an engineering student completing his final year of study. We were married the following year in a simple ceremony at New York's City Hall. Henceforth responsible for my increasingly needy mother, Jorn and I nevertheless managed, with the help of our growing family, to live a good life.

My brother's death, however (as I have said many times), took me forty years to "get over," forty years before I was able to speak about him. One year after his funeral, when—according to Jewish tradition—it was time to put a stone on his grave, I ordered one inscribed with a fragment by the Greek poet Menander in what is surely the only Greek inscription in that large Jewish cemetery: ὅν οἵ θεοί φιλοῦσιν ἀποθνήσκει νέος—"Whom the gods love dies young."

Notwithstanding her perennial hypochondria, her lifelong conviction that her death was imminent (she refused even to take out a two-year magazine subscription for fear that it would be wasted), and a series of strokes that began in her mid-seventies, my mother lived until a month before what would have been her eighty-seventh birthday. More and more isolated, in her later years she came to depend on a shifting group of home health aides for care and companionship. Increasingly deaf yet refusing to wear hearing aids (our son once suggested that we *"get Oma an ear trumpet"*), she continued to demand what she felt was her right to my and my family's full attention. Though proud of my academic career, she never approved that my field of study was literature rather than something she considered more respectable, like political science or medicine. She appreciated my husband and loved her grandchildren deeply in her way. But her main focus remained—as it always had been—on *her* needs, *her* desires, *her* disappointments and dissatisfactions.

Only at the very end, after she became almost wholly immobile and could no longer function with a single aide, was it necessary to place her in a nursing home. She lived just three months after entering, hating every moment, even though we retained her familiar companions for several hours each day. On October 4, 1999, her heart finally gave out and she died, still longing for "home," which for her would always be the Zwingenberg of her childhood.

CHAPTER 8

Aftermaths

THE FIVE CHILDREN OF MORITZ AND MARTHA SCHACK are now gone. Margot, the youngest, died first, in 1979, wasting away from lung cancer, which she insisted to the end had nothing to do with her years of smoking. Leo followed in 1998, depressed and distraught, having lost all his *joie de vivre* after the death of his beloved wife, Erna. My mother, Irma, the eldest, followed her brother by just one year, passing her final years in an increasing state of misery and debility. Suzy's extended and painful battle with colon cancer ended in 2008. Lina/Len—increasingly demented yet telling her favorite jokes to the very end—lived longest, dying three months before what would have been her ninety-ninth birthday, on September 11, 2014.

At Len's simple memorial service at the Ethical Culture Meeting

House in Teaneck, New Jersey, her daughter, Claire, presided and delivered the main eulogy. Beginning with a witty and affectionate portrait of Len's sociability, her delight in off-color jokes, and her deep love of art and opera—she had been a dedicated volunteer with the San Diego Opera for many years, and a devotee of both Metropolitans in New York, the Opera and the Museum—Claire abruptly changed tone. "But," she said quietly, "She was a terrible mother."

There was silence in the hall. Claire continued, enumerating the many characteristics of her mother that I (the oldest of the cousins) had observed through the years. Len had little interest in children, not even her own. Her attention and time were focused primarily on friends, casual acquaintances, and the organizations she worked for, while her children—though never lacking in essentials—were often otherwise ignored or belittled. She was generous to her extended family, having, through her constant efforts, been the person most responsible for rescuing Margot and Suzy from Europe, but she could also be careless or unthinking about punctuality, about her children's safety, and about others' emotional needs.

I had not planned to speak at the memorial, having written a rather lengthy account of Len's early life to distribute to the attendees. But Claire's words required more. I stood up and walked to the podium.

"They were all terrible mothers," I said, "all four sisters." Again, the hall hushed, everyone attentive. "In different ways," I said. "But none of them knew how to be mothers." I saw my cousins Paulette and Linda—Suzy's and Margot's daughters—nod slightly as they listened.

"But let me try to explain," I said, "not to excuse them but to try to understand what made them so." And I described their history, which of all present only I knew in any detail. I spoke of Irma's, Leo's, and Lina's separation from their parents during the First World War, when they were little more than babies, of their father's long Russian imprisonment and his return home as an invalid, of their mother's frailty and difficulty in mothering five children, especially in light of the family's continuing poverty. Yet the children seemed to do well, despite the overt anti-Semitism of some teachers and village officials. Their daily lives throughout the 1920's resembled those of their schoolmates, although they often turned to aunts or uncles for sympathy and assistance when their parents were too overwhelmed to help them.

I spoke of how the Nazi assumption of power changed things forever.

Although Leo and Lina had left Germany for good soon after 1933, and my parents had followed just a few years later, thereby escaping personal and direct persecution, to the ends of their lives all five siblings were haunted by that early history and what followed. For my mother, life proved to be an especially painful betrayal. Instead of marriage to the dynamic and charismatic man of her dreams, she married my father: by nature an unambitious aesthete and political theorist, quiet, soft-spoken, dryly witty but reclusive. Instead of the exciting career she had anticipated as the reward for her early school stardom, she was—in post-Depression America—barely employable, subject to the same market forces that left so many others in poverty. Then, after the war ended, there came the devastating news from Europe of the deaths of parents, aunts, uncles, and cousins, followed a few years later by the premature deaths of her husband and young son. These events served only to cement further her conviction that life was fragile and cruel. That she suffered from lifelong depression is not surprising. What is noteworthy is that, notwithstanding her frequent talk of suicide, she remained a woman of firm opinions and strong self-protective instincts.

Suzy and Margot, too young to leave when Hitler came to power, had remained with their parents in Zwingenberg through the first six years of escalating Nazi actions against Jews. Only in early 1939, after the brutalities of *Kristallnacht* made their probable future in Germany all too clear, were they sent to their brother in France, never again seeing their parents. Although both survived to form their own families, both displayed the effects of their forced uprooting—and in Suzy's case her capture and imprisonment—until their deaths. Margot's alcoholism and self-disregard and Suzy's lifelong rigidity and self-discipline—the strict weekly schedule from which nothing could cause her to deviate—were no doubt differing symptoms of their early dislocation and suffering.

Nor were they able to offer much emotional sustenance to their children. Always attentive to our physical requirements (food played an important role in our family and all the sisters were excellent cooks), they were generally inattentive to or perhaps even unaware of our emotional needs, treating our worries and concerns as trivial and not worth attention when measured against their own youthful life-and-death experiences. So we learned early not to tell them what was bothering us, and to rely for comfort or counsel on our friends, neighbors, and teachers rather than our parents.

Now I, the eldest, am the family matriarch and conservator of family history, because, unlike her siblings, my mother always spoke openly and graphically about what had happened to the families left behind. Only I knew any details, so perhaps I am also in a sense another prisoner of memory. Absorbed since childhood by my mother's recollections, I have now devoted countless hours over twenty years to excavate what I can of the truth and to write about it. My cousins' knowledge of events was more impressionistic than specific, although the number engraved on Uncle Otto's arm offered vivid testimony to his prior suffering. Yet my cousins all felt in different ways the effects of the damage done to our parents by their early deprivations and the continuing effects of their losses. Of the dozen children born to the Schack sisters and brother, only seven are still alive. My brother Peter's death was the first.

How have their lives played out?

Barely old enough to enlist, my cousin Bob, Len and Fred's eldest child, joined the army at seventeen to serve in Vietnam, notwithstanding his mother's deep involvement in the antiwar movement and vehement opposition to his enlistment. That he returned home, after two tours, to vote for the peace candidate, Dick Gregory, represented, I suppose, a form of atonement and a concession that he may not have made a wise choice. Married, though without children, he and his wife lived in Lower Manhattan's pre-gentrification Soho for most of their lives, together with several large terraria of snakes. What Bob did for a living in his early years remains something of a mystery, but in middle age he bought a bar on Avenue A in the East Village. A heavy smoker, like his father, he too succumbed to lung cancer at the relatively early age of sixty-four.

After years of battling with her mother, Margot's daughter Linda, at fourteen or fifteen, was placed in a residential school for "problem" children, where she lived until her graduation from high school. At eighteen she became pregnant by a somewhat older man in the midst of divorce proceedings. The baby was a boy; two years later, they had another son and eventually married. Yet when her boys were still young, she left her husband to relocate to San Diego, where her parents and Len (always her favorite aunt) had settled. With her were her two sons, their scoutmaster, and one of his sons. There she and the boys remained for several years, until the relationship with the scoutmaster ended. Eventually Linda and the boys (now both teens) returned east. She married again, this time settling near Atlantic City, getting an accounting degree and a job with an accounting firm, and devoting all her extra time and energy to an East Asian dog rescue organization she founded and administered. Another heavy smoker, she died of COPD at sixty-seven.

Her younger brother, Steve, more or less dropped out of the family orbit. After two unhappy marriages and two painful divorces (both wives having left him), he moved west, transferred by AT&T where he worked as a phone installer. Within a few years he claimed disability and, taking early retirement from his job, left San Diego, moved to Flagstaff, Arizona, and eventually settled somewhere in rural Colorado. In his early years in the West, he had taken responsibility for an abandoned teenaged boy, and when Steve became an invalid in recent years, that "boy," now with a family himself, cared for Steve until his death this past summer of brain cancer.

At the age of eighteen, my cousin Paulette, Suzy and Otto's firstborn, developed ulcerative colitis, an autoimmune gastrointestinal disease, and underwent a colostomy. The primary cause was probably genetic (something no one understood at the time), but development of the disease may have been exacerbated by the constant tension at mealtimes, her mother insisting from Paulette's early childhood on her remaining seated at the dining table (sometimes late into the night) until she had fully consumed everything on her plate. Grateful to her doctors and nurses, Paulette subsequently became a nurse herself. She met her husband at a support group for colitis sufferers and survivors of gastrointestinal surgery, which he too had experienced.

Four of us took refuge in school, finding relief only after we left home for college.

Claire, Len and Fred's middle child, seemed at odds with her mother from early childhood, receiving her principal solace from books—often shutting herself in her room alone for hours. In college, however, and as she went on to build a life and family of her own, she began to thrive, marrying an academic and raising two boys, while establishing a career in counseling and remaining active in the Ethical Culture world of her early years.

Len and Fred's youngest child, Michael, still a boy when his parents moved to San Diego, seems to have escaped the worst familial tensions, possibly because of his unawareness of his family's history as well as the easier pace of California life. After graduating from UCLA, he had a stable career as a writer in California's growing aerospace industry, married, and raised two sons.

Suzy and Otto's son Marvin also found success in school as well as in business, having been lucky enough to join one of the first successful computer software start-ups. As business director, he acquired considerable wealth, retired early, and devoted himself to his passion for photography while continuing to invest in promising technologies. Though he married early, he and his wife were childless. Always his parents' favorite, he remained close to them until their deaths.

I too found solace through education and a new family. From childhood I knew two things about myself: that whatever success I would later have, whatever mark I might make, would come through school. That, after all, was what I was best at. I felt, too, that it was my responsibility to reconstitute a home and family, to restore as much as I could of the losses we had suffered. And now at eighty-one, a professor emerita of Yeshiva University, happily married until his recent death to the Danish husband I met so long ago in Copenhagen, proud mother of three children and grandmother of six, I feel I did both. Not that I was either an ideal professor or ideal parent. But the rewards of both have been immeasurable.

As for the Mexican cousins, Leo's and Erna's children, too, searched for stability in differing ways. All were educated in French or American schools in Mexico City, but then emigrated—two permanently, one part-time. The oldest, Gerardo, married and divorced twice, his first wife the daughter of Mexican German-Jewish refugee parents with whom he had three children, his second an Italian clinical psychologist from Milan whom he met in Mexico, with whom he had two more. An engineer, Gerardo accepted a position in Switzerland, and he and his second wife moved permanently to Europe. The second marriage, however, did not last, and his wife and daughters returned to live in Milan. Now retired in Lugano, Switzerland, Gerardo maintains contact with all of his five children and their families, Mexican and Italian.

Leo's and Erna's second child (named Martha for her grandmother but always called Marthita), adopted religious orthodoxy when just a teenager. Refusing to eat the non-kosher food served at home, she survived during her teen years on cans of tuna fish and pre-packaged kosher foods imported from the United States. When it came time for college, she chose to attend the only Orthodox Jewish institution of higher education for women outside of Israel. At Stern College, a branch of Yeshiva University in New York, she immersed herself further in traditional Jewish life and study. While a student, she was introduced to her future husband, another Mexican Jew, who was "learning" at a very Orthodox Brooklyn Yeshiva. (For Orthodox Jews, "learning" refers to religious study, while "study" refers to secular subjects only.) After their marriage, she and her husband settled in Mexico City, where he served as a *mohel* (ritual circumciser). Both became deeply engaged with Mexico City's large Orthodox community but spent considerable time each year in Israel. Martha died suddenly and unexpectedly in 2011 during a cardiac stent implantation. I've always felt, however, that she died of a broken heart, brought on by the death of her forty-four-year-old elder son from lung cancer two years earlier.

The youngest of my Mexican cousins, Ricardo, studied medicine in Mexico, specializing in psychiatry. He and his first wife (a Canadian Catholic of Czech descent) moved to southern Texas, where for many years he treated Mexican immigrants in Waxahachie, near the border. Devoted to fast cars and motorcycles, both of which he collected, he was a known dirt track racer. An article in *Stock Car Racing* magazine, published sometime in the 1980s or 1990s, focused on the anomaly of a Mexican-Jewish "Dirt Track

Doctor" (as the article was titled) in a sport not known for its appeal to either Jews or well-educated professionals. A tragic motorcycle accident in which his young son was badly injured brought his marriage to an end. Now retired and happily remarried after many years alone, he maintains a close relationship with his son.

Of our children—though belonging to the "third generation" born so many years after the events narrated here—few have more than cursory acquaintance with the story of those tragic years of the 1930's and 1940's, although none of us could avoid passing on to our children the many effects of the damage done to our parents and thus to us. Perhaps our grandchildren (the "fourth generation") will be entirely free from that history. Most seem to feel little personal connection to their great-great-grandparents or great-grandparents, or to the "ancient" miseries of the mid-twentieth century, although when they reach the teen years they often are interested in hearing about the events in general terms.

It goes without saying that, for all Jews, memory of the Nazi genocide will forever be a source of great pain.

IF YOU TRAVELED IN GERMANY IN THE TWENTY or thirty years following the Second World War or encountered German citizens elsewhere, you may well have had experiences like mine. For Germans and most other Europeans the war remained vivid and present for decades after its end. The murder of millions on the battlefield, in the bombed and plundered cities, in the prison and extermination camps, and throughout the occupied countries had left most people of Germany's former enemies with deep hatred of Germans and, often, a longing for some kind of revenge. Germans, on the other hand, felt guilt but also anger and confusion when, in traveling abroad, they encountered citizens of formerly occupied nations, especially those who openly reminded them of the Nazi cruelties against their countrymen and, not infrequently, themselves. These accusations could take the form of direct or indirect attack, via rough verbal confrontations or snide remarks. Sometimes people even spat at—or on—them.

My own understanding of this German sensitivity arose from two experiences, one in Germany, one in New York. The former occurred on a beautiful summer day in the mid-1980s, when my husband, teen-aged daughters, and I accompanied my half-sister, Lotte, on an excursion through the Odenwald mountain range. We had driven to the Bergstrasse from Lotte's home in Mannheim to show our daughters my mother's birthplace, Zwingenberg. From there we continued along the Neckar River and through the lovely Hessian countryside, enjoying the splendid views from various stopping points along the road. Our goal was the *Schloss Hirschhorn*, a hotel and restaurant located in a seventeenth-century manor that had survived intact amid the ruins of the original medieval castle. There, from the high point of the terrace restaurant overlooking the beautiful Neckar Valley, we each ordered ice cream. After eating our elaborate confections, we entered the gift shop, our daughters, like young girls everywhere, hoping to purchase a souvenir.

While they were engrossed in making their selections, Lotte and

I spoke with the proprietor. "Where are you from?" she asked. We told her, and I asked if she had ever been to America.

"No," she replied, "And I will never go there, nor will I travel again outside of Germany."

"Why?" I asked, somewhat taken aback by her vehemence.

"Because," she said, "everyone hates us for what Germany did during the war, and I no longer want to be attacked by foreigners." As she said this, she looked simultaneously belligerent and ashamed. I remained silent, not knowing how to respond, for I knew that what she said was true. Germans, with their terrible history, their current affluence, and their often arrogant ways, were hated and mocked throughout Europe. We made our purchase—a doll, elaborately dressed in a witch's costume and riding a broom—and began our long drive back to Mannheim.

The second incident occurred in New York. One of our Danish nephews was spending a year as a graduate student in Massachusetts and brought a German fellow graduate student to our house for a weekend. Fritz (let me call him) hoped to buy a camera from B&H, one of the well-known photo equipment shops in lower Manhattan, and on Sunday morning he rode the subway downtown to do so. What he was unaware of, however, was that most of New York's fine camera shops were owned and operated by Hasidic Jews, many from Poland, and many of them former concentration camp victims with numbers branded on their arms. Despite the fact that his salesman was helpful and congenial, once Fritz caught a glimpse of that number he panicked and fled without a word. Back at our house, he tearfully told the story, confessing that both he and most of his friends, though born long after the war's end, felt overwhelmed by shame over their countrymen's crimes. I tried to comfort him; after all, he had not been alive at the time these things had occurred and bore no responsibility for them. But he was inconsolable. How can one go through life as a pariah, he wanted to know? How can he face those who suffered so because of his countrymen's actions? Was it possible to atone?

And that question was faced not only by Fritz. How was it possible even to attempt to atone and once again be accepted among the fellowship of human beings? After the war, that was the central moral issue for the entire German people, although its burden fell most directly on West Germany, compelled by the occupying American, British, and French to acknowledge German guilt. In the eastern part of the nation, by contrast, all responsibility for wartime atrocities was denied. First occupied by the Soviets and later as a communist satellite state, East Germany (the DDR) disclaimed any responsibility for Nazi Germany's many crimes and offered no restitution for either life or property. East Germany's argument was that the Communist Party had from the outset opposed and fought against the Third Reich and thus had nothing to do with Nazi crimes. In truth, of course, few East Germans had been communists until after the Soviet occupation, and the Nazis from the east were often even crueler than those from the west.

Not that atonement was possible for the seventy-five million dead in Europe—approximately fifty million civilians, among them six million Jews, and twenty-five million military personnel—although what came was usually welcomed. Forgiveness was too much to ask for, all agreed, but perhaps there might be some form of compensation.

A simple but direct form of compensation was some degree of financial restitution to survivors and their heirs. In 1953, West Germany slowly began to accept restitution claims (*Wiedergutmachung,* literally "make things better again")—though at first only to former German citizens who themselves had suffered in the camps and from forced labor or had had properties confiscated or stolen or pensions abrogated. Gradually it came to include the restoration of properties, including bank accounts and owed pension payments, to those former German citizens who had unwillingly emigrated or been declared stateless upon exile or deportation, as well as generous support for the new state of Israel.

Unhappily for those originally from East Germany, no compensation emerged for them until after the unification of the two Germanys. Similarly, it was not until after the fall of the Iron Curtain that any effort was made to compensate Holocaust victims from the once-occupied countries of Eastern Europe.

The granting of compensation has been a long and continuing process, and with the aging and death of survivors (the small, remaining remnant are now largely in their nineties or older) the payments will necessarily end. However, numerous refugees, including my mother, depended on those monthly checks from Germany to support them in their later years.

In more recent years Germans have also made notable attempts at memorialization within Germany itself. Probably the most famous are two in Berlin: Daniel Libeskind's notable addition to the Jewish Museum (opened in 2001) and the stark and perplexing *Holocaust Memorial to the Murdered Jews of Europe* (*Denkmal für die ermordeten Juden Europas*), designed by the architect Peter Eisenman and the engineer Buro Happold (inaugurated in 2005).

The two are strikingly different in their effects. The museum addition, with its disconcertingly irregular floor and walls, attempts to create in visitors a sense of disorientation similar to that supposedly experienced by the Nazis' displaced victims. Its wrenching collection of Holocaust memorabilia—much of it only vaguely glimpsed shoes, hair, handbags, photos—illustrates the tragic fact that these ordinary artifacts are the only surviving remains of all those lives lost. *The Holocaust Memorial to the Murdered Jews of Europe* is situated just beyond the Brandenburg Gate, on the former site of Hitler's Reich's Chancellery that was later replaced by the Berlin Wall separating East and West Berlin. Consisting of 2711 coffin-like *stelae*, variously positioned (some upright, some tilted or turned) but arranged in a grid on a large field, the *Memorial* seems to evoke ideas of death—but whose? None of the *stelae* have any inscriptions; none are identified as other than part of an anonymous mass. Although the architect declined to endorse any explicit interpretation, most viewers make the association with mass death. As *New Yorker* critic Richard Brody said, in a 2012 critique, "The memorial evokes a graveyard for those who were unburied or thrown into unmarked pits, and several uneasily tilting stelae suggest an old, untended, or even desecrated cemetery."[79]

In another form of atonement, towns large and small have sponsored the restoration of synagogues destroyed on *Kristallnacht*, in 1938, or in wartime bombings, although many are now museums of German-Jewish life before 1933 rather than active houses of worship. And there have been other efforts to memorialize the victims of the Nazis, including *Gedenkmal*: memorial tablets placed on public buildings throughout Germany listing the names and dates of all from the community imprisoned and killed by the Nazis.

Most notable, perhaps, is the movement characterized by the installation of *Stolpersteine* (translation "stumbling stones"), a project conceived by a non-Jewish Cologne sculptor, Gunther Deming. Ralph Blumenthal of the *New York Times* has called it "the world's largest monument."[80] Brass-covered concrete "stones," engraved with names, birth and death dates, and the circumstances—when known—of deportation and death, are set into the sidewalks in front of the final voluntary residences of all Nazi victims to commemorate the former inhabitants. Not only Jews, these victims were a heterogeneous group: "*Jews, Roma and Sinti, Homosexuals, Dissidents, Jehovah's Witnesses, and victims of euthanasia who were deported and exterminated.*"[81] The installation of *Stolpersteine*, begun in Germany and Austria, has gradually spread to other countries directly victimized by the Nazi killing machine, including the Netherlands and parts of Eastern Europe.

Despite their popularity (more than 75,000 *Stolpersteine* have, as of 2019, been installed in more than twelve hundred towns and cities throughout Europe), there has been some controversy about their installation, both within Jewish communities and among non-Jews. These criticisms generally focus on the stones' insertion into the pavement, where they may be trodden upon, as were the victims themselves. However, for the most part the memorial stones have been welcomed, although their insertion requires current homeowner or family permission.

Formal recognition of the murdered Jews of my mother's birthplace, Zwingenberg, came with the founding in 1999 of the *Arbeitskreis Zwingenberg Synagoge* ("Working Committee for the Zwingenberg Synagogue") by Dr. Friz Kilthau, a retired engineer and local historian, and a few other residents of the town. Created with the sole intention of rescuing the former synagogue from the private ownership that had followed *Kristallnacht* and turning it into a museum of pre-war Bergstrasse Jewish life, the group gradually turned its attention to other forms of memorialization as well. These have often succeeded although, as of 2020, all efforts to purchase the former synagogue from its owners have failed, and it remains in private hands.

In a letter to my mother sent in the mid-1990s, Dr. Kilthau tried to establish contact with her to learn about her family's fate. Her immediate response to me, when I brought it to her, was *"Throw it in the trash!"* I, however, was curious and answered him, beginning a correspondence and friendship that continues still. His first book about the Bergsträsse Jews, *Mitten unter Uns*, based the section on the Rothensies-Schack family primarily upon information I supplied him. And my own account of my grandparents' life in Zwingenberg under the Nazis relies considerably on information he discovered during his archival explorations.

Since the 1970s there had been a bronze *Gedenktafel* (memorial plaque) on the wall near the entrance of the old City Hall. It originally consisted, however, only of a brief, general statement remembering the Nazis' victims as a group. The members of the *Arbeitskreis* began a campaign for a new plaque that would list each of the village's seventeen victims individually by name. Over time their campaign succeeded, and on May 7, 2006 an additional *Gedenktafel* was dedicated, with each of the murdered individuals named. I was unable to attend the dedication ceremony, but I sent a speech that Dr. Kilthau read aloud to the assembled guests and residents in which I attempted to express my ambivalence about the town itself:

> *I try to imagine what my grandparents, Moritz and Martha Schack, and my great-aunt and great-uncle, Clara and Jakob Wolf, would say if they could learn of today's event. I never knew them, but I have often tried to visualize their final years, as the ordinary things of life were taken from them: their jobs and the means of subsistence; in the case of my grandparents, their children (all of whom survived); their synagogue—which (as Fritz Kilthau learned) my grandfather was forced to sell; their homes; and, finally, their lives.*

What would they say on this occasion? I imagine that they simply could not believe it to be true. Of course, not all their neighbors were among their persecutors. There were indeed those who risked their own lives by secretly placing food at my grandparents' door when they would otherwise have starved. And I know from my grandparents' letters, written after their forcible relocation to Frankfurt, how much they and their families missed the familiar surroundings of home. After all, Martha and Clara had been born in Zwingenberg, as had their ancestors for hundreds of years before them.

But time goes on, and new circumstances succeed the old. Now the Schacks and the Wolfs will forever be remembered in the town in which they spent most of their lives, their names engraved on this plaque and publicly displayed on the Rathaus. I am grateful to those of you who fought to achieve this moment. Yet I cannot help but mourn for the tortured and truncated lives of all those—not only my own family—who are today being remembered. It is some consolation, however, that another generation of Zwingenbergers evidently mourns too, as this memorial testifies.

Two years later, at the urging of the *Arbeidskreis Zwingenberg Synagoge*, Zwingenberg applied for installation of *Stolpersteine* as memorials to all the town's victims. On July 3, 2012, the "stones" were ceremoniously installed in the pavement in front of the former residences of the ten Jewish families and one family of Jehovah's Witnesses who had been deported and killed. Among them were my grandparents, Moritz and Martha Schack, whose two stones lie in front of Obergasse 3, and my grandmother's sister Clara and her husband Jakob Wolf, with stones at Obergasse 5. Although I was unable to attend the ceremony, my half-sister Lotte and her family were present. Though no blood relation to the Schack family, she always felt a strong connection.

I wrote the following to be read at the dedication:

> *On behalf of all the living descendants of my grandparents, Martha and Morris Schack (their only living child, Lina, now 96, grandchildren, great-grandchildren, and great-great grandchildren), I want to thank the Mayor and City Council of Zwingenberg, the members of the Artbeitskreis Zwingenberger Synagoge, and most of all Dr. Fritz Kilthau, for their efforts to keep alive their memories and those of Martha's sister and her husband, Clara and Jakob Wolf. I regret being unable to attend today's ceremony.*
>
> *At the time of the dedication of the Namenstafel in 2006, I wrote of my grandparents' continuing attachment to Zwingenberg and the pain of their forced exile from it. My mother, too, retained that attachment, remembering fondly her youth and friends there (though my younger aunts, Suzanne and Margot, who lived there throughout their childhood in the 1930's, had, understandably, no such*

fondness). But as I wrote to Fritz when he asked me to send a few words for today's occasion, the older I get (and I am now about 20 years older than my grandparents were when they died) the more unthinkable it seems to me that what happened in Germany from 1933 to 1945 could have happened. In my research on my family's history, I have been following the lives of my two grandmothers (my father's mother, too, was murdered), and—now a grandmother myself six times over—I find that thinking about their tortured last years and trying to grasp their suffering becomes more and more painful.

Remembering, however, is important. I am aware of the controversy that has attended the laying of Stolpersteine elsewhere, and I share some of that ambivalence. Let us hope, however, that these Stolpersteine, laid in loving memory of the former Jewish citizens of Zwingenberg, do not simply become an accustomed (and thus invisible) part of the landscape but serve as a continual reminder to everyone who sees them of the danger to ordinary people when madness prevails and the innocent are the victims.

So that is what remains of my mother's parents: a grave in the New Jewish cemetery in Frankfurt, with the body of my grandmother, Martha Schack, *née* Rothensies; an inscription of name and dates of my grandfather, Moritz Schack, although not his body, which lies somewhere in the ash pits of Auschwitz; and two concrete cubes covered by inscribed plates of polished brass installed on the pavement in front of their former front door:

Here lived MORITZ SCHACK / *Born 1883 / Involuntarily left his home village / deported in 1939 to Frankfurt / in 1942 to Theresienstadt / Murdered in Auschwitz.*

Here lived MARTHA SCHACK / *born Rothensies in 1885 / Involuntarily left her home village / deported in 1939 to Frankfurt / humiliated and deprived of her rights / escaped to death / Frankfurt 1941.*

Photo Gallery

Martha Schack (late 1930s) (Yad Vashem)

The Zwingenberg synagogue before Kristallnacht

The Kristallnacht destruction of Clara and Jakob Wolf's shop attracts attention the following day. (House second from right, November 10, 1938)

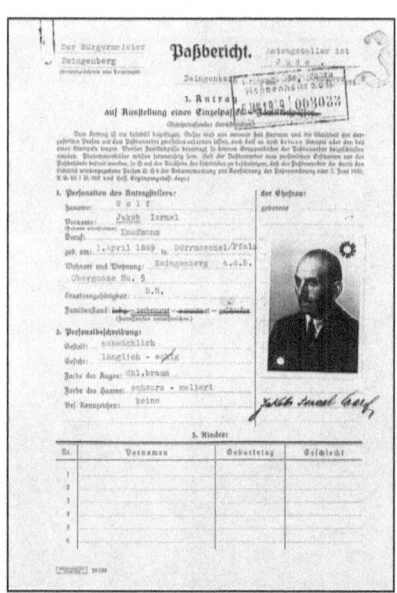

December 28, 1938, passport application for Jakob Wolf. The middle name "Israel" was made mandatory for all male Jews in Germany by January 1, 1939. Jakob and Clara Wolf filed these applications as soon as Jakob returned from six weeks in Buchenwald concentration camp.

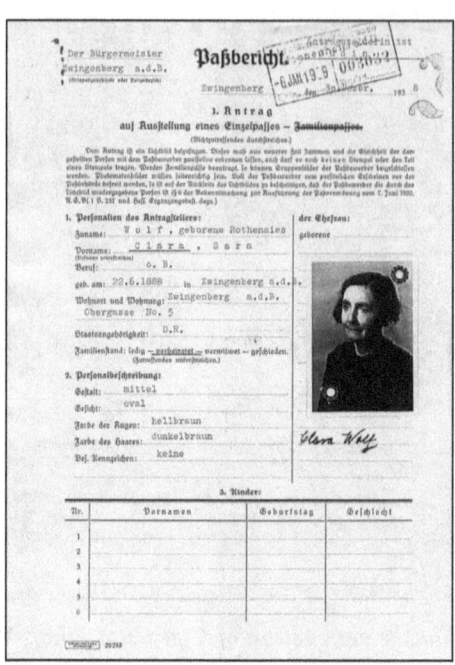

1938 passport application for Clara Wolf. The middle name "Sara" was made mandatory for all female Jews in Germany by January 1, 1939.

Leo Schack, his wife Erna, and sister Suzy in Marseille

Leo and baby Gerardo shortly after their arrival in Mexico City (1942)

Leo and children (Marthita and Gerardo), in Mexico City

Suzy and Otto Goldschmitt (front row) and other Displaced Persons in rehabilitation after release from Nazi imprisonment. Note, Otto is still wearing his concentration camp jacket.

Suzy and Otto's wedding, Marseille, 1946

The Glück Auf Miner's Symbol, Good luck. The traditional miner's greeting is not only encountered on street signs, but also in poems and songs.

Hanna Glückauf in Amsterdam

A few friends at the Amsterdam boarding house. Hanna, Werner, and Julius Glückauf (front row)

A favorite pastime at the boarding house

The apartment building in Amsterdam on Zuider Amstellaan (now Rooseveltlaan), where the Glückauf family lived and ran a boarding house.

Marriage of Werner Glückauf and Selma Mingelgrün in 1939. Both perished in Auschwitz in 1942.

Selma, Hanna, and Werner Glückauf in Amsterdam

Erich Glückauf (front row left) with other leaders of the FDJ (Freie Deutsche Jugend), the East German official youth organization (1946)

Erich Glückauf (top right) receiving the Karl Marx order of the DDR for his work promoting the communist and workers' movements

Paul Glückauf and Lina Schack, partners in the Silver Star Restaurant on Lafayette Street in lower Manhattan

Menu boards for Paul and Lina's short-lived restaurant, the Silver Star (1938–1939)

Margot Schack in New York

Margot Schack

Irma and Paul Glückauf in Washington Heights (1939–1940)

Sisters and sister-in-law—Ilse Kratz (née Glückauf), Lina Scarano, Irma Gluckauf

On Joan's six month birthday. Front row (left to right), Hannah Lehman (née Reichenberg), Lina, Hedy Futran. Back row, Irma and Paul.

Ilse (née Glückauf) and Kurt Kratz

Paul with his closest friend, Herbert Gordon, in front of our building at 461-471 Audubon Avenue in Washington Heights

Paul, Irma, and baby Joan Glückauf

Mother and daughter, Irma and Joan

Viola and Walter Kassel in Los Angeles

Joan and her beloved bunny. In the background is P.S. 189, which Joan and Peter attended from kindergarten to eighth grade.

Joan and Peter, with Uncle Fred Scarano, photographer

Our little family—Paul, Irma, Joan, and Peter in the Amsterdam Avenue playground, now named for Raoul Wallenberg (1946)

Peter Michael Gluckauf

*Joan and Peter on the steps of
George Washington High School (c. 1953)*

Aunt Bessie Steiner's 85th birthday party (August 16, 1962) at the Gruen's house in Riverdale, The Bronx. Rear row: Suzy, Margot, Paulette (Suzy and Otto's daughter), Carola Gruen; Front row: Fred Scarano, Linda (Margot and Henri's daughter), Lina, Otto Goldschmitt, Aunt Bessie.

The five Schack siblings (mid-1960s)— Lina, Margot, Leo, Irma, Suzy

Lina and Irma, with Margot standing, shortly before Margot's death (San Diego, 1978)

Lotte (right), her daughter, Petra (center) and "Die Oma" Oestreicher, who saved her "Mischling" granddaughter, Lotte, from deportation during the Nazi period.

My grandparents' gravestone in the Neue Jüdische Friedhof (New Jewish Cemetery) in Frankfurt am Main

The memorial plaques outside the Zwingenberg Town Hall

Endnotes

Prologue

1. *Miracle Fair: selected poems of Wisława Szymborska* (W. W. Norton and Company Inc., 2001)
2. Marianne Hirsch, *The Generation of Postmemory: Writing and Visual Culture After the Holocaust* (New York: Columbia University Press, 2012).
3. Eva Hoffman, in *After Such Knowledge: Memory, History and the Legacy of the Holocaust* (New York: Public Affairs, 2004), outlines the responsibility of the so-called "second generation"—my generation and hers—to record and promulgate the narrative of our parents' experiences: "The guardianship of the Holocaust is being passed on to us. The second generation is the hinge generation in which received, transferred knowledge of events is being transmuted into history, or into myth. It is also the generation in which we can think about certain questions arising from the *Shoah* with a sense of living connection" (Introduction, p. xv).

Chapter 1

4. Both accounts can be found in Norbert Mischlich, "Die Israelitische Gemeinde" in *700 Jahre Stadtrechte 1274–1974. Chronik von Zwingenberg an der Bergstraße. Hrsg.: Geschichtsverein und Magistrat der Stadt Zwingenberg.* Zwingenberg 1974. Although both accounts reflect the prevailing anti-Semitism (the Jew as stupid or as clown), the second is more sympathetic to the plight of the person being interrogated.
5. See Chapter 6 for a brief account of the brothers' lives in upstate New York.
6. The bankruptcy notice, from the Zwingenberg professional register of March 10, 1928, is cited by Fritz Kilthau, *Mitten unter uns: Zwingenberg an der Bergstraße von 1933 bis*

1945[In the Midst of Us: Zwingenberg an der Bergstraße from 1933 to 1945]. Sonderband 21 der Geschichtsblätter für den Kreis Bergstraße (Verlag Laurissa, Lorsch), p. 81. Much of my knowledge of events in Zwingenberg and the Bergstrasse during the Nazi period derives from Kilthau's painstaking research.

7 *Wayward Threads* (Evanston, Ill: Northwestern University Press, 1997, pp. 3–4)

8 Fritz Kilthau and Johannes Mingo, "Der Jüdische Friedhof in Alsbach an der Bergstrasse." *Commission for the history of the Jews in Hesse* (Wiesbaden, 2001). (Available in an English translation by Richard B. Morton, "Beth Olam, House of Eternity: A visit to the Jewish Cemetery in Alsbach on the Bergstrasse." *Arbeitskreis Zwingenberger Synagoge*, September 2004).

9 This and all other direct citations of my mother's words throughout this book are from a brief autobiographical essay she wrote, dated April 14, 1982.

Chapter 2

10 Franz-Josef Schmit, *Die Geschichte der deutsch-jüdischen Familie Glückauf* [*The History of the German Jewish Family Glückauf*], (Emil-Frank-Institut: Jahresbericht 2011/2012), 2.

11 Wilhelm Mentrup, Testimony cited by Franz-Josef Schmit, *Entschädigung für Julius und Johanna Glückauf* [*Compensation for Julius and Johanna Glückauf*]. *Nach den Akten der Regierung zu Arnsberg, Landesarchiv* NRW, Abteilung Münster, Signatur: 161772.

12 *Der Stürmer, Deutsche Volksgesundheit aus Blut und Boden*, New Year's issue 1935, cited by Charles B. Flood, *Hitler: The Path To Power* (Boston: Houghton Mifflin, 1989), 282. http://fcit.coedu.usf.edu/holocaust/ resource/ document/ DocStrei. See also http://www.calvin.edu/academic/cas/faculty/streich3.htm, a slightly edited version of Chapter 3 of Randall Bytwerk's book, *Julius Streicher: The Man Who Persuaded a Nation to Hate Jews* (New York: Stein & Day,

1983), 63.
13 Stadtarchiv Nürnberg GSI 134 „Stürmer"-Kartei, Serie I Nicht zur Vervielfältigung oder vollständigen, teilweisen oder modifizierten (z.B. übersetzten) Personen / Sachen (Karton 1 - 28) © Stadtarchiv Nürnberg, Marientorgraben 8, 90402 Nürnberg, Deutschland. (Stand: 15.08.2012) (Published in another location or in a different medium [sic].)
14 This and the asterisk at the end of the next paragraph direct the reader to notes supposed to be Talmudical citations. They actually come from *The Talmud Unmasked*, a deeply antisemitic book published in Russian (in St. Petersburg) in 1892, in German in 1894, and in other Eastern European languages throughout the 1890's. An English edition was published in 1939. The Internet offers many editions and translations, and the book remains a staple of of radical right-wing Roman Catholic antisemitic propaganda.
15 See Vicky Caron. *Uneasy Asylum: France and the Jewish Refugee Crisis, 1933–1942* (Stanford Studies in Jewish History and Culture, 1999).

Chapter 3

16 Fritz Kilthau, *Mitten Unter Uns*, 40.
17 Kilthau cites a report in the *Bergsträsser Bote* (March 11, 1933) of an interview with Hermann Göring: "*Schutz der Juden gesetzlich gewährleistet... Weiter habe der Minister erklärt, die Sicherheit des Lebens und das Eigentum der jüdischen Staatsbürger, die sich gegenüber der Regierung loyal verhielten, sei gesetzlich gewährleistet.*" [*Mitten unter Uns*, 42] ["Protection of the Jews guaranteed by law ... Furthermore, the Minister has stated that the safety of life and property of Jewish citizens who were loyal to the government was ensured by law."]
18 *Mitten unter Uns*, 128
19 *Ibid*. 45.
20 *Bergsträsser Bote*, August 29, 1935, cited in *Mitten unter Uns*, 47.
21 As an example, one Zwingenberg teacher, reported to have

patronized a Jewish department store in Darmstadt, was fined 50 RM. *Mitten unter Uns*, 48.

22 *The Survivors of the Shoah Visual History Foundation* was a non-profit organization founded by Steven Spielberg in 1994 to record and collect video testimonies of Holocaust survivors and other witnesses (many of them by then in the last years of their lives and few now still alive). Now called the USC Shoah Foundation, its more than 50,000 interviews, conducted from 1994 to 1999, have since 2005 been located at the University of Southern California. *http://sfi.usc.edu/*

23 The frustrating and unending quest for food is one of the main themes of the extraordinary diaries of Victor Klemperer, written in Dresden during the years of Nazi rule. *I will Bear Witness: A Diary of the Nazi Years* (New York: Random House, 1998–1999). *Volume I* covers the years 1933–1941.

24 Norbert Mischlich, "Die Israelitische Gemeinde" [The Jewish Communities], in *700 Jahre Stadtrechte 1274-1974: Chronik von Zwingenberg an der Bergstrasse* (1974) 380 (Kilthau, *Mitten Unter Uns*, 48)

25 Henny Rauch, cited in *Mitten unter Uns*, 82

26 Kilthau, *Als die Synagogen branten: Die Reichsprogramnacht 1938 im Kreis Bergstrasse* [*While the Synagogues Burned: The Reichsprogram Night in the Bergstasse District*] (2008), 48–52.

27 Kilthau, *Mitten unter Uns*, 49–52. This kind of action, known as *Reibpartien* or *Reibactionen* ("scrub parties") was a common form of humiliation, forcing Jews (often elderly) to clean public places in the most demeaning way possible

28 *Mitten unter Uns*, 51-2

29 Talmud Bavli, Berakhot, 28b]. *Mitten unter Uns*, 54, cites Norbert Mischlich, "Die Synagogue in Zwingenberg, a.d.B." In *Geschichtsblätter Kreis Bergstrasse*, 10, Heppenheim 1977, 250ff.

30 Kilthau, *Als die Synagogen branten*, 56. In 1938, 6000 RM would have been the equivalent of about 2,400 U.S. dollars, about one half to one third of the cost of an ordinary res-

idence. After the war, the buyer had to pay the same price again to the current owner although the original synagogue was partly destroyed. Today, although still privately owned, the synagogue is a cultural monument. Its original façade, however, was never restored.

31 *Mitten unter Uns*, 82.

32 "The cost of the certification, the conveyance and the registration, the real estate transfer tax and the deed tax and any capital gains tax are charged to the seller." Fritz Kilthau, *Zur Geschichte der Synagogen von Zwingenberg and der Bergstrasse*, Arbeitzkreis Zwingenberger Synagoge (March 2014), 29.

33 Zwingenberg: 11-15-1938: "*This morning Martha arrived safely in Vilbel; she wants to visit the grandfather, who is ailing. Of course it's not so surprising, as he is 94 years old. If she has time, she will visit Clara and Julius Strauss in Frankfurt. Jakob has also gone to see how things are in Frankfurt. They seem to be pleased with the life there. Heartfelt greetings and kisses. Your Clara.*"

34 *Studienkreis*, Ref. p. 46. http://www.alemannia-judaica.de/reinheim_synagoge.htm

35 Joan Crawford, Joan Blondell, Joan Fontaine, Joan Caulfield, Joan Bennett among them.

36 According to Suzy's Shoah Foundation testimony, the family in Marseille learned about Martha's death via America. Presumably Clara's letter as well as other mail from Germany, now at war with France, was not getting through to Marseille, still in the French Free Zone.

37 Moritz Schack's second wife's name was provided to me by Monica Kilgreen of the Fritz Bauer Institute in Frankfurt. Additional information came from Markus Schmidt of the Frankfurt Registry Office (Bethmannstraße 360311 Frankfurt am Main: "*The parents of Selma Schack née Strauss were Joseph Strauss (born 03.04.1853 in Grebenroth/Untertaunus) and Betti Strauss née Weinberg (born 14.01.1847 in Storndorf). Their marriage was on 03.12.1876 in Egenroth, Kreis Wiesbaden. Their last residence was Storndorf.*"

[38] Ferdinand Levi, cited in *"Und Keiner hat für uns Kaddisch Gesagt...": Deportation aus Frankfurt am Main 1941 bis 1945 [And No One Said Kaddish for Us:Deportation from Frankfurt am Main 1941 to 1945.]* (Stroemfeld Verlag, Jewish Museum, Frankfurt, 2005, pp. 307–308.)

[39] *Mitten unter Uns*, 82

Chapter 4

[40] Cited by Donna E. Ryan, *The Holocaust and the Jews of Marseille: The Enforcement of Anti-Semitic Policies in Vichy France* (Urbana and Chicago, Ill: University of Illinois Press, 1996), p. 82.

[41] Operation Salli, the three-pronged Axis invasion of Free France in November 1942, included an Italian invasion from the South.

[42] Salomon Reichenberg lived the remainder of his life in England where, after the war, he opened a fashionable and successful leather goods store.

[43] The identity of the third person is unclear. Is Leo referring to himself and his two brothers-in-law? But Sally is purportedly in England.

[44] Ryan, p. 138. Ryan writes extensively about the refugee aid agencies.

[45] "JDC Arranges Sailing of 700 Refugees for North and South American Countries."Jewish Telegraphic Agency 15 Oct 1941. *http://archive.jta.org/article/1941/ 10/15/2854341/ jdc-arranges-sailing-of-700-refugees-for-north-and-south-american-countries.*

[46] G. Garretto, *Serpa Pinto: Pueblos en la Tormenta* (Ediciones Quetzal, S.A., Mexico D.F. 1943). p. 13, 194–195, translation by Gerardo Schack, the child in the anecdote.

[47] Jeanne D'Arc Day is celebrated on May 30. Note that Suzy's scheduled arrest was five months before the Germans occupied Southern France.

[48] Rivesaltes was a military camp in the eastern Pyrenees. In 1942, 2,251 Jews, including 110 children, were transferred from there to the Drancy transit camp, from where they

were sent to Auschwitz and murdered.
49 The Todt Organisation was named after its founder, Fritz Todt, an engineer and senior Nazi official, and was responsible for numerous and varied engineering projects throughout the entire German Reich, both at home and abroad. It was notorious for its use of forced labor, and during the years from 1942 until the end of the war, under the leadership of Albert Speer, it oversaw a slave-labor operation of approximately 1.4 million prisoners, many of whom did not survive the war.
50 *The Holocaust Encyclopedia* website describes in detail the history and conditions of the Bremen-Farge camp. http://www.ushmm.org/wlc/en/article.php?ModuleId=10007390
51 Opened in September 1939 near the village of Les Milles in Aix-en-Provence, Camp des Milles was a French internment camp. Built to intern German and Austrian refugees living in Marseille and its environs, its prisoners included a number of well-known artists, writers, and other intellectuals (among them Lion Feuchtwanger, Alfred Kantorowicz, Golo Mann, and Max Ernst). After 1941, it served as a transit camp for Jews, primarily men, and a starting point for deportation first to Drancy and then Auschwitz, of all Jewish males living in Marseille or even trying to pass through Marseille in transit to a safer port. Held there at one time were Suzy's husband, Otto Goldschmitt, as well as Leo's brother-in-law, Louis Reichenberg. See André Fontaine, *Le camp d'étrangers des Milles: 1939–1943* (Edisud: Aix-en-Provence (1989) and Donna F. Ryan, *The Holocaust and the Jews of Marseille* (Urbana and Chicago: University of Illinois Press (1996).
52 Lina had married Fred Scarano, a New York born Italian American, on July 3, 1944. Fred was with the Army Air Force in Italy, serving as an airplane technician.

Chapter 5

53 Erich Glückauf, *Begegnungen und Signale: Erinnerungen*

54 *eines Revolutionärs [Encounters and Signals: Reminiscences of a Revolutionary]* (Berlin: Verlag Neues Leben, 1976).

55 Franz-Joseph Schmit, *Die Geschichte der deutsch-jüdischen Familie Glückauf [The History of the German Jewish Gluckauf Family]*. (Wittlich: *Annual of the Emil-Frank-Institute* 2011/2012), pp. 12-20

56 Bob Moore, *Victims and Survivors: The Nazi Persecution of the Jews in the Netherlands*, 1940–1945. (London: Arnold, 1997). Most of my understanding of Dutch Jewish life both before the German occupation and during the war derives from Moore's excellent book.

57 Moore, p. 37.

58 Moore, p. 31.

59 Erich's version of his arrest differs only slightly. He says that he had gone to a cinema for an arranged meeting with the local comrade, when he was seized and arrested by two Dutch policemen (*Erinnerung*, p. 340). His description of his imprisonment and release follows.

60 Cited (and abbreviated) by Franz-Josef Schmit, "Erich Glückauf – Jude und Kommunist aus Wittlich," *volksfreund.de* <http://www.volksfreund.de/nachrichten/region/wittlich/aktuell/pogromnacht./Heute-in-der-Wittlicher-Zeitung-Erich-Glueckauf-Jude-und-Kommunist-aus-Wittlich; art 8137, 2963221.

61 *Begegnungen und Signale*, p. 340.

62 *Begegnungen und Signale*, pp. 238; 340–343.

63 Erich Glückauf, *Lebenslauf*, Berlin den 25. Marz, 1954. Bundesarchiv copy sent me by Franz-Josef Schmit.

64 See *Die Geschichte der deutsch-jüdischen Familie Glückauf*, 9. n. 22.

65 Many questioned the memoir's assertions, which often seemed somewhat distant from the truth, emphasizing (perhaps exaggerating) Erich's contributions while downplaying those of others. Evidently, the remainder of the press run was deliberately destroyed shortly after publication.

66 Some contempt for Polish, Russian, and other Eastern European Jews for their often rural ways, traditional religious orthodoxy, and lack of secular education was widespread

among German Jews, who prided themselves on their modernity and assimilation. In this way, ironically, German Jews echoed the prejudices of their anti-Semitic persecutors.

66 Walter Isaacson, *Kissinger: A Biography* (New York: Simon and Schuster, 2005), p. 37.

67 Moore, p. 42

68 Moore, pp. 48–49, citing Herzberg, A.J. *Kroniek der Jodenvervolging* 1940–45 (Amsterdam, Querido, 1985), p. 19. For a detailed account of various (usually unsuccessful) Jewish strategies for escape, see Moore, pp. 42–50.

69 Moore, p. 53. The development of occupation policies regarding the Dutch Jews is described in detail in Moore, Chapter 4, "Isolation" (pp. 62–79).

70 Moore, pp. 71-2.

71 See Moore 79ff.

72 Not until June 30, 1942, were Jews alone explicitly forbidden to be on the streets after 8 PM

73 Moore, p. 100.

74 See Marnix Croes, "The Holocaust in the Netherlands and the Rate of Jewish Survival," *Holocaust and Genocide Studies* (Winter 2006) 20 (3), 474–499. "[O]nly 27 percent [of Dutch Jews] survived the occupation. Yet in Belgium, 60 percent of the approximately 66,000 Jews survived, and in France, 75 percent of the approximately 320,000 Jews escaped death at the hands of the Nazis."

75 Begegnungen und Signale (pp. 403-4)

76 See Walter Wimmer and Karlheinz Pesch, "Erklärung zu Dem Gutachten über Das Buch Des Genossen Glückauf." ["Explanation of the Report on the Book by Comrade Glückauf"]. *Bundesarchiv Berlin NY 4200/9 [the Glückauf estate papers)*, 24 March 1977. Franz-Josef Schmit posits that at least some of the objections arise from personality clashes and personal enmities, as well as the fact that Erich had attacked Herbert Wehner as being a traitor, when at the time described Wehner was still a party loyalist. Nonetheless, that the book on which he had expended so much effort in his final years was banned by the party to which he had devoted his life must, as Schmit writes: "have finally broken

Erich G's heart," and he died less than two weeks later. (Schmit letter to me, January 10, 2012)

77 A common children's game, whereby one strokes the baby's hand while naming each of the items (Thaler [a silver coin], Maler [painter], cow, calf, tail, etc.) and ends by tickling the palm of the baby's hand while saying one of many German versions of *tickle, tickle, tickle*. My thanks to Martina Rohde and Daniela Tobias of *Jekkes Engaged in Worldwide Social Networking* for the information.

Chapter 6

78 Mika Adler, in the Israeli film *The Flat*. Written, directed and co-produced by Arnon Goldfinger. ARTE (Israel, 2011), in cooperation with Arnon Goldfinger Productions.

Chapter 8

79 Richard Brody, "The Inadequacy of Berlin's 'Memorial to the Murdered Jews of Europe.'" *The New Yorker* (July 12, 2012).
80 Ralph Blumenthal, "In Berlin, Unraveling a Family History," *Personal Journeys, New York Times* (June 22, 2016).
81 Cited from the English translation of the official web page of Gunther Deming's *Stolpersteine* project. http://www.stolpersteine.eu/en/

Acknowledgements

This book would not exist without the contributions and support of many others. When I began exploring my family's history before, during, and after the Third Reich, Yeshiva University kindly provided me with a student assistant, a native German speaker, Robert Nowbakht, who patiently transcribed and loosely translated many of the family letters on which Chapters 3 and 4 are based. Nor could I have written Chapter 5 without the assistance of my late half-sister, Lotte Dukamp, who transcribed all the letters from our common grandmother, which were written in the early twentieth-century German script that is largely illegible except to those who learned it in school.

I am also deeply indebted to two German scholars whose unsolicited research on my family filled in many blanks in my parents' and grandparents' biographies. One is Dr. Fritz Kilthau, a resident of my mother's native village of Zwingenberg an der Bergstrasse, on whose support and friendship I have relied almost from the start of my project. Fritz's painstaking quest to learn the fates of the Jews of the entire Bergstrasse region during the Nazi period provided much of the background for the chapter on my maternal grandparents. The other is Dr. Franz-Josef Schmit, whose participation in a group project to remember the lost Jews of the small city of Wittlich in the Rhineland (his home and my father's birthplace) led to his interest in my father's family. Both generously shared with me the results of their own research and often helped me find answers to questions that arose in the course of my investigations. In addition, Jürgen Poth, a singer and folklorist from my maternal grandfather's place of origin, kindly sent me local documents about my family that he had gathered for a forthcoming performance about the town's former Jews.

I am grateful to all the colleagues and friends who read or listened to parts of my manuscript and helped guide its progress: Professors Joanne Jacobson and Simon Gaunt, as well as the members of the NY Meds (our long-running Columbia University based Medievalist Seminar) who were willing, for a session, to abandon the Middle Ages for a visit to Nazi Germany: Professors Christopher Baswell, Susan Crane, Sealy Gilles, Charlotte Gross, Robert Hanning, Ronald Herzman, Francis Ingledew, Sarah Novacich, Sandra Pearson Prior, Anne Schotter, Sylvia Tomasch, and Jocelyn Wogan-Brown.

I thank my aunts and uncle (all now deceased) who, as long as I can remember, shared their memories with me. Thanks, too, to my cousins Gerardo Schack, who shared with me what he remembered about the voyage on the Serpa Pinto and his parents' lives in France and Mexico, and Paulette Reda and her son Scott for giving me access to the USC Shoah Foundation testimonies of her parents, parts of which I have incorporated directly into my narrative.

I am especially grateful to my old friend from Harvard Graduate School, Professor George M. Logan, who so generously read and reread my manuscript, helping guide its evolution and continually encouraging me to forge on.

Last but not least, I thank my immediate family. My late mother, whether intentionally or not, kindled my obsession with our family's experiences during the Weimar and Nazi regimes and made this book possible by rescuing the family photos and saving every letter that arrived from Europe. To my daughters, Berit and Marit Haahr (writers themselves and my first readers), thank you for your unfailing support and willingness to read and comment on my manuscript in its several manifestations. To my son, Paul Haahr, thanks for your helpful advice throughout on the technical and visual aspects of the book. Finally, I want to express unending love and gratitude to my late husband, Jorn Haahr, my beloved partner for almost sixty years, for his unstinting support and encouragement throughout the long years of research and writing.

About the Author

The child of German Jewish refugees, Joan Gluckauf Haahr was born and grew up in New York City's Washington Heights, a place of refuge for many German Jews. After receiving her Ph.D. in English Literature from Harvard, she taught for over forty years at Yeshiva College, where she also served as long-time chair of the English Department. She has lived for many years in Riverdale, the Bronx, where she and her husband raised their three children.

www.ingramcontent.com/pod-product-compliance
Lightning Source LLC
Chambersburg PA
CBHW030849170426
43193CB00009BA/548